HOTEL FRONT OFFICE TRAINING MANUAL

श्री गणेशाय नमः

ॐ नमः शिवाय

HOTEL FRONT OFFICE TRAINING MANUAL

Revised and Enlarged Edition

Suvradeep Gauranga Ghosh

AMAN PUBLICATIONS
NEW DELHI

Published by
Rajiv Jain for Aman Publications
LG-4A, Ganpati Bhawan,
4675-B/21, Ansari Road,
Darya Ganj, Delhi - 110002
PH: 23255012, 23282127
E-mail: sshjbs@yahoo.com

First Published 2005

Revised and Enlarged Edition 2010

Reprint **2020**

ISBN: 81-8204-065-5
ISBN: 978-81-8204-065-6

SOLE DISTRIBUTOR
JINDAL BOOK SERVICES
LG-4A, Ganpati Bhawan,
4675-B/21, Ansari Road,
Darya Ganj, Delhi - 110002

Jacket Designed by :
S.M. Graphics

Printed by:
Sachin Printers, Delhi, India.

"This Work is Dedicated To

My

Nearest & Dearest Uncle

Late Shri PRADIP NANDY

Whose

Blessings Will Be Always There

For Me

In

All Spheres of Life"

"Special Thanks

To

My Family

For Their Continuous

Support and Best Wishes"

PREFACE

The **"Hotel Front Office Training Manual"** published in the year 2005 was an immense success in the market. The manual was widely appreciated not only by the faculties but was also appreciated a lot by the student fraternities being the most student friendly practical book launched in the market.

Now after five years of the launch of the book, a need has been felt to upgrade it with the latest information on the hotel industry and functioning of the hotel front office. The revised and enlarged edition of the book has basically concentrated towards addition of sections such as overview of the Indian Hotel Industry, new technical terms in front office, latest photographs & illustrations and discussion on revenue management.

As the young students of hospitality and hotel management will be the main readers of the manual, the revised edition of the manual takes care to give them a good amount of theoretical and practical knowledge in the operations of the front office department of a hotel. The student fraternity always feel the need for a training manual which is purely a training manual and not a theory text book which gives them no information about the practicalities of the front office but is only a mere collection of facts.

The revised edition has a comprehensive coverage on the hotel industry of India and gives important facts and figures on present development and future prospects of the travel, tourism and hotel industry.

It is widely appreciated by all the front office professionals that one should have a sound general knowledge for working efficiently at the hotel front office. Keeping in to view the requirements of the front office personnel, the general knowledge section of the training manual has been updated with the latest industry jargons, knowledge about the tallest hotel buildings, currencies of the countries of the world. The revised edition also discusses about various unusual hotel accommodations and also covers various illustrations on types of hotel rooms and front office equipments.

In all, the revised and enlarged edition of Hotel Front Office Training Manual promises to live up to the expectation standards of the teaching as well student fraternity of the country.

I also hereby declare that the views expressed by me in the book is purely mine and not of the company in which I am working.

Happy Reading!!!

Suvradeep Gauranga Ghosh

ACKNOWLEDGEMENTS

I express my sincere gratitude and thanks to the following intellectuals under whose guidance the entire concept of writing and compiling this book have been developed:

Shri Rakesh Tandon	:	(Managing Director, IRCTC) For his blessings and best wishes.
Dr. Nalin Shinghal,	:	(Director-Tourism & Marketing, IRCTC) For his guidance and support towards bringing this book.
Shri. Vinod Asthana	:	(Director - Catering Services, IRCTC) for his best wishes.
Shri. V.R. Gupta	:	(Director - Finance, IRCTC) for his best wishes.
Shri. Arvind Neherwa	:	(Assistant Manager - Catering) For his guidance in the technical structuring of this book.
Shri. Rajiv Jain & Shri. Sanjeev Jain	:	(Aman Publications, Delhi) For their continuing support and sincere efforts in publishing of the manual and it's marketing it in the country
Shri. Sudeep Nandy (My Brother)	:	For his sincere efforts in the proof reading and formatting of the text book.
All members of IRCTC family	:	For their support and encouragement

Contents

UNIT – I

THE HOSPITALITY AND LODGING INDUSTRY

UNIT – I

THE HOSPITALITY AND LODGING INDUSTRY

LEARNING OBJECTIVES

- ❖ To Study The Travel and Tourism Industry and its present Trends and Developments in India.
- ❖ To Study The Hospitality Industry As A Part of The Travel and Tourism Industry.
- ❖ To Study The History and Development Of The Lodging Industry.
- ❖ To Study The Classification of The Organized Hotel Industry.
- ❖ To Study The Classification of The Unorganized Supplementary Accommodation Industry.
- ❖ To Study The Classification Of The Semi-organized Intermediate Accommodation Industry.

CHAPTER 1

THE TRAVEL AND TOURISM INDUSTRY

TRAVEL AND TOURISM

The Travel and Tourism Industry is perhaps one of the largest and fastest growing industries in the whole world due to the increase in the inflow of tourists in various countries, due to increase in business between the nations, increasing spending power of the people, curiosity to visit new countries and learn new cultures and improvement in the means of communication.

Tourism has become a popular global leisure activity. In 2008, there were over 922 million international tourist arrivals, with a growth of 1.9% as compared to 2007. International tourism receipts grew to US$944 billion in 2008, corresponding to an increase in real terms of 1.8%.

The Travel and Tourism Industry has many dimensions such as Hospitality Industry, Transportation Services and the Events and Activities.

(For Detailed Look at the Lodging Industry, Please Refer Figure 1.1).

DEFINING TOURISM

Tourism is travel for various purposes such as recreation, leisure or business . The World Tourism Organization has defined **tourists** as people who "undertake travel to and stay in places outside their usual environment for more than 24 hours and not more than one consecutive year for leisure, business and other purposes not related to the exercise of an activity remunerated from within the place visited".

The United Nations classified three forms of tourism in 1994, in its "Recommendations on Tourism Statistics:

- Domestic tourism, which involves residents of the given country traveling only within this country.
- Inbound tourism, involving non-residents traveling in the given country.
- Outbound tourism, involving residents traveling in another country.

TYPES OF TOURISM

Leisure Tourism was associated with the onset of Industrial Revolution in Europe. United Kingdomthe first European country to promote leisure time to the increasing industrial population.

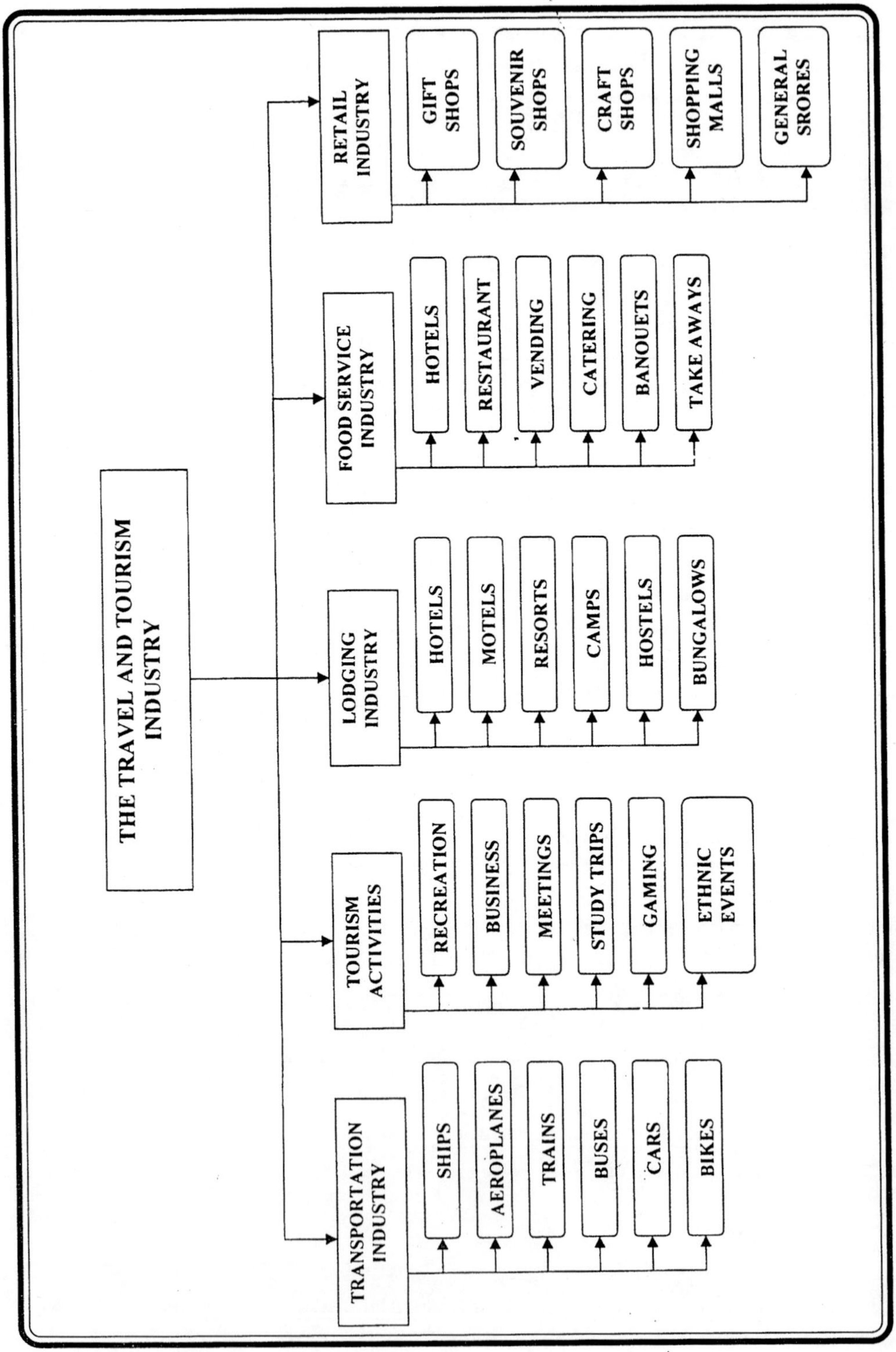

Fig. 1.1: The Travel and Tourism Industry and its Dimensions

Initially, this applied to the owners of the machinery of production, the factory owners and the traders which comprised the new middle class. Cox & Kings was the first official travel company to be formed in 1758.

Mass Tourism developed with the invent of globalization and improvements in technology which allowed the transport of large numbers of people in a short period of time to places of leisure interest, so that greater numbers of people could begin to enjoy the benefits of leisure time.

Special Interest Tourism includes various forms of tourism such as ecotourism, cultural tourism, adventure tourism, sports tourism, geo-tourism, heritage tourism, religious tourism, medical tourism, space tourism, wildlife tourism and war tourism.

Medical tourism is a type of tourism in which people travel from one country to another for various medical treatment and surgery. There is a significant price differential between countries of West and Southeast Asia such as India, in terms of medical procedures.

Educational tourism is a type of tourism in which the main focus of the tour or leisure activity includes visiting another country to learn about the culture, such as in Student Exchange Programs and Study Tours, or to work and apply skills learned inside the classroom in a different environment, such as in the International Practicum Training Program. This type of tourism has developed since time immemorial , because of the growing popularity of teaching and learning of knowledge and the enhancing of technical competency outside of the classroom environment.

Creative tourism is a type of cultural tourism which is an engaged, authentic experience that promotes an active participation of the traveller in the culture of the host community through interactive workshops and informal learning experiences.

Sustainable tourism is a form of tourism in which all resources are managed in such a way that economic, social and aesthetic needs are fulfilled while maintaining cultural integrity, essential ecological processes, biological diversity and life support systems. Sustainable development implies meeting the needs of the present without compromising the ability of future generations to meet their own needs.

Ecotourism is a form of tourism which is responsible tourism to fragile, pristine, and usually protected areas that is determined to be low impact and (often) small scale. It helps educate the traveller; provides funds for conservation; directly benefits the economic development and political empowerment of local communities; and fosters respect for different cultures and for human rights.

Recession tourism is a travel trend which has been identified by American entrepreneur Matt Landau (2007) is a recent tourism phenomenon. Recession tourism is defined by low-cost, high-value experiences taking place of understanding of the specific cultural features of a place.

Dark tourism is a type of unusual tourism in which the tourists visit to various dark sites such as such as battlegrounds, scenes of horrific crimes or acts of genocide.

CHAPTER 2

HOSPITALITY INDUSTRY: A DIMENSION OF THE TRAVEL AND TOURISM INDUSTRY

DEFINING THE HOSPITALITY INDUSTRY

The word ***"Hospitality"*** means a friendly treatment, which is offered to a stranger. The concept of Hospitality has been diversified to a huge extent after the process of globalization, which has taken place in most of the countries of the world.

The Hospitality Industry can be defined as "a dimension of the travel and tourism industry encompassing the lodging and foodservice industry."

The hospitality industry is a several billion dollar industry that mostly lies on the availability of leisure time and disposable income. A hospitality unit such as a restaurant, hotel, or even an amusement park consists of multiple groups such as facility maintenance, direct operations comprising of food and beverage attendants, housekeeping staff, porters, kitchen workers etc.), management, marketing, and human resources.

The hospitality industry covers a wide range of organizations offering food service and accommodation. The hospitality industry is divided into sectors according to the skill-sets required for the work involved. Sectors include accommodation, food and beverage, meeting and events, gaming, entertainment and recreation, tourism services, and visitor information

The **Hospitality Industry** is broadly classified into:

- The **Lodging Industry** that includes hotels, motels, casinos, resorts, parks, hostels and other type of accommodations.
- The **Foodservice Industry** that includes restaurants, fast food counters, kiosks, bars, tea and coffee houses, snack bars, institutional food service catering and so on.

The Lodging and Foodservice industry has tremendous capacity to generate business and revenue for the hospitality organizations and the countries at large.

DEFINING THE LODGING INDUSTRY

The Lodging Industry can be defined as "a dimension of the hospitality industry which strives on the vision and mission of providing accommodation services to the bonafide travellers."

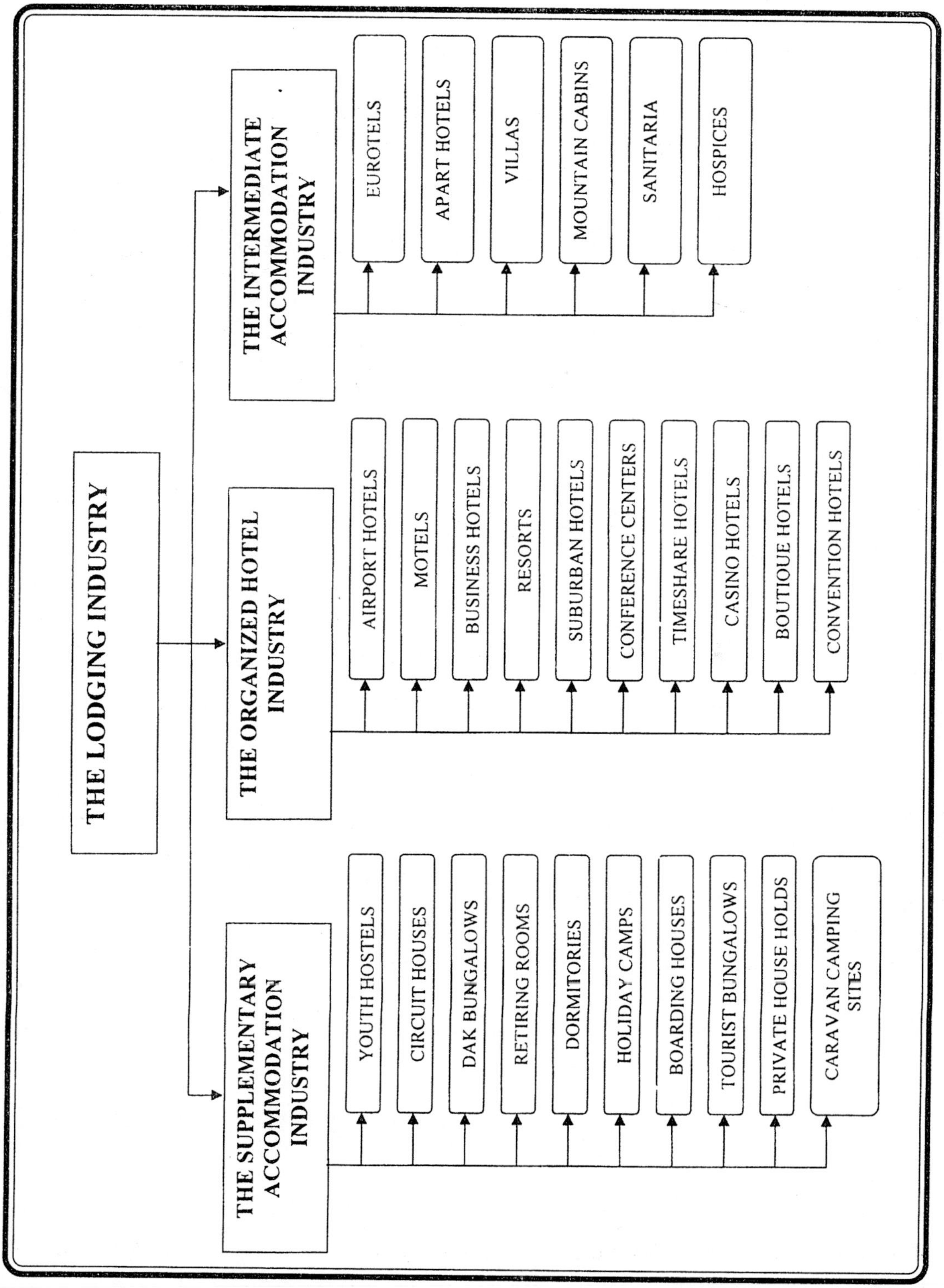

Fig. 2.1: The Lodging Industry and its Dimensions

The lodging industry is further classified into:-

- The **Organized Hotel Industry**
- The **Unorganized Supplementary Accommodation Industry**
- The **Semi-organized Intermediate Accommodation Industry**

(For Detailed Look at the Lodging Industry, Please Refer Figure 2.1).

A large number of tourists are traveling around the world and so their ever-increasing demands for accommodation and food are providing opportunities to the Hospitality companies to invest and reap huge profits in this branch of the Hospitality industry.

So, the Hospitality industry gives enormous career opportunities for hardworking and optimistic human resource to flourish and emerge successful as hospitality professionals in the hospitality industry.

Thus, the amount of scope and career opportunities provided by the hospitality industry and its future potential for growth has made it a very popular industry in the world.

CHAPTER 3

THE HISTORY AND DEVELOPMENT OF THE LODGING INDUSTRY

The lodging industry is perhaps the oldest commercial industry of the world and is a fast growing industry with a lot of career opportunities.

The establishment of money during the sixth century B.C. gave the opportunity to people to trade and travel. Thus, the origin of hotel can be traced back to the sixth century B.C which was in the form of "**Inns**" which were the first type of hotels to cater to the lodging requirements of the travellers. These inns were managed by the husband and wife team who provided the travellers with overnight accommodation by allowing the travellers to sleep on the floor and make their own beds. They also provided food and wines and some other types of facilities. Thus, the entire services were provided by the husband and wife teams along with some type of recreational facilities such as music, dance and some types of indoor games.

The beginning of **Industrial Revolution** in **Europe** introduced the new idea in the business of inn-keeping as traveling become more frequent after the development of other means of transportation such as the railways and ships. The **Industrial Revolution** also gave a rise to a new dimension of travel known as the business in which people started traveling from one place to another for their purpose of business.

In England, in earlier days, public houses called ***"Inns"*** were constructed for the noble and elite class of guests. At the same time low and mid-budget properties called ***"Taverns"*** were also constructed for catering to the needs of the common people.

In France, finer lodging establishments called ***"Hotelleries"*** were constructed to cater to the needs of the rich and noble class of people while "cabarets" were constructed for catering to the needs of the common people.

Similarly, other native form of hostelry also became popular in other parts of the world such as ***"Riokan"*** in Japan, ***"Paradors"*** in Spain and ***"Pousadas"*** in Portugal.

England was the first country to use the term ***"Hotel"*** to these commercial lodging establishments in the year 1760 A.D. In the United States of America, the lodging establishments were called ***"Inns"*** of ***"Coffee Houses"***.

U.S.A was the first country where the real growth of hotels took place when the first building for hotel purposes was built in the year **1794** called the "**City Hotel**" in **New York**. This was followed by an era of competition in the field of the hotel industry as many beautiful hotels were constructed at that time.

The concept of operation of the chain of hotels was introduced in the field of the hotel industry with the beginning of the first commercial hotel by **Ellsworth Statler** in **1908 A.D**. called ***"The Buffalo Statler"***.

In **1930**, there was a **"Great Economic Depression"** in **United States** and **Europe** which sank the business of the hotel industry into an all time low. The effects of the Depression in United States were so severe that about 85% of the hotels in United States went either into receivership or through some form of liquidation.

After the Great Economic Depression which hit the lodging industry very badly in United States, there was a speedy recovery in this industry during and after the World War II.

IMPORTANT CALENDAR EVENTS IN THE HISTORY OF HOTEL INDUSTRY

YEAR	EVENT
1794 A.D.	The first commercial building for the hotel purposes called the "The City Hotel" was constructed in New York, U.S.A.
1829 A.D.	"Tremont House", the first class hotel was constructed in Boston, U.S.A.
1875 A.D.	The most expensive hotel of its day called "The Palace" was built in San Francisco.
1908 A.D.	Ellsworth Statler started the first chain of hotels called "The Buffalo Chain of Hotels".
1915 A.D.	The international chain of hotels were started.
1930 A.D.	The Economic Depression led to the decline of the hotel industry.
1945 A.D.	There was an increase in the number of hotels after World War - II.

CHAPTER 4

THE PRESENT DEVELOPMENTS IN THE TRAVEL AND TOURISM INDUSTRY OF INDIA

Hospitality, as an industry segment in itself, is a US$ 3.5 trillion service sector within the global economy.

In India, the tourism and hospitality industries are witnessing a period of exponential growth.

The year 2007 also marked the fifth consecutive year during which India has witnessed double-digit growth in foreign tourist arrivals.

Along with the rise in foreign tourist arrivals, foreign exchange earnings have shown a robust growth of 25.6% during January-October 2007 to touch US$ 6.32 billion as against US$ 5.03 billion during January-October 2006.

Tourism has now become a significant industry in India, contributing around 5.9 per cent of the Gross Domestic Product (GDP) and providing employment to about 41.8 million people.

As per the World Travel & Tourism Council, the tourism industry in India is likely to generate US$ 121.4 billion of economic activity by 2015 and Hospitality sector has the potential to earn US$ 24 billion in foreign exchange by 2015.

Additionally, India is also likely to become a major hub for medical tourism, with revenues from the industry estimated to grow from US$ 333 million in 2007 to US$ 2.2 billion by 2012.

The booming tourism industry has had a cascading effect on the hospitality sector with an increase in the occupancy ratios and average room rates.

While occupancy ratio is around 80-85 per cent – up nearly 10 percent from three years back, the average increase in room rates over the last one year has hovered around 22-25%.

It is pertinent to mention in this context, that according to recent estimates, there are a total of 110,000 rooms in India, as against a total requirement of approximately 250,000 – demonstrating the untapped potential that continues to exist in this industry.

With a view to stimulating domestic and international investments in this sector, the government has implemented the following initiatives:

- 100% FDI under the automatic route is now permitted in all construction development projects including construction of hotels and resorts, recreational facilities and city and regional level infrastructure.

- 100% FDI is now permitted in all airport development projects subject to the condition that FDI for up gradation of existing airports requires FIPB approval beyond 74%.
- A five year tax holiday has been extended to Companies that set up hotels, resorts and convention centers at specified destinations, subject to compliance with the prescribed conditions.
- Plans for substantial up gradation of 28 regional airports in smaller towns and the privatization and expansion of Delhi and Mumbai airports.

The aforementioned initiatives have resulted in increasing FDI inflows being witnessed by this industry. For the period April 2000 to November 2007, a total of US$ 636 million in foreign direct investments was channelised towards development of hotels and tourism.

CHAPTER 5

THE CLASSIFICATION OF ORGANIZED HOTEL INDUSTRY

DEFINING THE TERM HOTEL

A hotel can be defined as "an establishment whose primary purpose is to provide accommodation services to a bonafide traveller and other services such as food and beverage services, housekeeping services, laundry services and uniformed services."

The Main Criteria for the Classification of the Hotels

- Classification on the basis of **Size or Number of Rooms.**
- Classification on the basis of **Location.**
- Classification on the basis of **Type of Clientele.**
- Classification on the basis of **Length of Stay.**
- Classification on the basis of **Levels Of Service.**
- Classification on the basis of **Management and Affiliation.**
- Classification on the basis of **Ownership of Guests.**

CLASSIFICATION OF HOTELS ON THE BASIS OF SIZE OR NUMBER OF ROOMS PRESENT

There are generally two aspects of the classification of hotels on the basis of size or number of rooms present. They are:

According to the Indian scenario:

- **Small Hotels** These hotels have less than **25** rooms.
- **Medium Hotels** These hotels have **25** to **100** rooms.
- **Large Hotels** These hotels have **100** to **300** rooms.
- **Very large Hotels** These hotels have more than **300** rooms.

According to the American scenario:

- ❖ **Small Hotels** These hotels have less than **150** rooms.
- ❖ **Medium Hotels** These hotels have **150** to **299** rooms.
- ❖ **Large Hotels** These hotels have **300** to **600** rooms.
- ❖ **Very large Hotels** These hotels have more than **600** rooms

CLASSIFICATION OF HOTELS ON THE BASIS OF LOCATION

The following are the various types of hotels on the basis of location:

Down Town Hotels

- ❖ These hotels are also called "**Commercial Hotels**", "**City Hotels**" or "**Business Hotels**".
- ❖ These hotels are located in the heart of cities and towns. *e.g.* **Blue Diamond (Pune)**, **Oberoi Grand (Kolkata)**.
- ❖ These hotels mostly cater to the businessmen, tour groups, individual tourists and small conference groups.
- ❖ Commercial hotels provide a wide range of room types such as single rooms, double rooms, junior suites, suites and other essential facilities such as conference rooms, cocktail lounges etc.
- ❖ Most of the commercial hotels have restaurants, coffee shops, business centers with secretarial, fax, internet, and Xerox facilities.
- ❖ Commercial hotels also offer room services, laundry-valets, uniformed services such as concierge and transport facilities such as airport pick up and drop.

Airport Hotels

- ❖ These hotels as the name suggests are located in the close vicinity to international and domestic airports of major cities and towns. *e.g.* **Airport Ashok (Kolkata)**, **Airport Centaur (New Delhi)**.
- ❖ These hotels cater primarily to airline passengers with cancelled flights and airline crew members.
- ❖ Generally the guests in these hotels stay for a very short duration which is usually one or two days.
- ❖ These hotels have well furnished guestrooms with restaurants and coffee shops and offer various other facilities such as airport pick up and drop through the hotel owned cars and buses which is very important for the passengers and crew members.

Resorts

- Resorts are hotels which are located in exotic locations such as beaches, hill stations, forests and so on and thus are famous for their scenic beauty. *e.g.* **Fort Aguada Beach Resort (Goa)**, **Vanya Villas (Ranthambore)**.
- The resorts mostly cater to the leisure travellers, families, holiday makers and vacationers who visit this special category of hotels to enjoy their vacations.
- The resorts provide most of the important facilities to the holiday makers such as accommodation, food and beverage services, valet services, uniformed services etc.
- The resorts have various recreational facilities such as tennis courts, golf courses, skiing grounds, amusement parks for children and so on.
- Thus resorts are a major attraction for the tourists who enjoy the breathtaking scenery in which these hotels are located.

Motels

- The term "**motel**" is an **American** concept and has originated form the word "**Motor Hotel**".
- These hotels are located on the national highways and other important roads and mostly cater to the various passer-bys on the highways and especially to the guests arriving at the hotel by automobiles.
- These hotels are not very large and generally have a fewer number of rooms but do have enough space for the parking of the vehicles of the guests and other visitors.
- These hotels generally provide inexpensive rooms with the basic facilities and amenities and do have food and beverage facilities.

Suburban Hotels

- The suburban hotels as the name suggests are hotels which are located on the outskirts of the cities and towns. E.g. **JAYPEE Palace (Agra)**.
- These hotels generally cater to the official and business groups who want to hold conferences and seminars in a peaceful and calm environment away from the cities.
- These hotels also provide extensive accommodation and food and beverage facilities and have huge conference rooms and seminar halls and also provide a wide range of conference and seminar equipments.

CLASSIFICATION OF HOTELS ON THE BASIS OF TYPE OF CLIENTELE

The following are the various types of hotels on the basis of clientele:

Down Town Hotels

These hotels are located in the middle of the cities and towns and cater to the business traveller, individual traveller, tourist groups. *(Has been discussed already)*

Airport Hotels

These hotels are located near airports and cater primarily to the passengers with cancelled and delayed flights and airline crew members. *(Has been discussed already)*

Resorts

These hotels situated in exotic locations such as hills, sea beaches and forests mainly cater to the tourist groups, families and other vacationers and holiday makers. *(Has been discussed already)*

Motels

These hotels are situated near highways and basically cater to the passer-bys, passengers and other transit guests with vehicles. *(Has been discussed already)*

Conference Centers

- Conference Centers especially cater to the conference, meeting and seminar attendees and provide overnight accommodation to these guests. *e.g.* **Hotel Ashoka (New Delhi)**
- These hotels provide various equipments required for conference and seminars such as audiovisual equipments such as Overhead projectors and LCD projectors, business centers with fax, Xerox and internet facilities, various seating arrangements, display screens, flipcharts and other important technical assistances required during the meetings and seminars.
- These hotels also provide other facilities such as food and beverage service facilities, laundry-valet facilities, uniformed service facilities and a host of other facilities such as transport and recreational facilities.

Convention Hotels

- Convention hotels are very large hotels especially constructed to cater to the needs of housing the convention attendees.
- Convention hotels have **1000** to **3000** rooms and thus are able to accommodate a large number of guests coming to attend conventions.
- Convention hotels are very common in United States of America and mostly attract the convention market of regional, national and international associations.

- Convention hotels offer a large number of business services to the guests such as secretarial assistance, fax machines, computers, laptops and so on.
- Convention hotels also provide other facilities such as food and beverage service facilities, housekeeping services and transport services.

Casino Hotels

- Casino hotels are a special class of hotels which cater to the needs of the guests who are interested in gambling. E.g. **Gamblers Paradise (Arizona, USA)**
- These hotels are very common in United States of America and offer a vast range of gambling facilities, with the casinos of the hotels operating 24 hours a day throughout the year and these are a major source of revenue for these hotels.
- These hotels attract the guest through theme parties and profligate shows and thus earn a large amount of revenue.
- Apart from gambling facilities, these hotels also provide accommodation with exclusive guestrooms and also provide a large range of food and beverage service facilities.

Suite Hotels

- These hotels according to the name have either all suite rooms or majority of the rooms as suites. E.g. **Grand Hyatt (New Delhi)**.
- These hotels cater to lawyers, elite class of businessmen, film personalities, politicians and various executives.
- Since these hotels mostly have suite rooms which have a sitting room and bedroom, the privacy of the guest is maintained.
- These hotels also offer a large number of other facilities to the guests such as food and beverage services, uniformed services, laundry-valet services and so on.

Boutique Hotels

- Boutique hotels are a few small hotels located throughout the country and are targeted to the rich class of businessmen and vacationers who visit the hotels for hideaway and getaway. E.g. **The Park, (Kolkata)**, **The Park (Vishakhapatnam)**, **De L'Orient (Pondicherry)**
- They have been categorized as boutique owing to their intimate size, idyllic settings, highly personalized service, individual size and outstanding attributes.
- Each of the boutique hotels offers a unique vacation experience and highly personalized service to the guests.

CLASSIFICATION OF HOTELS ON THE BASIS OF LENGTH OF STAY

The following are the various types of hotels on the basis of length or duration stay:

Extended Stay Hotels

- Extended Stay hotels also called "**Residential hotels**" are hotels where the travellers and tourists stay for a longer such as one month or so.
- These hotels are very similar to the suite hotels but the guestrooms of these hotels do offer kitchen facilities.
- These hotels generally provide elaborate world class services to the guests such as uniformed services and valet services and hence are targeted towards budget minded tourists who require reduced hotel service.
- These hotels generally have a more homely atmosphere and hence attract tourists for a long stay.

Semi-extended Stay Hotels

- Semi-extended hotels also called "**Semi-residential hotels**" are hotels where the guest stay for 3 to 5 days and are widely used by vacationers as well as business travellers.
- These hotels combine the features of extended stay hotels and transient hotels.

Brief Stay Hotels

- Brief Stay hotels also called "**Transient hotels**" are hotels where the guests come for a very short stay which range from a few hours to one night.
- These hotels are generally airport hotels where the flight passengers and airline crew members come for overnight stay.
- These hotels generally give discounts called "**leeway**" to the guests staying for a few hours and a reduced or discounted rate is charged form the guests.

CLASSIFICATION OF HOTELS ON THE BASIS OF OWNERSHIP OF GUESTS

The following are the various types of hotels on the basis of ownership of guests:

Condominium Hotels

- The concept of Condominium hotels was introduced in the year **1957** in **Europe**. E.g. **Sea Pines Plantation (South Carolina, USA)**

- According to the concept of condominium hotels, individual guests are encouraged to purchase the ownership of the individual units for the entire year.
- The guests have to inform the hotel management about the time of period of the year when they would visit and stay at the property and at the remaining time of the year, the guests can rent their unit through the hotel management.
- Hence, in condominium hotels, there is only a single owner for each of the unit or cottage of the hotel or resort.
- The entire concept of the condominium is costlier than timesharing and hence this concept could attract only few guests and thus resorts using this concept started incurring huge losses.

Timeshare Hotels

- The concept of Timeshare hotels was introduced in **Europe** in the year **1970** when the condominium hotels started incurring huge losses and were on the verge on extinction.
- According to the concept of timesharing, individual guests will purchase the ownership of a particular unit of a resort for a definite period of the year and will occupy the unit during that period.
- *(E.g. Mr. Kumar may purchase a particular cottage of a resort for the first three weeks of January during which he may stay at the cottage. Other individuals will purchase the ownership of the cottage for the remaining 48 weeks of the year.)*
- Thus, in timeshare hotels, there are multiple owners for a single cottage or unit of a resort or a hotel.
- The process of timesharing is far cheaper than the condominium concept and hence was more popular in the hospitality world.
- One of the unique advantages of the timesharing concept is that the owners of the units can easily trade their ownership time with other owners in other locations.
- In India few of the holiday resorts have started the concept of timesharing and are earning huge profits. E.g. **Sinclair's Resort (Darjeeling)**.

CLASSIFICATION OF HOTELS ON THE BASIS OF LEVELS OF SERVICE

World Class Service Hotels

- These are the top class hotels which are especially targeted to the elite class of guests who include commercially important persons, politically important persons, dignitaries and ambassadors as well other famous personalities and celebraties.
- World class service hotels offer excellent accommodation, food and beverage and uniformed services to the guests such as guestrooms with world class décor and finish , private

lounges and dinning rooms along with upscale restaurants, concierge services, valet parking services, dry cleaning and laundry valet services.

- Guestrooms of these are built in a modern fashion and are all well equipped with all supplies such as personalized stationery, beautiful sets of bathroom supplies including shaving sets, morning kits, herbal shampoos, soaps, lager sized bath towels, shower caps, bath robes and a large number of other amenities.
- One of the special feature of these hotels is the "**Club Floor**" or "**Tower**" which are separate floors or buildings constructed for very important guests to provide them with more comfortable accommodation and are more personalized and above all provide security as these floors or buildings have restricted entry for the staff as well as visitors to ensure complete privacy to the guests.
- The public areas of these hotels are well decorated with exquisite floorings and furnishings making these hotels a piece of art. There are 24 hours coffee shops, specialty restaurants, banquet halls and conference rooms in these hotels.
- The world class service hotels above all maintain a high ratio of staff members to guests which is generally 1 or even more than that.
- This high ratio of staff members to the guests helps them to offer highly personalized service to the guests ultimately leading to guest satisfaction.

Middle Class Service Hotels

- Middle class service hotels have the largest target market as they cater to the largest segment of the tourists which consist of businessmen, families and free individual travellers.
- Although the middle class service hotels have a good staff to guest ratio of about 0.75, they do not offer extremely personalized service to the guests as it becomes an expensive affair for the guests.
- The guestrooms of these hotels are equipped with the basic amenities and supplies required for a comfortable stay.
- These hotels may also offer uniformed service, food and beverage service and sometimes airport pick-up and drop service.
- These hotels have 24-hour coffee shops, restaurants, meeting rooms, banquet halls and also some recreational services.
- The stays at middle class service hotels are comparatively less expensive than the world class service hotels.

Economy or Limited Service Hotels

- Limited or economy service hotels are increasing in number day by day due to the requirements of the travellers for cheaper accommodations as compared to the world class and middle class service hotels.

- These hotels mainly cater to the budget minded travellers such as families with children, retired persons, tour groups as well as some traveling business people who require clean and inexpensive guestrooms with least amenities required for a modest stay.
- The economy class service hotels have less staff to guest ratio and generally do not provide elaborate food and beverage service and other types of service offered in the world class and middle class service hotels.
- Generally these hotels offer limited food and beverage service, some basic amenities in the guestrooms such as linen and soaps and sometimes may have small meeting rooms for conferences.

CLASSIFICATION OF HOTELS ON THE BASIS OF AFFILIATION

The following are the various types of hotels on the basis of affiliation:

Chain Hotels

- The chain hotels are hotels which are affiliated to one another and are owned or affiliated with other property. E.g. **Taj Group of Hotels**, **Oberoi Group of Hotels** etc.
- The chain hotels enjoy a large economies of scale as:
  - All the properties of the chain enjoy the benefit of advertisement and promotion as it is the brand which is being promoted rather than the individual property.
  - All of them have management information systems, reservation systems, national purchasing contracts, and common architectural designs.

Independent Hotels

- The independent hotels are hotels which do not have any recognizable ownership and also do not have any management affiliation like the chain properties. E.g. **Bristol (Gurgaon)**
- These hotels do not have to obey the rules and regulations which the properties of a chain have to follow to maintain their affiliation.

CLASSIFICATION OF HOTELS ON THE BASIS OF MANAGEMENT

The following are the various types of hotels on the basis of **management**:

Management Contracts

- The concept of management contract originated in **USA** in the year **1970** and was immensely successful thereafter.

- A management contract is a contract which is signed between an individual property owner (who does not have fair knowledge about the management of hotel) and a hotel management company to run the day to day administration and management of the hotel.
- In return, the hotel management company would get a commission called the "**management fee**" which is generally **1% - 8%** of the total revenue generated by the hotel and also sometimes an additional incentive fee which is a percentage of the net profit generated by the hotel property.
- Although a management contract gives total control of the hotel property to the hotel management company, but the legal and financial responsibilities lie ultimately with the owner.
- A chain acting as Management Company for a particular property has total control over the standards and quality of each property and this benefits both the chain as well as the owner.

Franchising

- The concept of franchising also developed in the year **1960** in **USA**.
- In franchising process, an individual entity builds a hotel property and enters into an agreement with a hotel company rather than operating as an individual property. In this case the individual entity is called "**Franchisee**".
- Thus, the hotel company called "**Franchisor**" agrees to grant the right to the franchisee to conduct the business according to the pattern established by the company.
- The individual owner gains a lot form the franchising agreement as the new property enjoys the name and reputation of the franchisor, receives assistance from the company regarding the technical know-how to run the property and above all also enjoys a central reservation system and sales and marketing assistance to run the property.
- The franchisee in return pays a set of fee to the franchisor which includes an initial franchising fee which a lump some amount and then royalty fee, reservation fee and marketing fee which are a percentage of the total room sales.
- Thus the process of franchising was extremely successful business strategy in the world of hospitality.

Referral Groups or Organization

- The concept of referral groups or organization was developed in **USA** in **1960s** by the independent hotel operators in order to compete with the chain hotels.
- In referral groups or organization, the independent hotels join together to form an association for a common purpose.
- Thus an independent hotel gained a broader level of exposure and a number of advantages by joining the referral group.

- Through the referral group, the independent hotel owner could obtain sales promotion benefits similar to those enjoyed by the properties of a chain.
- By joining the referral group, the independent had a brand-name image that could help in the marketing efforts and management of the independent property.
- The independent hotel properties of a referral group could also refer business to each other and thus they help each other in generating revenue.

CHAPTER 6

SUPPLEMENTARY AND INTERMEDIATE ACCOMMODATION

SUPPLEMENTARY ACCOMMODATION

Defining Supplementary Accommodation

Supplementary accommodation includes all the establishments of the unorganized sector of the accommodation industry which do not provide elaborate services that are provided by the organized hotel industry; but these establishments provide the basic services of accommodation and may or may not provide food services and other services.

CLASSIFYING THE SUPPLEMENTARY ACCOMMODATION

Youth Hostels

- Youth hostels generally offer clean and inexpensive shelter to the young people who are either out for exploring the city and the country or traveling independently or in groups on holiday or for educational purposes.
- These are the hospitality establishments where the young people from different nationality, community and castes come together to meet each other and know each other's culture and tradition.
- These establishments are managed by non-commercial organizations whose aim is the development of the youth tourism.
- The youth hostels are well equipped for the young people to prepare their own food and so the comfort in these hostels is modest.

Young Men Christian Association and Young Women Christian Association

- These associations run the chain of youth hostels around the whole world.
- They provide the young people with the basic facilities of food, clean beds and the concept of self service and community life.

Caravan Camping Sites

- These hospitality establishments are also called **camping grounds** or **tourist camps** or **open air hostels**.
- This concept of caravan camping sites initiated in the **Federal Republic of Germany** in the first half of 20th century.
- These camping grounds are well equipped to receive mobile form of accommodation used by tourists.
- Some of the camping grounds even have provision for cooking for the tourists.
- In India, camping sites are proposed to set up along important highways where there is more flow of the international tourists.
- In India, best camping sites are found in places like **Amritsar**, **Khajuraho**, **Hyderabad**, **Aurangabad**, and **Goa**.

Circuit Houses

- The circuit houses are tourist bungalows which cater to the high government officials.
- The accommodation of these houses is provided to the bonafide "**Tourist Card Holders**".
- These houses also provide the service of cooks and attendants and thus have a high degree of efficient management.

Dak Bungalows

- These establishments are constructed primarily to cater to the needs of the traveling officials on government duty.
- These are small rest houses with a limited number of rooms and are situated in areas which are important from the point of view of government duty.
- These establishments are moderately furnished and offer accommodation at a very low rate and also have provision for cooks and attendants.
- These establishments allow stay to the bonafide traveller and government officials holding tourist cards.

Dormitories

- The dormitories cater mainly to the students and low class tourists.
- These are big halls with a large number of individual beds for the travellers.
- Near each bed, there is a rack with a pigeon hole which can be locked. In these holes, the travellers can keep their valuable items safely.
- The toilets and bathrooms in these dormitories are common.

- Although, the dormitories are kept very neat and clean, they lack the element of privacy for the travellers.

Railway Retiring Rooms

- These rooms are owned by the railways and are situated in the railway stations.
- This is a type of accommodation service provided to the passengers holding confirmed and current reservation tickets.
- These rooms may or may not be air-conditioned and have an attached bath with them.
- The charges of these rooms are nominal and reasonable and the meals served to the travellers in the retiring rooms are generally sent from the railway canteen.

Traveler's Lodge

- These are modest hospitality establishments situated in the places of tourist interest.
- The rooms of the traveler's lodges are moderately furnished and may or may not be air-conditioned.
- These are generally self-sufficient establishments and provide rooms with attached bathrooms, dining room, laundry service, parking facilities and postal services and at times room service and car rental services.
- In **1969**, **India Tourism Development Corporation** took over the management of the traveler's lodge and thus accommodation charges in these traveler's lodges became more reasonable.

Holiday Camps

- These camps are situated outside the cities and towns and have the same objectives as those of the camping grounds.
- These camps have a permanent building with provision of entertainment and recreational facilities in addition to the holiday accommodation.
- The guests or the travellers can hire cots, utensils, fans, tents and mugs at these holiday camps.

Private House Hold

- Many people owning houses provide accommodation and sometimes even food to the travellers in return for money.
- A substantial number of bed accommodations are provided by the private households to the travellers.

Holiday and Conference Centres

- The holiday and conference centres are open to the general public groups.
- These holiday and conference centres do provide substantial facilities to the guests and travellers but these facilities need not be available for block arrangements.\

Breakfast Establishments

- These are special establishments which provide overnight accommodation and food to the travellers and the passer-bys and are generally located in towns and cities.
- These establishments are very popular in **U.S.A** and **Europe** and are also called **"Bed and Breakfast"** establishments.

Boarding Houses

- These establishments provide accommodation and meals at regular intervals to the residents.
- These establishments are generally managed by small enterprises for clients staying for certain duration.
- These establishments generally cater to the travellers and students and sometimes service personnel.
- These establishments are also called "**Guest houses**" or "**Private Hostels**".

Tourist Bungalows

- Tourist bungalows are supplementary establishments which provide inexpensive accommodation and other facilities to the travellers and tourists.
- These establishments are located in attractive tourist locations and sites such as near beaches, lakes, rivers etc. and are maintained moderately.
- These establishments generally cater to the middle class tourists and budget travellers and also for the youth of the country and those coming from overseas.
- These establishments generally provide all the basic facilities required to meet the needs of the domestic travellers as well as foreign travellers.
- These establishments are generally small in size with not more than 15 rooms for the travellers. But these establishments have extensive grounds, gardens, lawns, driveways, boating facilities, spacious lounges, extensive furniture and so on.

Forest Lodges

- The forest lodges are a special category of supplementary accommodation and generally cater to the tourist and travellers on a visit to a wild life sanctuary and hence are located adjacent to the forest sanctuaries.

- They are so constructed that they provide clear view of the forests to the residents from the guestrooms and also from the public rooms.
- The ground floors of these establishments generally have the kitchen block, dining hall, lounge reception and parking areas.
- The guestrooms are constructed in such a way so as to provide complete privacy to the guests.
- The lodges have a unique ambience which is reflected from the overall décor of these establishments. But these lodges do not disturb the natural habitats of the animals in the sanctuaries.

INTERMEDIATE ACCOMMODATION

Defining Intermediate Accommodation

Intermediate accommodation includes all the establishments of the semi-organized sector of the accommodation industry which do provide accommodation, food and beverage services and some other services but not as elaborate as the services that are provided by the organized hotel industry.

CLASSIFYING THE INTERMEDIATE ACCOMMODATION

Eurotel

- The Eurotels are very similar to the apartment houses and are very popular in **U.S.A.** and **Europe**.
- An important characteristic of the Eurotels is that they have multiple owners or co-owners and the co-owners can use another apartment in another place and another building through an exchange system between them agreed well in advance.
- These establishments are designed in such a way that the occupants are provided with all the facilities of a pronounced hotel nature.

Apart hotel

- The name of the apart hotels has been derived from apartments which is also a sort of accommodation. This concept of intermediate accommodation was developed in **Spain** in **1970**.
- These building are hotels because hotel services are provided to the guests and yet they are not hotels because the accommodation consists of an apartment which the guests who are also the owners can sell when desired.
- The owners of the apart hotels get full services from the apart hotel management and during their absence allow the hotel management to rent the units.

Villas, Chalet Bungalows

- Villa is an **Italian** concept which is a large country residence with an estate around it or adjacent to it.
- Chalet is a **Swiss** concept which means the farmers' residences which are generally wooden cottages with overhanging roofs. The chalets are generally smaller in size as compared to the villas.
- The Villas and Chalet Bungalows have now been converted into holiday homes where the guests hire accommodation and other facilities required during their stay. Some of them are even open to the people for sale.

Cabins in mountains and alpine clubs

- These types of establishments are generally situated in the mountains and other hilly terrains.
- They cater to the requirements of the mountaineers and tourists on a visit to mountains.
- The tourists stay in these establishments to enjoy mountain climbing and other winter sports such as skiing.

Sanitaria

- Sanitaria are establishments built or constructed and equipped appropriately for persons requiring rest during medical and therapeutic treatment.

Hospices

- The hospices were the primitive type of hotels which were built primarily to cater to the needs of the religious travellers.
- The owners of these establishments offers free accommodation and food to the religious travellers and thus these establishments were totally built for socially noble cause.
- In India, the hospices are known as "**Dharamshalas**".

CHAPTER 7

SOME UNUSUAL TYPES OF HOTELS

1) **Eco hotel** is a type of hotel that has made important environmental improvements to its structure and overall façade in order to minimize its impact on the environment. The basic definition of a green hotel is an environmentally-responsible lodging that follows the practices of green living. These hotels have to be certified green by an independent third-party or by the state they are located in.

An eco hotel must usually meet the following characteristics:

- ❖ Should depend on the natural environment
- ❖ Should have ecological sustainability
- ❖ Should have previous record of contribution to conservation
- ❖ Should have adequate provision of environmental training programs
- ❖ Should Incorporate cultural considerations
- ❖ Should have provision of an economic return to the local community

2) **Garden hotels** are hotels which have converted from large private residences having gardens designed by famous garden designers or are particularly notable for their gardens. Alternative uses have had to be found for castles, palaces, monasteries, mansions and country seats which have become financially unviable as homes, and their conversion into hotels has often been successful.

3) **Pop-up hotel** is a hotel which is temporarily established at a location for a short time before being moved. Such hotels may be built from pre-fabricated modules which are joined together on site or from collapsible structures such as tents or they may be fully mobile, being built on a large vehicle.

4) **Capsule hotel** is a type of hotel found in Japan with a large number of extremely small "rooms" (capsules) with an average size of 2m × 1m × 1.25m which are made of modular plastics of fiberglass. These capsules are stacked side by side and two units top to bottom, with steps providing access to the second level rooms. Luggage is stored in a locker, usually somewhere outside of the hotel. Washrooms are communal and most hotels include restaurants and other entertainment facilities.

5) **Destination hotel** is a type of hotel whose location, facilities and amenities make the hotel itself a destination for tourists, rather than merely a convenient place to stay while traveling through or visiting the area for other reasons. The destination hotels have extremely well designed and beautiful rooms, fine dining restaurants, recreational and entertainment and overall has a beautiful garden with stunning landscaping.

6) **Ice hotel** is a typical hotel which is a temporary structure and is made up of snow , sculpted blocks of ice, and some steel framing. Their lobbies are often filled with ice sculptures, and food and beverages are specially chosen for the circumstances. All of the ice hotels are reconstructed every year, and are dependent upon constant sub-freezing temperatures during construction and operation.
7) **Tree hotels** are hotels which are built with living trees as structural elements.
8) **Bunker hotels** are former nuclear bunkers transformed into hotels and are found in Switzerland.
9) **Cave hotels** are hotels built into natural cave formations, some with rooms underground.
10) **Underwater hotels** are special hotels which are constructed under the water and requires scuba diving for the guests to get access to the rooms.

UNIT – II
HOTEL ORGANIZATION AND THE ROOMS DIVISION

UNIT – II

HOTEL ORGANIZATION AND THE ROOMS DIVISION

LEARNING OBJECTIVES

- ❖ To Study the Concept of Hotel Organization.
- ❖ To Study the Various Operational Divisions of a Hotel.
- ❖ To Study the Importance of Rooms Division of Hotel.
- ❖ To Study the Duties and Responsibilities of Rooms Division Manager.

CHAPTER 1

THE HOTEL ORGANIZATION

DEFINING HOTEL MANAGEMENT

The people authorized by a hotel's owner to represent his or her interests are called "**hotel management**". In small properties, hotel management maybe represented by one person, whereas in big hotels the hotel management maybe represented by many persons.

The hotel management guides the daily operations and regularly gives news about the overall financial status of the hotel to the owner of the hotel.

The hotel management formulates the various policies of the organization and sets standard operating procedures for the various divisions and departments.

The major responsibility of a hotel management includes planning, organizing, coordinating, staffing, directing, controlling, and evaluating the overall activities of the hotel.

The top official of a single property is called the "**general manager**". The **general manager** supervises the overall functioning of the hotel and reports to the **board of directors** of the hotel. The **resident manager**, the **assistant general manager** and other departmental heads help him.

In chain hotel organizations, the management is usually the responsibility of the district, area, or regional executives and above all the board of directors.

Thus, with the help of efficient and well qualified staff; the hotel organization functions effectively and gives valuable guest services and earns revenue and profit at large.

DEFINING ORGANIZATION CHART AND ITS APPLICATION IN HOTELS

An "**organization chart**" is a schematic representation of the relationships between positions within an organization.

An organization chart shows where each position fits in the overall organization, as well as where the divisions of responsibility and the lines of authority lie.

"**Solid lines**" on the chart indicate the direct-line accountability. "**Dotted lines**" indicate the relationship that involve a high degree of cooperation and communication, but not a direct relationship.

An organizational chart should be flexible and should be reviewed and revised annually. Employee responsibility may change with the individuals assuming more duties depending on their strengths and qualifications.

The organizational structure depends on various factors such as the size of the hotel and the availability of the various facilities in the hotels such as restaurants, banquet halls, and conference centers.

Thus an organization chart clearly reflects the line of authority in an organization and thus helps in achieving the mission and goals of an organization at large.

CHAPTER 2

THE DIVISIONS OF A HOTEL

THE VARIOUS FUNCTIONAL DIVISIONS OF A HOTEL

Rooms Division

- The "**rooms division**" consists of departments and personnel essential for providing the services guests during their stay. In most of the hotels, this is the only division which collects the most revenue by selling guestrooms.
- The following are the main departments under the rooms division:
  - Front Office
  - Housekeeping
  - Uniformed Services

Food and Beverage Division

- The hotel's "**food and beverage division**" generally ranks second after the rooms division in terms of the total revenue.
- This division is responsible for the production of food and beverage and their service to the guests for catering to their needs.
- This division includes the various food and beverage outlets such as the restaurants, coffee shops, lounges etc.
- The food and beverage division also supports other hotel functions such as the room service, catering and the other banquet functions.
- Catered functions such as wedding and anniversaries, may also provide significant revenue opportunities for the food and beverage division.

Sales And Marketing Division

- The "**marketing and sales division**" is one of the most important divisions of a hotel since they are involved in the four main responsibilities: **sales**, **convention service**, **advertising** and **public relation**.

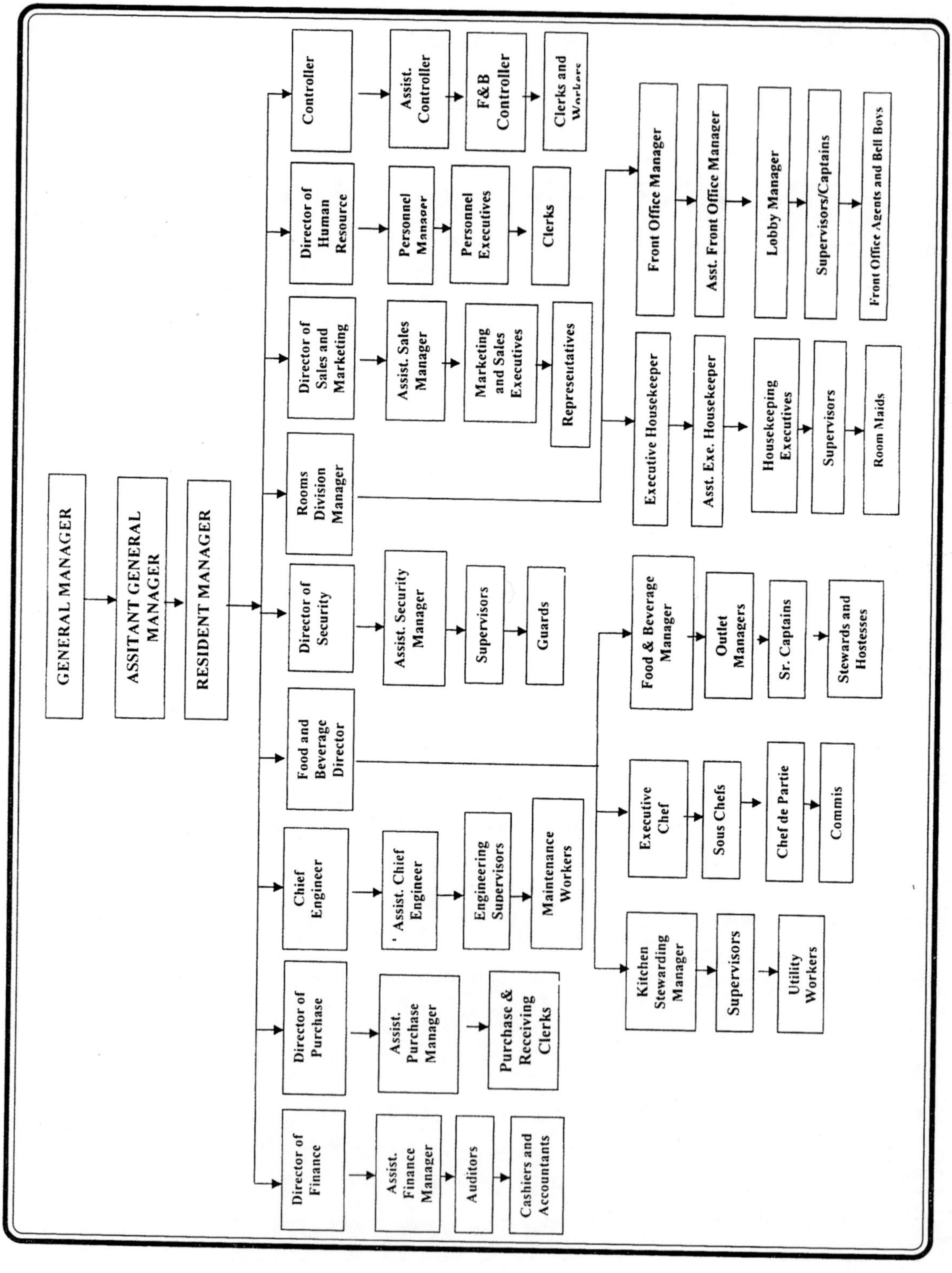

Fig. 2.1: Organizational Hierarchy of a Large Hotel

- The marketing employees of a hotel attract guests towards the hotel, research the marketplace, competing products and guests' needs and their satisfactions at large.
- Sales staffs on the other hand try to create the sale of the hotel products to guests and groups.

Accounting Division

- The hotel's "**accounting division**" monitors the financial activities of the property.
- The accounting activities typically involve paying pending bills, payment of the salary and wages and preparing various financial reports.
- In addition, the accounting division is also responsible for making the bank deposits, securing the various cash loans and keeping a proper control on the various financial activities of a hotel.

Human Resource Division

- The "**human resource division**" is perhaps the most important division in any organization as this is the only division that deals with the manpower planning, recruitment and selection of staffs for the various departments of a hotel.
- Besides, the human resource division is also responsible for the training and development of the staffs and also keeps a track on their performance during their job and thus awards and punishes them suitably.

Security Division

- The "**security division**" plays a very important part in the hotels, as they are responsible for providing total security to the guests, as security is the most vital factor for the comfortable stay of the guests.
- The security staffs include in-house personnel, contract security officers, or retired police or defense officers.
- Security responsibility may include patrolling the property, monitoring with special equipments and in general ensuring that the guests, visitors as well as the employees feel secure in the hotel.

Engineering and Maintenance Division

- The "**engineering and maintenance department**" is responsible for maintaining the property's structure and grounds, as well as its electrical and mechanical equipments.
- This division also has the responsibility of the maintenance of the swimming pools, sanitation, parking area cleanliness and the fountain operation.

(For Detailed Look of The Hotel Organization, Please Refer Figure 2.1).

CHAPTER 3

AN INTRODUCTION TO THE ROOMS DIVISION OF A HOTEL

The "**Rooms Division**" of a hospitality property is a very important active and revenue generating division and plays a vital role in earning a large amount of revenue for the hotel.

In small hotels, rooms division is generally not found and instead, there are separate departments of front office and housekeeping.

But, in large and very large hotels, the front office and housekeeping departments have been clubbed together to form the "**Rooms Division**".

The Rooms Division generally consists of **three** departments, namely:

Front Office Department

The "**Front Office Department**" consists of various sections that deal with the reservation requests, registration and information services to the guests on their arrival in the hotel.

Housekeeping Department

The "**Housekeeping Department**" also called the "**Accommodation Operations Department**" consists of various sections that deal with the general cleanliness and maintenance of the guestrooms and other public areas of the hotel besides providing valuable guest services such as laundry services.

Uniformed Service Department

The "**Uniformed Service Department**" consists of staffs that provide special uniformed services to the guests such as parking of the vehicles of the guests on their arrival in the hotel, opening the door of the hotel for the guests and special information services.

The **Rooms Division Manager** who is also called the "**RDM**" heads the Rooms Division.

The **Rooms Division Manager** is assisted by the **Front Office Manager** for managing the operations of the front office department and is also assisted by the **Executive Housekeeper** for managing the operations of the Housekeeping Department.

As the Rooms Division contributes about 2/3rd of the revenue earned by most of the hotel from the sale of the guestrooms, the division has a great importance in the overall profitability of the hotel.

Thus, most of the large and very large hotels around the world who earn a large amount of revenue from the sale of the guestrooms have a well organized rooms division consisting of front office, housekeeping and uniformed service with a sound and strong brigade of managers, supervisors and grass root level employees who are well committed to improve the overall performance of the division and make it more productive for the entire hotel property.

(For Detailed Look of The Rooms Division, Please Refer Figure 2.2).

Front Office Department

- To sell guestrooms, register guests, and assign guestrooms.
- To coordinate the various guest services.
- To maintain an accurate room status.
- To handle the complaints of the guests.
- To maintain the guest accounts and monitor the credit limits of the guests.
- To route the various incoming calls of the guests though the telephone exchange
- To generate the various management reports required for assessing the overall performance of the hotel.

Housekeeping Department

- The housekeeping department is one of the most important departments of the rooms division.
- This department is responsible for the general up keeping and maintenance of the various guestrooms of a hotel.
- This department is also responsible for the cleanliness and maintenance of the various other public areas within a hotel such as banquet halls, the various offices, and lobby as well as the various conference halls of the hotel.
- The housekeeping department also provides a large number of other services to the guests such as evening service, valet service and laundry and dry-cleaning services.

Uniformed Service Department

Bell Attendants	:	Persons who provide baggage service between the lobby area and the guestroom.
Door Attendants	:	Persons who provide baggage service and traffic control at the hotel entrance.

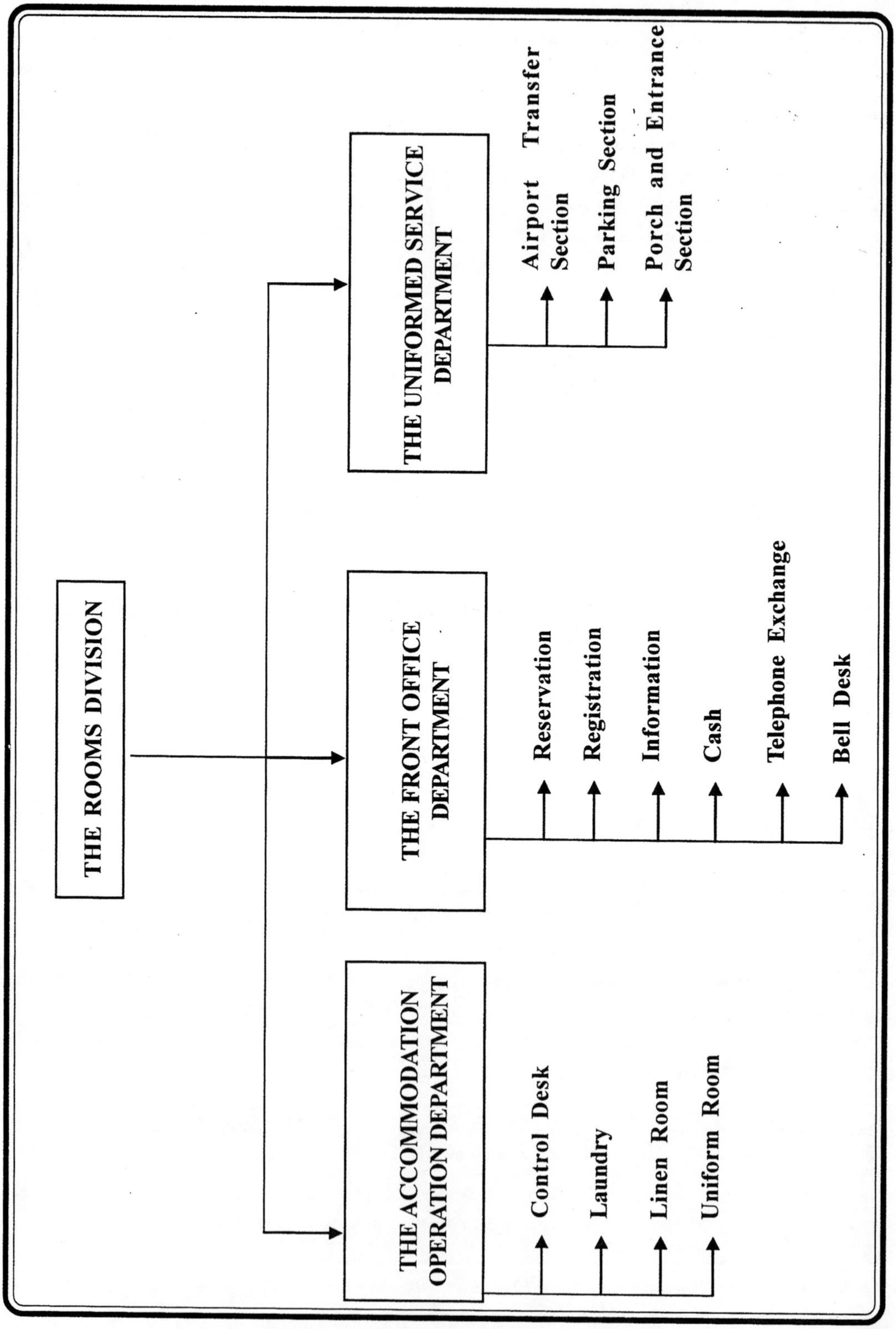

Fig. 2.2: The Rooms Division and its Departments

Valet Parking Attendant	:	Persons who provide parking service for the guests automobile.
Transportation Personnel	:	Persons who provide transportation services for the guests.
Concierges	:	Persons who assist the guests by making restaurant reservations, arranging for transportation, and getting tickets for theatres, sporting or other special events.

CHAPTER 4

THE ROOMS DIVISION MANAGER

- The "**Rooms Division Manager**" is the head of the Rooms Division and is so the ultimate boss of the front office department.
- The Room Division Manager manages the operations of the Front Office, Housekeeping and Uniformed Service Department.

JOB DESCRIPTION OF ROOMS DIVISION MANAGER

Job Position Title : ROOMS DIVISION MANAGER

Job Category : Managerial

Reports To : General Manager

Position Summary : Directly supervises and manages all the front office staff and ensures the proper completion of all the activities of the front office. Co-ordinates intra-departmentally as well as interdepartmentally with in the hotel for the proper achievement of the goals and mission of the hotel.

Hours of Operation : Eight hour shift each day or according to the policy of the hotel management.

Duties and Responsibilities

- Actively participates in the recruitment and selection of the front office personnel.
- Prepares the working schedules of the front office supervisors and other executives with in the department.
- Supervises the working of the executives as well as other staff in each shift. Keeps an accurate track of the amount of contribution of the front office department in the total business of the hotel.
- Prepares monthly and annual forecasts of the total revenue to be generated by the front office from the sale of rooms.
- Operates the front office department within the allotted budget for the department.
- Resolves all the guest complaints and problems effectively and follows up the same.

Educational Qualification	:	Four years Degree or Three years Diploma in Hotel Management and Catering Technology from a recognized university or an institute.
Experience	:	Minimum five years of hotel experience with two years experience as a front office supervisor.

UNIT – III
FRONT OFFICE AND ITS SECTIONS

UNIT – III

FRONT OFFICE AND ITS SECTIONS

LEARNING OBJECTIVES

- ❖ To Understand The Concept of Front Office.
- ❖ To Understand And Study The Functions Performed By The Front Office Department of A Hotel.
- ❖ To Understand The Various Sections of The Front Office Department.
- ❖ To Study The Job Description of The Personnel Involved In The Overall Management of The Front Office - Department of A Hotel.
- ❖ To Understand The Essential Qualities That Should Be Present In A Front Office Personnel.
- ❖ To Gather Information About Various Equipments Used In Front Office Operations.
- ❖ To Gather Information About The Various Room Categories, Rates and Plans Offered In Hotels Around The World.

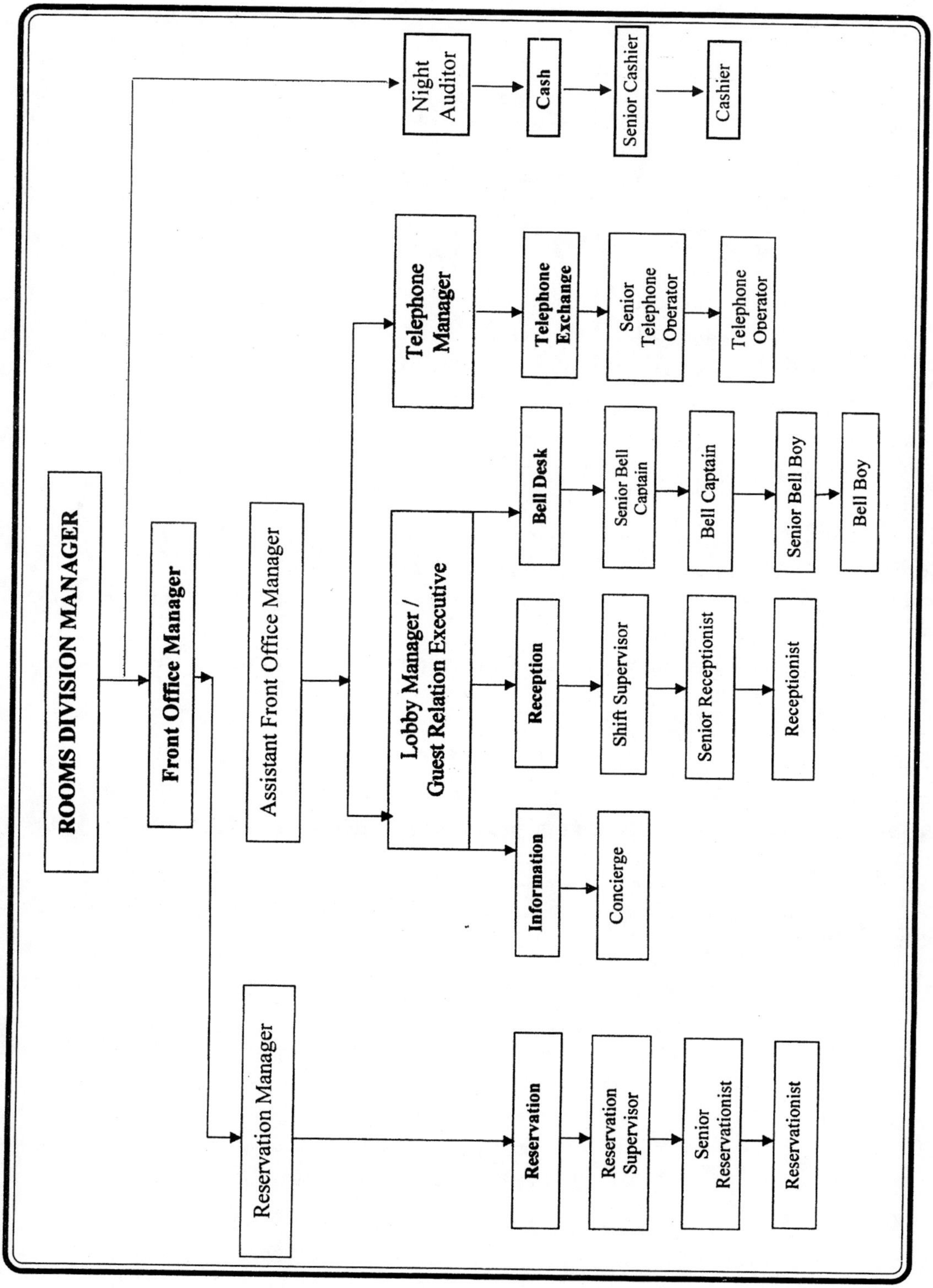

Fig. 1.1: Herarchy of the Front Office Department of a Large Hotel

CHAPTER 1

AN INTRODUCTION TO THE FRONT OFFICE

DEFINING FRONT OFFICE OF A HOTEL

- Front Office can be defined as "a front of the house department located around the foyer and the lobby area of a hospitality property".
- Hence as these departments are located around the foyer area of the hotel and are visible to the guests, patrons and visitors, they are collectively called "Front Office".
- Front office is one of the major operational and revenue producing departments of the hotel which generates two third of the revenue earned by a hotel from the sale of the guestrooms.
- Front office is involved in providing valuable services to the guests during the entire guest cycle consisting of Pre-arrival, Arrival, Occupancy and Departure.

(For A Detailed Study of the Hierarchy of the Front Office Department of a Large, Small and Medium Hotel, see Figure 1.1, 1.2 and 1.3).

DIFFERENCE BETWEEN THE TERM "FRONT OFFICE" AND "RECEPTION"

The Front Office

- The term "**front office**" is best explained by reference to the physical layout of hotels of varying size.
- In a world class hotel, it may be seen that a large number of departments grouped around the **foyer area** of the hotel to deal with the guests not only on arrival and departure but also throughout their stay.
- Because they are situated in the **foyer area**, which is easily accessible to the guests, for convenience they are grouped together under the term "**front office**".

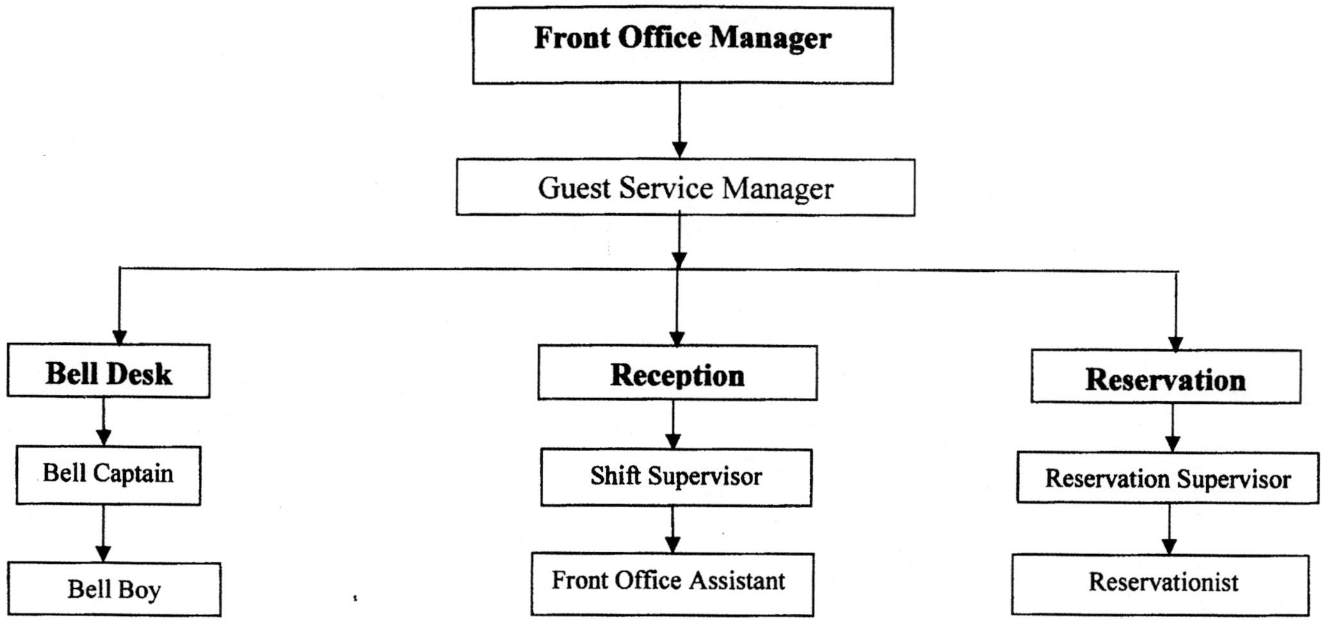

Fig. 1.2: Herarchy of the Front Office Department of a Medium Sized Hotel

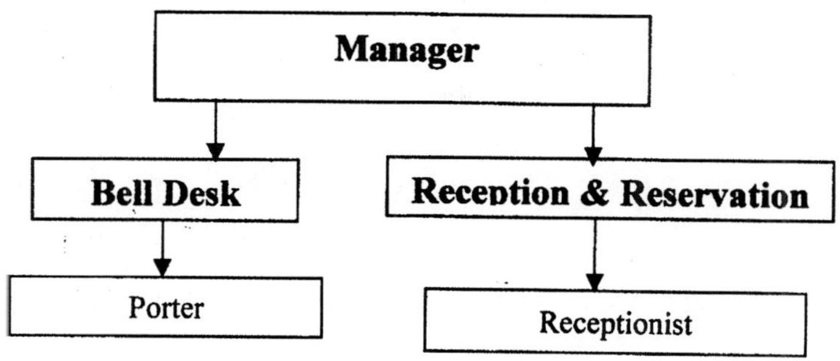

Fig. 1.3: Herarchy of the Front Office Department of a Small Hotel

The Reception Desk

- The "**reception desk**" is one small part of the total front office and therefore in a world class type and size of hotel, forms a single department within the complete front office.
- But in small hotels with less strength of staffs, there may be only one or two staffs in this department dealing with the guests during their arrival, departure and stay. So, it will be wise to group them under the term "**reception**".

CHAPTER 2

FUNCTIONS PERFORMED BY FRONT OFFICE

THE VARIOUS FUNCTIONS OF THE FRONT OFFICE

Receiving and Processing Reservations

- The front office plays a vital role in the receiving and processing of reservation requests from the guests.
- Reservations are also very detailed and taken for many different lengths of time, so they must be recorded accurately as mistakes may be extremely embarrassing and could irritate the guests.

Welcoming the Arriving Guests

- The front office also performs the important responsibility of welcoming the guests on their arrival at the hotel property.
- By carrying this task out the guests coming to the hotel property with or without reservation will feel relaxed and at ease which would result in creation of a positive image of the hotel in the minds of the guests.

Filling of the Arrival and Departure Register

- The legal formality of registration must be fulfilled by the receptionist who sees that all customers supply the details required for a record that may be inspected by the police from time to time.
- Useful marketing about the guests as elicited from the guests are noted down in the arrival and departure register which includes his personal and financial information.

Providing Information Services

- The reception desk is the focus of the hotel to many guests and therefore the receptionists should be able to answer all types of enquiries not only about the hotel but also about the surrounding area and its activities.

- Most of the hotels nowadays have a concierge desk in which useful information about the hotel and about the city is provided to the guests.

Preparing and Updating the Folios of the Guest

- The bill that is presented to a guest on departure involves many items of expenditure that have been incurred by the customers in the different departments of the hotel right throughout their stay.
- Thus, all these transactions between the hotel and the guests have to be properly recorded on to one bill accurately so that the guest is neither overcharged nor undercharged.
- Billing must be carried out swiftly so that the guest's bill is always instantly ready should the guest wish to check-out.

Dealing with Complaints and Handling Them

- The front office also plays a vital role in handling the complaints of the guests during their stay in the hotel.
- The receptionist must therefore be prepared to handle all types of complaint, sometime from the customers who will be in an emotional state of mind and should try to solve the complaint with his skills and techniques.

Marketing and Selling the Hotel

- The front office also plays an important role in the marketing and selling of the hotel and its facilities at large.
- The receptionists should not only be able to sell the rooms but they must also be aware of the facilities of the other departments within the hotel so that they are able to sell them effectively.
- This is known as "**in house sales**" and is a means of encouraging guests to make use of the hotel's facilities such as the restaurant.

Providing Security Services

- Hotels may have several different types of security problems which receptionists must be aware of and prepared to play their parts towards preventing.
- They will be keen to see that customers pay for their stay at the establishment and will operate a deposit system so that less customer leave the hotel without paying their bill.
- They will operate a safe custody system so that the guests may leave their valuables and they may well operate the room key systems, sometimes with the benefit of computerized keys, ensuring that only the correct guest receive the key to his or her bedroom.

Communication And Coordination With Other Departments

- Communication is extremely essential for the proper co-ordination between the various departments of a hotel and thus for the efficient service of the hotel at large.
- As reception is the department that is recording the guest's requirements when they make their reservations it is up to the staff there to inform the other departments of the hotel of the details and the state of the business.
- The reception also contains all the means of communication, so logically it becomes the co-ordination center of the business.

Maximising Occupancy Through Revenue Management

- Occupancy is a statistical term used to describe how full or occupied are the rooms in the hotel. One of the major aims of reception is to maximize the number of rooms sold therefore bringing in as much revenue to the business as possible.
- The front office applies useful revenue management strategies to maximize the sales of the guestrooms of the hospitality property during the period of low sales as well as during the period of high sales.

CHAPTER 3

COMPONENTS OF FRONT OFFICE

THE MAJOR SECTIONS OF FRONT OFFICE

Reservation

- The "**reservation section**" is a very important section of front office as this section deals with the important job of booking rooms for the free individual traveller guests as well as groups.
- The staffs of the reservation department take bookings from the guest through various ways such as letters, fax, telephones as well as e-mail.
- The staffs of the reservation department maintain accurate room inventory information and also maintain an up-to-date inventory list of the available rooms for the various dates.
- The reservation staffs also take various group bookings such as airline crew bookings as well as other corporate group bookings and thus earn valuable revenue for the hotel.

Reception Or Registration

- The "**reception**" or the "**registration department**" is one of the most important sections of the front office as this staff of this section remains in direct contact with the guest right from the time of their arrival till their time of departure.
- The reception staffs welcome the guests on their arrival at the hotel and register them in the hotel and assign guestrooms to the guests in the hotel.
- The reception staffs assign rooms to guests coming with reservations as well as guests coming without reservation.
- The reception staffs also deal with the various problems of the guests during their stay at the hotel.
- Thus the reception staff maintain a thorough guest contact during the stay of the guest at the hotel in order to ensure that the guest do not face any sort of problems during their say at the hotel.

Cash

- The "**cash section**" of the front office also plays an important role as this section maintains the various accounts of the guest during their stay at the hotel.
- The cash section of the front office ensures that all the expenditure incurred by the guests during their stay at the hotel is properly recorded in the accounts of the guests.
- The cash section also ensures that the various accounts of the guest are accurate and complete regularly by the process of night.
- The cash section also prepares various reports such as daily operations report, occupancy report as well as manager's report and various other reports important from the point of management.

Bell Desk

- The "**bell desk**" is also an important department which is generally included as a section in the front office of the hotel.
- This is also a very important section of the front office as the bell attendants are the first staffs with who the guests are in contact the moment they enter the lobby of the hotel.
- The bell attendants help the guests to in the transportation of the luggage from the lobby to the guestrooms as well as from the guestrooms to the lobby during the arrival and departure of the guests.
- The bell attendants also perform various other important duties such as supplying magazines and newspapers to the guestrooms as well as paging the names of the guests on paging boards in the lobby as well as in other public areas.
- The bell attendants also sell stamps to the guests on demand as well as do various jobs for the guests within the hotels as well as outside of the hotel on request.

Telephone Exchange

- The "**telephone exchange**" is also a very important section of the front office as it performs the important job of directing the various incoming as well as outgoing telephone calls of the hotel.
- The telephone exchange staffs also compile the bills of the guests incurring various STD as well as ISD call charges.
- The telephone exchange also performs the very important function placing the various wake-up calls for the guests on request.

Information

- The "**information section**" is also an important part of the front office as this section plays an important role in providing valuable information to the guests regarding the hotel, city and the country at large.
- The information section has a concierge as its important part whose main duty is to provide various travel related information as well as other types of information to the guests as well as booking tickets for the guests in various concerts as well as various other important events going around in the city.

CHAPTER 4

MANAGEMENT TEAM OF FRONT OFFICE

JOB DESCRIPTION OF FRONT OFFICE MANAGER

Job Position Title	:	FRONT OFFICE MANAGER
Job Category	:	Managerial
Reports To	:	Rooms Division Manager/General Manager
Position Summary	:	Directly supervises and manages all the front office staff and ensures the proper completion of all the activities of the front office. Co-ordinates intradepartmentally as well as interdepartmentally with in the hotels for the proper achievement of the goals and mission of the hotel.
Hours of Operation	:	Eight hour shift each day or according to the policy of the hotel management.

Duties and Responsibilities

- ❖ Actively participates in the recruitment and selection of the front office personnel.
- ❖ Prepares the working schedules of the front office supervisors and other executives with in the department.
- ❖ Supervises the working of the executives as well as other staff in each shift.
- ❖ Keeps an accurate track of the amount of contribution of the front office department in the total business of the hotel.
- ❖ Prepares monthly and annual forecasts of the total revenue to be generated by the front office from the sale of rooms.
- ❖ Operates the front office department within the allotted budget for the department.
- ❖ Resolves all the guest complaints and problems effectively and follow ups the same.

Educational Qualification	:	Four years Degree or Three years Diploma in Hotel Management and Catering Technology from a recognized university or an institute.
Experience	:	Minimum five years of hotel experience with two years experience as a front office supervisor.

JOB DESCRIPTION OF LOBBY MANAGER/GUEST RELATION EXECUTIVE

Job Position Title	:	LOBBY MANAGER/GUEST RELATION EXECUTIVE
Job Category	:	Managerial
Reports To	:	Front Office Manager or General Manager
Position Summary	:	Supervises the overall functioning of the various sections of the front office including reception, reservation, bell desk and telephone exchange.
Hours of Operation	:	Eight hour shift each day or according to the policy of the hotel management.

Duties and Responsibilities

- Takes the attendance of the front office staff and checks their grooming at the beginning of each shift.
- Trains the various staff of the front office in providing guest service.
- Welcomes the VIP guests with garlands and offering welcome drinks on their arrival.
- He maintains a detailed knowledge of the room status and reservation status and answers the various e-mails and letters of queries from the guest.
- He also keeps a detailed knowledge of the various services and facilities available in the hotel so as to inform the guests about the same.
- He anticipates the various incidents of guest dissatisfaction and tries to solvethe problems of the guests within the policy laid down by the hotel management.

Educational Qualification	:	Four years Degree or Three years Diploma in Hotel Management and Catering Technology from a reputed and affiliated university or college.
Experience	:	Minimum two years of hotel experience with one year experience as a front office supervisor.

CHAPTER 5

ATTRIBUTES OF FRONT OFFICE PERSONNEL

A High Sense of Personal Grooming

- ❖ Uniforms of the front office personnel must be clean and neatly pressed.
- ❖ Hairs of the front office personnel should be well groomed.
- ❖ Nails of the front office personnel should be properly trimmed
- ❖ It is essential for the front office personnel to take a bath regularly and use a soft deodorant.
- ❖ Jewellery should be restricted for the ladies and should be banned for males.

A High Sense of Personal Hygiene

- ❖ The front office personnel should have a clean appearance that is essential for the proper projection of good image of the hotel in front of the hotel.

A Strong Feeling of Self Confidence

- ❖ It is extremely essential that front office personnel should have the self confidence to meet the guests coming from different countries and different culture and language and make them feel comfortable in the hotel.

Excellent Communication Skills

- ❖ The front office personnel should be well versed with English which is the official language of the world and should be also aware of the local language of the place where the hospitality property is located.
- ❖ Hence, it becomes important for the front desk agent to know a foreign language in order to deal with the guests coming from different countries.

Diplomatic in Approach

- It is again an essential quality of the front office personnel to have a diplomatic approach towards the guests in order to diffuse any type of tension, which may occur due to the poor service of the hotel.

A Good Memory and Ability to Remember Names and Faces of Guests

- It is rare attribute present in very few of the front staffs and this ability differentiates the good front office staff from the average because the guests feel extremely happy if they are being addressed by their names.

Good Manners

- This is supposed to be the basic quality that should be present in all the staffs of the hospitality industry.
- Good manners are the essence of hospitality and will thus attract more guests and will thus maintain the good will of the hotel and the industry at large.
- Thus, good gestures on behalf of the front office personnel help in creating a good image on the guests coming to the hospitality property.

Physical Fitness

- Front office operations require that the front office personnel should be physically fit and active so that they are able to serve the guest with smile and pleasure.

Improvisation and Decision Making Ability

- The front office staff should have the ability to improvise and solve the various problems of the guests requiring quick decision making ability and at the same time take care that the interest of the organization is not at stake.
- Thus, rapid improvisation skills help the front office agent to making quick decisions according to the demand of the situation.

CHAPTER 6

EQUIPMENTS USED IN FRONT OFFICE OPERATIONS

EQUIPMENTS USED IN FRONT OFFICE

- A large number of factors play a very important role in the choice of equipments to be kept or installed in the front office of a hotel to carry out the day to day administration and management of the department.
- The factors include the system of operations prevailing in front office, the size of the hotel, the level of automation and the budget of the hotel.
- A big hotel having a high budget will definitely choose an automated front office with fully automated or computerized equipments.
- A big hotel having limited budget will opt for a semi-automated front office with semi-automated equipments.
- A small hotel with limited budget will choose a non-automated system of front office operations with non-automated front office equipments.

LIST OF MANUAL EQUIPMENTS USED IN FRONT OFFICE OPERATIONS

Room Rack

- The "**room rack**" is a large front office equipment located just behind the front desk.
- The room rack is a wooden framework designed and contains a metallic array of pockets which contain a large number of room rack slips for showing the reservation and housekeeping status of each guestroom of a property.
- The room rack slip contained in the metallic pockets shows the type of room (Double, Twin, King, Suite), the occupancy status of the guestroom (Occupied, Vacant, Not Cleared) and the name of the guest registered in the guestroom.
- The current occupancy status of the guestrooms is indicated by the colored strips inserted in the pockets of the room rack.

- It is the joint effort of the front desk and housekeeping to timely update the room rack in order to have an accurate room status position.

Information Rack

- The "**information rack**" is another important devise positioned in the front desk and is used by the front desk agent to track the various in-house guests of the hotel.
- The information is a revolving devise that contains information about the various guests presently registered in the hotel with the name of the guests alphabetically arranged in the rack and the information taken from the upper portion of the folios of the guests.
- The information contained in the information rack are name of the guest, number and type of room occupied, rate of the guestroom, date of arrival and departure and the billing instructions.

Mail and Message Rack

- The "**mail and message rack**" is a wooden framework containing an array of pigeonholes with each pigeonhole used to store the various mails and messages received for an in-house guest.
- Previously, the mail and message rack used to contain the keys of the guestrooms in the pigeonholes and was thus called the "**mail, message and key rack**".
- But nowadays, the mail rack has been isolated from the key rack and has been moved behind scenes to present a more professional appearance and at the same time ensuring the security of the mails and messages of the guests of the hotel.

Key Rack Or Key Drawer

- The "**key rack**" or the "**key drawer**" is an important front office equipment located underneath the counter of the front desk.
- The key rack as the name suggests, is a wooden or metallic framework containing an array of slots used for keeping the keys of the guestrooms in sequential order of the guestrooms present in the hotel.
- This rack is maintained by the front desk in hotels where metal or hard keys are used and is thus an essential front desk equipment for such hotels.

Folio Well or Folio Bucket

- A "**folio well**" or "**folio bucket**" is also an important equipment used in the front desk cash section.
- This equipment contains a large number of slots where the folios are arranged sequentially according to the room number.

- The folio well is used by the front office cashier to store and track the folios of the various registered guests of the hotel and is used to maintain the folios safely for future use and reference.

LIST OF SEMI-AUTOMATED EQUIPMENTS USED IN FRONT OFFICE OPERATIONS

Posting Machine

- The "**accounting posting machine**" is a very essential equipment used in the semi-automated front office system for posting the various charges in the accounts of the guests.
- The posting machine is generally used to calculate the totals of the guest accounts, departments and transactions.
- The mechanical features of the accounting posting machine are arranged in such a logical sequence that the job of posting the charges into the various guest accounts becomes very easy.
- The line pick-up keys ensures that the posting machine is not over printing a line as the operator indicates where the accounting posting machine should start the calculation and should start printing.
- There is a key pad in the account posting machine which is used by the cashier or the operator to enter the room numbers of the guests, department key (*e.g. room, tax, food*) and also the type of transaction (*e.g. debit, credit, transfer*)

Cash Register

- The "**cash register**" is a semi-automated equipment used optionally by the front desk.
- The cash register is generally used by the front desk to record the various sales of sundries at the front desk such as stamps, newspapers, candy etc.
- The various required mechanical features present in the cash register include a key pad, category key (*stamps, newspapers, candy*) and amount entering key.

Wake-up Devices

- The "**wake-up device**" is a very important device used by the front desk or the telephone exchange of non-automated or semi-automated hotels to remind the staffs of awakening the guests at requested times.
- The most famous and common wake-up device is known as the James Remindo Timer which is an alarm clock with pull-out pins.
- Many hotels also use a simple alarm clock for awakening the guests. The guests' requests for wake-up calls are recorded in a wake-up sheet with the information of time, room number and name of the guest.

- In fully automated systems, the telephone exchange automatically places the various requests of the guests for wake-up calls by automatic-voice-recorded wake-up messages. This feature is of great help when many guests have to be woken up at the same time in the hotel.

Credit Card Imprinter

- The "**credit card imprinter**" is is used especially when the guests present credit cards at the time of their arrival or departure to settle their bill.
- The credit card imprinter makes an imprint of the credit card used by the guest as a method of payment.

Typewriter

- The "**typewriter**" is very important semi-automated equipment used for preparing various documents related to the front office operations and also related to the guests.
- The front office employees use typewriters to prepare guest reservation confirmation letter, to prepare the registration card of the guest and also to conduct the other word processing jobs of the department.

LIST OF FULLY-AUTOMATED EQUIPMENTS USED IN FRONT OFFICE OPERATIONS

Credit Card Validator

- The "**credit card validator**" is an automated front office equipment used by the front office cashier to check the validity of the credit card presented by the guest as a mode of payment at the time of arrival or departure of the guest.
- This equipment is a computer terminal linked to a credit card data bank, which holds information concerning the validity of the credit card of the guest.
- The credit card equipment assures the hotel management that the guest has credit balance high enough to cover the projected charges and it also verifies that the card presented by the guest is not a stolen property.

Time Stamping Machine

- The "**time stamping machine**" is a mechanical or an electronic device which is used extensively by the front office of a hotel record the check-in and check-out time of the guests, delivery time of any mail or message for the in-house guests.
- This device imprints the date and time on a piece of paper either electronically or mechanically and is thus an important equipment for carrying out the operations of the front office leading to guest satisfaction.

Fax Machines

- The full form of **FAX** machine is "**Facsimile Automated Xerox**" machine and is an important electronic equipment used in the front desk for communication purposes.
- This is a facsimile reproduction equipment that operates through telephone lines and are used extensively by the front office to receive and send official documents important from the point of view of the guest or the hotel management at large.
- While sending a fax message, the operator dials the destination fax machine number and then sends the fax message by inserting the message page in the machine.
- It is important that the destination fax machine should be switched on when the fax message is sent from the hotel.

Call Accounting System

- A "**call accounting system**" is a fully computerized telephone system which allows the proper billings of the outgoing calls of the guests.
- This type of automated telephone system has been introduced in a large number of hotels nowadays due to the reason for providing improved services to the guest.
- The call accounting system is called "**APBX**" or the "**Automated Private Branch Exchange**" and is used in the hotel telephone exchange section of the front office department to automatically trace and bill the outgoing calls made by the guests during their stay at the hotel.

Computer

- All the automated hotels around the world are excessively using computers for the day to day operations, administration and management.
- Computers are also used widely in the front office departments of the hotels for the purpose of reservation, registration, accounting and auditing.
- Computers are efficient to operate and are extremely user friendly and thus help the employees to store and retrieve important data of the guest from time to time to carry out the various guest services.

ILLUSTRATION OF SOME TYPES ROOMS FOUND IN HOTEL

TWIN ROOM

DOUBLE ROOM

CHAPTER 7

KNOWLEDGE ABOUT ACCOMMODATION PRODUCTS

SOME SPECIAL ROOM TYPES AND CATEGORIES AND THEIR ABBREVIATIONS

Single Room (SGL or S)

A "**Single Room**" is a room which has a single bed. This type of room is normally assigned to one person.

Double Room (DBL or D)

A "**Double Room**" is a room which has a double or *a* composite bed. This type of room is normally assigned to two persons.

Triple Room

A "**Triple Room**" is a room which is assigned to three persons. It may have two or more beds.

Quad Room

A "**Quad Room**" is a room which is assigned to four persons. It may have two or more beds.

King Room (K)

A "**King Room**" is a room with a king-size bed. It may be occupied by one or more persons.

Queen Room (Q)

A "**Queen Room**" is a room with a queen-size bed. It may be occupied by one or more persons.

HOLLYWOOD TWIN ROOM

TWIN DOUBLE ROOM

TRIPLE ROOM

KING ROOM

QUEEN ROOM

JUNIOR SUITE ROOM

Twin Room (T)

A "**Twin Room**" is a room which has two single beds. This type of room is also normally assigned to two persons.

Twin Double Room

This is a room which has two double beds separated from each other. This type of room is normally assigned to four persons. These rooms are normally assigned to families and are therefore called "**Family Room**".

Hollywood Twin Bed Room

This is a room which has two single beds with a single head board common for both.

Parlor

A "**Parlor**" is a sitting or a living room and generally not used as a bedroom.

Studio Room

A "**Studio Room**" is a parlor with a studio bed or a couch. *(A bed which can be converted into a sofa during the day)*

Suite Room

A "**Suite Room**" consists of a parlor with connected with one or more bedrooms.

Junior Suite Room

A "**Junior Suite Room**" is a large room with a partition separating the living room from the bedroom.

Duplex

A "**Duplex**" is a set of rooms not situated on the level and connected by a staircase. Generally the parlor is at the lower level and the bedroom is at the upper level.

Efficiency Room

A room that has some sort of kitchen facilities attached to it is called an "**Efficiency Room**". These types of rooms are usually found in resorts and residential hotels.

LIVING ROOM OF A SUITE

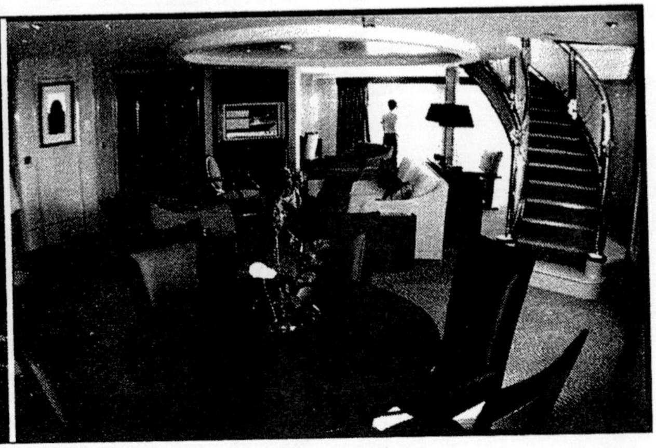

DUPLES SUITE

EFFICIENCY ROOM

LANAI

CABANA

Hospitality Room

A "**Hospitality Room**" is a room which is used by a guest to entertain his own guests and usually charged on an hourly basis.

Penthouse Suite

A "**Penthouse Suite**" is a set of rooms situated on the terrace level part of which may be opened to the sky.

Adjoining Rooms

"**Adjoining Rooms**" are two or more rooms having a common wall but no connecting door in between.

Adjacent Rooms

"**Adjacent Rooms**" are two or more rooms with private connecting doors permitting access between rooms without having to go into the corridor.

Cabana

A "**Cabana**" is a room adjacent to the swimming pool area with or without sleeping facility and has generally facilities to change and having light showers.

Lanai

A "**Lanai**" is a room with a good view. It generally has a balcony overlooking the garden or the swimming pool. These are generally found in resort hotels.

DIFFERENT TYPES OF ROOM RATES USED IN THE HOTEL INDUSTRY

Rack Rate

"**Rack rate**" is the maximum possible room rate which is charged from the guest by the hotel for overnight accommodation.

Discount Rate

"**Discount rate**" is a room rate which is less than the rack rate charged by the hotel from the guests when the hotel gives discounts or concessions on the stay of the guests.

Seasonal Rate

The "**seasonal rate**" is charged from the guests visiting hotels having extreme climatic conditions such as in resorts.

TYPES OF DISCOUNTED RATE

Corporate Rate or Commercial Rate

The rate offered to companies that provide frequent **(CVGR)** business for the hotel or its chain.

Promotional Rate

The rate offered to individuals who may belong to an affinity group such as **American Automobile Association** or **HRACC** or **FHRAI** to promote occupancy.

Incentive Rate

The rate offered to guests in affiliated organizations such as travel agencies and airlines due to potential referral business. The rate may also be offered to promote future business; it is often extended to group leaders, meeting planners, tour operators, and others capable of providing the hotel with additional room sales.

Group Rate

The rate offered to groups, meetings, and conventions using the hotel for their functions.

Family Rates

A rate offered to only family with children sharing the same room.

Package Plan Rate

A rate that includes a guestroom in combination with other events or activities.

Day Rate

This is a special type of room rate which is charged only for the guests who usually check-in and check-out the same day.

Crew Rate

This type of rate is usually charged to the airline crew members who do not stay in the hotels for a long duration.

Weekend Rate

This is a special type of room rate which is charged for the guests who visit the hotels during the week-ends. (*the rate is generally the highest during the week-ends*)

Government Rate

This type of room rate is generally charged by government guest houses and circuit houses to the guest for providing them with overnight accommodation and food. (*the rate is generally lower than the private establishments as the target market is generally the government employees*)

Extra Bed Rate

This type of rate is generally applicable to the families demanding an extra bed for their spouse. It is generally of the rack rate charged by the hotel.

Crib Rate

This type of rate is applicable to the children below 5 years.

MEAL PLANS USED IN THE HOTEL INDUSTRY

1.	**EUROPEAN PLAN (EP)**	:	Room charge + Early Morning Tea.
2.	**CONTINENTAL PLAN (CP)**	:	Room charge + Early Morning Tea + Continental Breakfast.
3.	**AMERICAN PLAN (AP)**	:	Room charge + Early Morning Tea + Breakfast + Lunch + High Tea + Dinner. This plan is also called the "**Full Board Plan or Full Pension**".
4.	**MODIFIED AMERICAN PLAN (MAP)**	:	Room charge + Early Morning Tea + Breakfast / High Tea + Lunch / Dinner.
5.	**BERMUDA PLAN (BP)**	:	Room Charges + Early Morning Tea + American Breakfast.
			This plan is also called the "**Half Board Plan or Semi Pension**"

USES OF THE INTRODUCTION OF THE VARIOUS TYPES OF PLANS IN THE LODGING INDUSTRY

- These plans allow the guest to opt for the types of meals they would like to have in the hotels during their stay.
- These plans make it easier for the hotels to charge the guest on the basis of a package stay.
- These plans are much more cost effective as the guest generally gets a discount on his bill during his or her stay as these plans are much cheaper as compared to having the meals separately in a hotel.

European Plan

- This plan is mostly used in all the types of hotels and especially the city or the down town hotels.
- This plan is the cheapest as it only includes the room charges and early morning tea.
- This plan mainly caters the busy executives and the other commercially important persons who are out of the hotel throughout the day for their business activities.

Continental Plan

- This plan is also called the "**bed and breakfast plan**" as it is mostly used in motels and the bed and breakfast hotels.
- This plan is very cheap as it only includes the room charges, early morning tea and continental breakfast.
- This plan mainly caters the roadside travellers and other transient guests.

Bermuda Plan

- This plan is mostly used in the American motels and other small roadside hotels.
- This plan is the more heavier and expensive than the European and the Continental Plan as it includes the room charges, early morning tea and American breakfast.
- This plan mainly caters the tourists, vacationers and the conference attendees who stay within the hotel throughout the day for their activities.

American Plan

- This plan is mostly used in the resorts and suburban hotels.
- This plan is the most expensive as it includes the room charges, early morning tea, breakfast, lunch, evening tea and dinner.

- This plan mainly caters to the tourists, vacationers and the conference attendees who stay within the hotel throughout the day for their activities.

Modified American Plan

- This plan is mostly used in the resorts and various hotels.
- This plan is cheaper than the American Plan as it includes the room charges, early morning tea, breakfast or evening, lunch or dinner.
- This plan mainly caters to the tourists who are out of the hotel during the day for sight seeing and during the night for night safaris.

UNIT – IV

THE RESERVATIONS SECTION

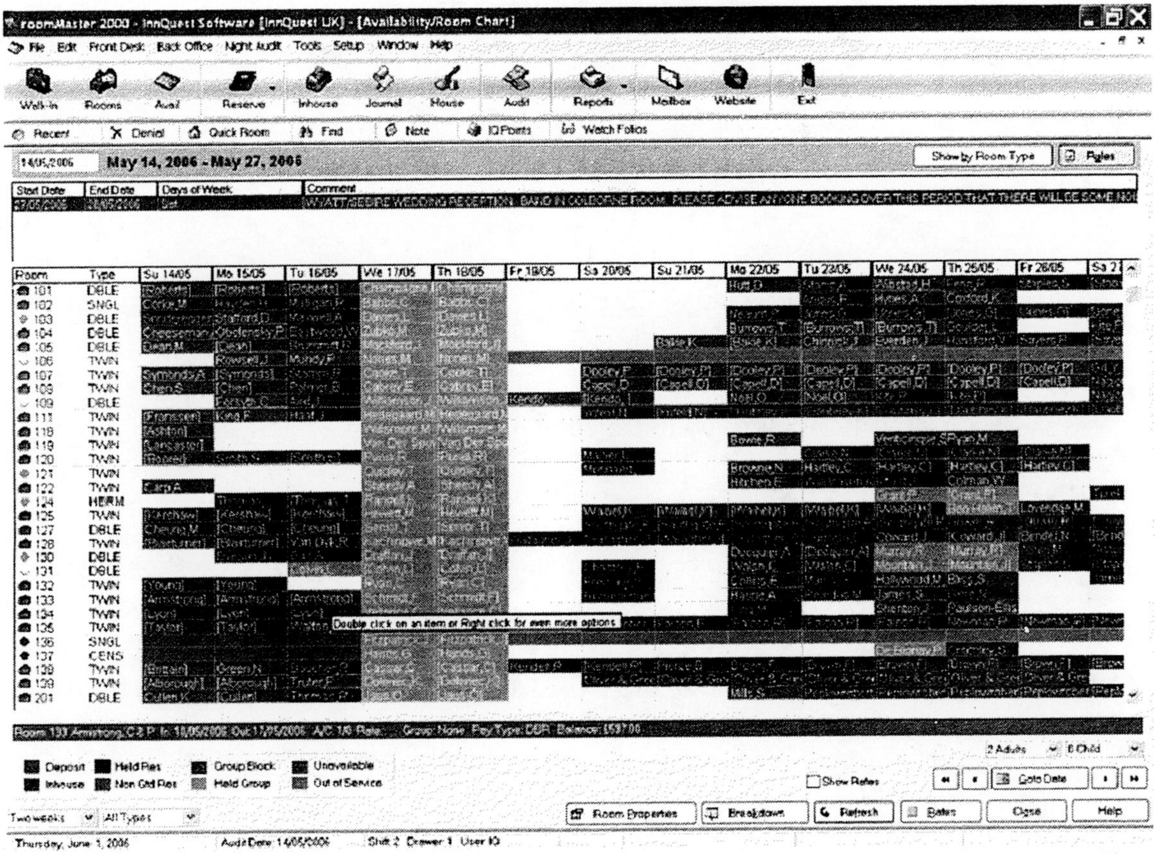

UNIT IV

THE RESERVATIONS SECTIONS

PART A (THEORY)

PART B (PRACTICAL FORMATS)

LEARNING OBJECTIVES

- ❖ To Study The Definition, Process and Sources of Reservation.
- ❖ To Understand The Types of Reservation.
- ❖ To Study About The Staff Working in Reservation Section.
- ❖ To Learn About The Various Formats Used In Reservation Section.

CHAPTER 1

AN INTRODUCTION TO THE RESERVATION SECTION

DEFINITION

The **"Reservation Section"** is a vital part of the front office department of a hotel and it plays an important role in the sale of guestrooms by taking future room bookings and thus generating revenue for the hotel.

ORGANISATION

- The Reservation Manager heads the reservation section.
- He is assisted by the **Senior reservationist** and **Reservationists.**

Reservation Manager

↓

Senior Reservationist

↓

Reservationist

LOCATION

The reservation section is located at the back of the front office in a hotel.

Main Functions of the Reservation Section

- Receiving the reservation request from the guest.
- Checking the room availability for accepting the reservation request.
- To process the reservation request either for accepting or denying the same.
- Communicating the reservation confirmation to the guests and keeping a record of the same.
- Processing reservation modifications and cancellations according to the request of the guests and also according to the availability of guestrooms.
- Ensuring full occupancy of the guestrooms of the hotel by taking future reservations.
- Processing individual and group reservation separately.

Importance of the Reservation Section

- The reservation section gives the hotel a chance to equate the guest inquiry with the rooms' availability and thus, gives the hotel sufficient time to arrange and prepare for the most suitable accommodation for the guests.
- The section also forecasts and gives good indication of the level of business that the hotel might get in future.
- Thus, to a great extent the hotel can forecast the future revenue generation keeping in mind the reservation business.
- The reservation section also helps the hotel in scheduling and reorganizing the staff that the front office and other departments might need for the future period.
- The reservation section also helps the hotel to equate the needs of the guest with the available product.
- Thus, the main importance of the reservation section is that it sells the main perishable product of the hotel i.e. room and increase the chance of revenue earning for the hotel.

CHAPTER 2

MODES OF RESERVATION

MODES OF RESERVATIONS

VERBAL	WRITTEN
e.g. Telephone	e.g. Letter
	Telex
	Fax
	E-mail

VERBAL MODES

The following are the verbal modes in which a reservation request reaches a hotel:

Telephone

- Prospective guests may telephone the hotel directly.
- This is the most common method of direct reservation communications.

WRITTEN MODES

The following are the written modes in which a reservation request reaches a hotel:

Mail

- Written requests for reservations are common for group, tour, and convention business.
- Generally, mail requests are sent directly to the reservation department of the destination property.

Telex, Cable, Fax, E-mail and Others

- Telex is often used to communicate the international reservation requests.
- Cable, fax and other methods of communication account for a small proportion of total reservation transactions.

CHAPTER 3

CHANNELS OR SOURCES OF RESERVATION

The following are the channels and sources of reservation of hotel guestrooms:-

Property Direct

- ❖ The hotels and motels are the main sources or channels of reservation for guests as the guests can directly approach the property for the process of reservation of guestrooms.
- ❖ Thus, the guests can personally visit the hotels and motels for reservation or may even contact these properties through telephone, fax, e-mail etc.

Travel Agents

- ❖ The travel agents are also important channels or sources of reservation for the hospitality properties.
- ❖ The travel agents are intermediary retail agents who sell rooms, airline seats and other products and services to the travellers.

Corporate Travel Departments

- ❖ Most of the big corporate organizations have a separate travel departments consisting of hired professionals who arrange and cater for the travel and accommodation requirements of the travellers.

Hotel Representatives

- ❖ All the hospitality properties have sales representatives who approach various market segments and give the sales presentations of the products and services offered by the hotels.
- ❖ Thus, these sales representatives also generate a large amount of revenue for the hotel.

Tour Operators

- ❖ The tour operators are also intermediary agents who sell accommodations to the travellers.

- The tour operators are wholesalers who purchase the rooms, airline tickets and other products from the various principal suppliers and form a package and finally sell these packages either to the travel agents or to the guest directly.
- Thus, the price quoted by the wholesalers is always less than the price quoted by the travel agents.

Intersell Agencies

- The intersell agencies are multiple product handlers such as hotel rooms, airlines and car rental who act as intermediary agents for the hotels and help these hospitality properties to sell their products such as rooms along with the airline seats which they sell to the travellers.

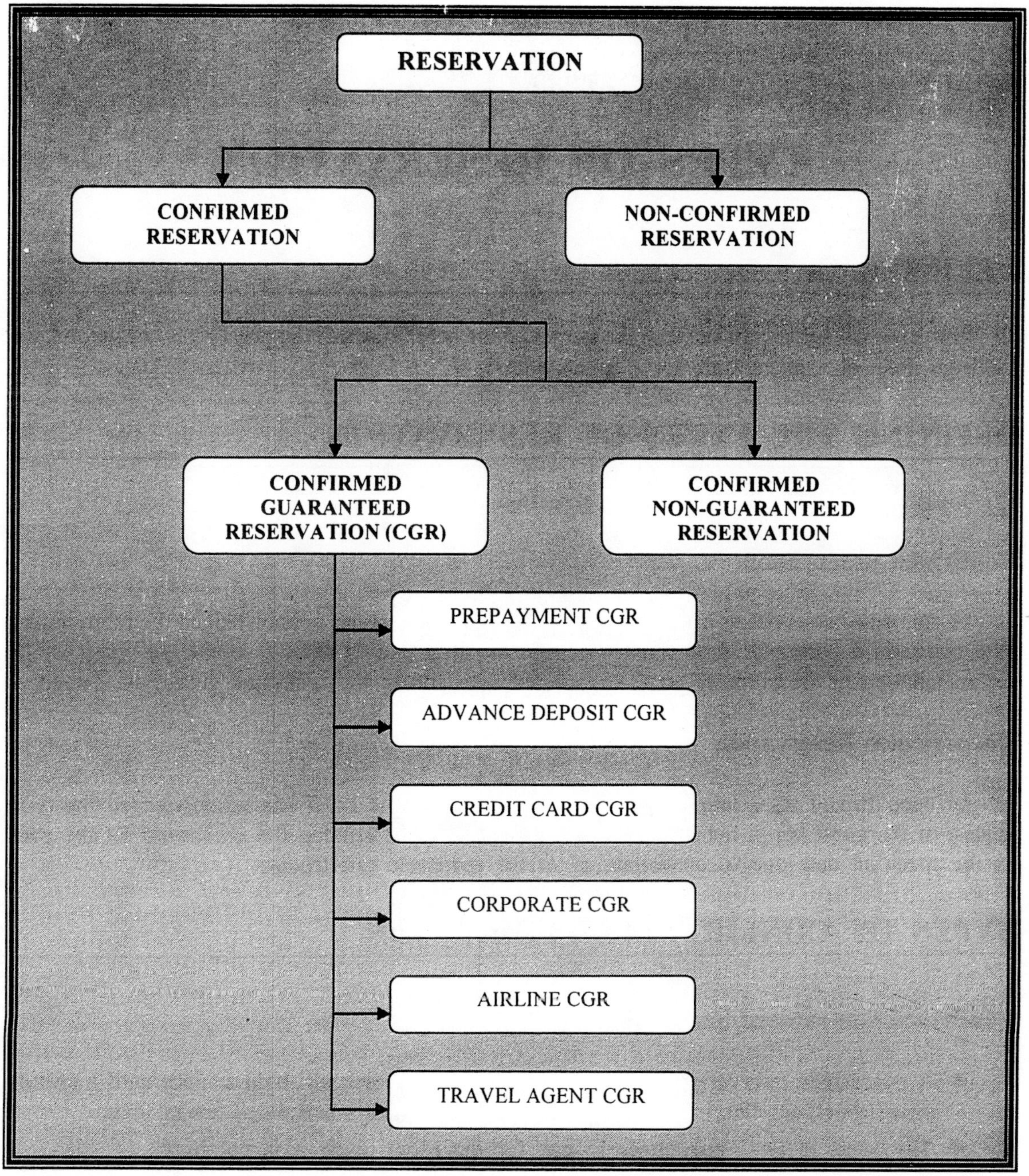

Fig. 4.1: Types of Reservation

CHAPTER 4

TYPES OF RESERVATION

DEFINING RESERVATION

"It is a mutual agreement between the guest and the hotel in which the guest hires accommodation from the hotel at a given time for a given time".

DEFINING THE TYPES OF RESERVATION

Broadly, the reservations have been classified into:

Confirmed Reservation

"A confirmed reservation is a reservation in which the hotel has acknowledged the room request of a guest on a particular date for a specified duration and is able to assure the guest of the accommodation in the property on the requested date and in the requested guestroom category".

Unconfirmed Reservation

An unconfirmed reservation is a reservation in which the hotel has acknowledged the room request of the guest but is not able to assure the guest about holding the guestroom for the guest on the specified date due to unavailability of the requested guestroom.

TYPES OF CONFIRMED RESERVATION

Confirmed Guaranteed Reservation

- A guaranteed reservation assures the guest that the hotel will hold a room until a specific time (check-out time) of the day following the guest's scheduled arrival date.
- The guest in turn, guarantees to pay for the room, even it is not used.
- Thus, the guaranteed reservations provide some protection for the hotel's revenue even in the case of no-show, a situation in which a guest makes a reservation but does not register or cancel.

(For a detailed look on the types of Reservation. See Figure 4.1).

TYPES OF GUARANTEED RESERVATION

Prepayment

- A prepayment guaranteed reservation requires that a payment in full be received before the day of the arrival of the guest.
- This type of reservation is the most desirable form of reservation and is used at the resorts.

Credit Card

- A credit card guaranteed reservation is a type of guaranteed reservation in which a credit card company ensures that the lodging properties will receive payment for the no-shows.

Advance Deposit

- An advance deposit guaranteed reservation requires that the guest should pay the hotel a specified amount of money as deposit (one night's room rent) before arrival.
- Thus, if a guest holding an advance deposit guaranteed reservation fails to register, the hotel may retain the deposit and cancel the reservation for the guest's entire stay.

Travel Agent

- In a travel agent guaranteed reservation, the travel agent guarantees the guest's reservation.
- Thus, in case of a no-show, the hotel generally bills the travel agency for the payment and the travel agent must then collect from the client or the guest.

Voucher or Miscellaneous Charge Order

- **The** Airline Reporting Corporation (ARC) **issues the voucher or the miscellaneous charge order.**
- Thus, in this case the ARC guarantees payment to the hotel if the travel agency defaults on payment or if the guest is a no-show.

Corporate

- A corporate guaranteed reservation involves a corporation or a company entering in to a contract with the hotel and will accept the financial responsibility for any no-show business travellers the company sponsors.

CONFIRMED NON-GUARANTEED RESERVATION

- A non-guaranteed **reservation assures the guest that the hotel will hold a room until a stated reservation cancellation hour on the day of arrival.**
- This type of reservation does not guarantee that the property will receive payment for no-shows.
- Thus, if the guest does not arrive by the cancellation hour, the hotel is free to release the room for sale.
- If the guest arrives after the cancellation hour, the hotel will accommodate the guest if a room is available.

CHAPTER 5

SYSTEMS OF RESERVATION

- The Hotels around the world have developed different systems of processing and recording reservation requests from the guests depending on their level of operations, number of rooms and budget.
- This chapter discusses the various systems of reservation found in the hotels of the world
- The following are the various systems of reservation in the hotel industry: -

HOTEL DIARY SYSTEM OF RESERVATION

- The "**hotel diary system of reservation**" is found in hotels which are small in size and thus, have limited number of guestrooms with them. (15-20 rooms)
- This system consists of a booking diary which is maintained by the reservation office and is used for taking down the reservations for the coming or future period.
- The booking diary has got 365 to 366 pages which mark the days of the year.
- Each page is for each day of the year for which guestrooms of the hotel will be reserved.
- Thus, the reservations are taken for the requested date in reservation and then transferred to the diary according to the date of arrival of the guest.
- The diary also contains various other information which is taken from the guest at the time reservation such as duration of stay, room type, plan requested, name of the guest, PAX, mode of payment and special instructions.

Advantages

- It is useful for small hotels.
- All the information is available at one place together and so the chance for losing information is very less.

Disadvantages

- As the diary is big and heavy, its movement is difficult.
- Cancellations and amendments can create problem and disturb the sequence of the diary.

(For A Detailed Look of The Hotel Diary, Please See Topic - 1 In The Practical Section).

WHITNEY SYSTEM OF RESERVATION

- The "**Whitney system of reservation**" was a very popular system of processing reservation in large hotels which had non-automated operating system.
- The Whitney system of reservation consists of a large wooden rack called the "**Whitney Rack**" which has **14** to **16** columns.
- Each of these columns has a number of metallic pockets for storing the reservation information in Whitney slips.
- The first column is the broadest and stores the reservation of the present month of the present year.
- The next 11 columns denote the forthcoming eleven columns of the present and the next year.
- The last 2 columns are for the subsequent years to come.
- Thus, the reservation information is transferred to the Whitney slips from the reservation form and then, the Whitney slips are arranged according date of arrival in the columns.

Advantages

- It is useful for taking reservations in large hotels.
- Cancellations and amendments are very easy as the slips can be easily referred.

Disadvantages

- The Whitney slips may be lost and the reservation information can be lost.

CENTRAL RESERVATION SYSTEM

- The "**central reservation system**" is a fully computerized network of reservation used by the players of the hospitality industry across the world.
- The central reservation system operates through the satellite and is based on the principle of **WAN (Wide Area Network)**.
- The central reservation system operates through "**Central Reservation Offices**" which are also called "**CROs**".

TYPES OF CENTRAL RESERVATION SYSTEM

Affiliate Central Reservation System

- The "**affiliate central reservation system**" is the central reservation network formed by the properties of a particular hotel chain.

- The reservation system operates through the central reservation offices which are located within the properties of the chain, outside the hotel in the same city and also in cities where the particular chain is not having any such property.
- Thus, through the central reservation system, a guest can book his reservation from one city to another as well as from cities where the chain has no properties.
- Thus, it is important for the participating properties of the chain to give their room availability to the central reservation offices from time to time.
- Sometimes, independent properties also participate in the affiliate reservation system of a particular chain in order to gain the benefit of the central reservation network and so these independent properties are called **"Overflow Facility"**.

Non-affiliate Central Reservation System

The association of the independent properties in order to gain the same benefits of the affiliate central reservation system forms the non-affiliate central reservation system.

The non-affiliate central reservation system also works in the same way as the affiliate central reservation system.

INSTANT RESERVATION SYSTEM

- The **"Instant Reservation System"** is also a fully computerized reservation network and is also based on the principle of **Wide Area Network**.
- The **Instant Reservation System** operates through the **Instant Reservation Offices,** which are also called **IROs**.
- The Instant Reservation Offices are always located in the hotels of the chain forming the **IRS**.
- The **IRO** is a separate office other than the hotel's own reservation office and the **IRO** takes or accepts the reservation request of all the other participating properties of the reservation network except the property in which it is located as the reservation office of the particular property takes its reservation requests.
- The **IRS**, thus, has got a limited coverage and thus is used by hotel chains, which cannot afford to establish a central reservation system due to heavy installation expenditure.

CHAPTER 6

TOOLS OF ROOM AVAILABILITY

ADVANCE LETTING CHART

❖ The "**Advance Letting Chart**" was a famous system of recording reservation used in small hotels which do not have computerized system of reservation.

❖ The chart is maintained on a monthly basis and is also called the "**Room Letting Chart**" or the "**Conventional Booking Chart**".

❖ The chart has **31** columns in which the dates of the month are arranged horizontally while the guestroom number and types are arranged vertically for reservation.

❖ Each individual reservation is completed by showing line with arrows with the name of the guest written on the line with block letters while each group reservation is shown by boxes with the name of the group written in block letters.

Advantages

❖ The chart is used in small hotels there are limited number of rooms and where the guests stay for a longer duration.

Disadvantages

❖ It is not easy to find out how many rooms are booked and how many rooms are available for sale at a glance from the chart.

(For A Detailed Look Of The Advance Letting Chart, Please See Topic -2 In The Practical Section).

DENSITY CONTROL CHART

❖ The "**Density Control Chart**" is used in large hotels with a large number of guestrooms, which do not have computerized reservation system.

❖ In this chart the various categories or types of guestrooms available in the hotel are grouped separately and displayed on a chart.

❖ Thus, if a hotel has 25 double rooms, each of the guestrooms would be shown on the chart.

- This chart is designed on the principle that each reservation reduces the availability of the rooms and each cancellation increases the availability of the rooms.
- In this chart, the dates of the month are arranged horizontally in **31** columns while the numbers of rooms of specific type are written in descending order.
- Thus, strokes are put in the boxes against each of the rooms and the numbers of strokes put in continuation denote the reservation of a particular guestroom for the future period.

Advantages

- It is easier to complete with strokes.
- It allows one to see at a glance just how many rooms of particular type one has left.
- It makes it easier to handle overbooking for maximizing occupancy.

Disadvantages

- While completing the density chart with strokes, it is easier to make mistakes, and more difficult to check them, since one has no idea which stroke represents which guest.
- The density chart is useful only in hotels with standard rooms. Attempts to use the chart in older hotels have caused problem especially with regular guest asking for a specific room, as it is not at all easy to guarantee while using a density chart.

(For A Detailed Look of The Density Control Chart, Please See Topic -3 In The Practical Section).

ROOM STATUS BOARD

- The "**room status board**" is a chart, which shows the rooms booking position for one year on continuous basis.
- The statuses are shown under three categories: **sold out, on request** and **free sales** by three different colored plastic discs.
- "**Sold out**" condition means that no rooms are available for further reservation for that period or date.
- "**On Request**" condition means that the rooms can be blocked subject to cancellation and the guest is given this status of wait list.
- "**Free Sales**" means that the guestrooms are available for sale for the requested dates.
- The free sale changes to on request and further to sold out and with the cancellation the status changes from sold out to on request and further to free sales.

COMPUTERISED ROOM STATUS DISPLAY

❖ In most of the automated hotels nowadays, the room availability information is managed by the computers which display the electronic room availability chart in the visual display units or the monitors.

❖ Thus, the reservation agents are able to know the room booking positions of the hotel in the computers itself.

CHAPTER 7

PROCESSING INDIVIDUAL AND GROUP RESERVATION

PROCESSING INDIVIDUAL RESERVATION REQUESTS

- All the hotels follow a systematic procedure for processing the reservation requests of the individual guests or **FITs**.
- The hotel receives the reservation enquiry from the guests and then matches the reservation enquiry with the availability of the required guestrooms on the requested dates.

STEPS OF PROCESSING INDIVIDUAL RESERVATION

- The hotel at first receives the reservation enquiry from the guest through telephone, fax, letter or through personal meeting.
- The reservation personnel then enquire about the dates of arrival and departure of the guest to and from the hotel.
- Then the reservation agent enquires about the type and number or rooms requested by the guest on the specified date.
- Then the reservation agent matches the reservation request of the guest with the availability of the accommodation product and this is done with the help of tools of availability such as **Advance Letting Chart** or **Density Control Chart** or **Room Status Board** or **Computer**.
- If the reservation request does not match with the room availability, the reservation agent suggests alternative dates or guestroom types to the guest.
- If the reservation request matches with the room availability, the reservation agent proceeds further with the processing of the reservation requests and takes other details of the reservation enquiry such as the name of the guest, his designation, his company address, time and arrival details which may cover the flight number and its time of arrival, billing instructions given by the guest, person requesting the reservation for the guest, special instructions given by the guest and any other information relevant from the point of view of the reservation. All the above information about the reservation is recorded in reservation form or slip.

- Finally, the reservation agent gives a confirmation number to the guest, which is the proof of the confirmation of the reservation by the hotel.

(For A Detailed Look of The Reservation Form, Please See Topic -4 In The Practical Section).

PROCESSING GROUP RESERVATION REQUESTS

- Most of the hotels around the world have a large number of guests coming in groups and these groups are of major importance to the hotels from the point of view of the revenue generation.
- The various types of groups visiting hotels are airline crewmembers, corporate groups for seminar, conference or convention, educational groups of students or professionals, travel groups of vacationers or holidaymakers or religious travellers.
- Thus, the hotels take great care while handling the reservation requests of the groups as the groups give a huge magnitude of revenue to the hotels.

STEPS OF PROCESSING GROUP RESERVATION

- The hotel at first receives the reservation enquiry from the group either through the group leader or through the intermediary agent by telephone, fax, letter or through personal meeting.
- The reservation personnel then enquire about the dates of arrival and departure of the group to and from the hotel.
- Then the reservation agent enquires about the type and number or rooms requested by the group on the specified date.
- Then the reservation agent matches the reservation request of the group with the availability of the accommodation product and this is done with the help of tools of availability such as **Advance Letting Chart** or **Density Control Chart** or **Room Status Board** or **Computer**.
- If the reservation request does not match with the room availability, the reservation agent suggests alternative dates or guestroom types to the group.
- If the reservation requests matches with the room availability, then the reservation agent discusses with the group leader or the intermediary agent about the number of rooms to be kept aside for the group as "**Block**" and then decides the cut-off date with the reservation agent which is agreed upon date between both the parties according to which the group leader or the intermediary agent has to reserve all the guestrooms of the block by the cut-off date and after the date specified, the hotel is free to release all the unreserved rooms of the block in the general room inventory pool.
- The reservation agent then, proceeds further with the processing of the reservation requests and takes other details of the reservation enquiry such as the name of the group, name of the group leader and the group members, number and type of guestrooms requested, date and time of arrival of the group, date and time of departure of the group, meal plans

accepted by the group, mode of settlement of the bill by the group and special instructions by the group to the hotel.

- Finally, the reservation agent gives a confirmation number to the group leader or the intermediary agent involved in the process of the group reservation.
- The reservation agent then sends the letter of confirmation of the group reservation to the group leader or to the intermediary agent.

CHAPTER 8

AMENDMENTS, CANCELLATIONS AND OVERBOOKING

RESERVATION MAINTENANCE

- ❖ Thus, it is very important for the reservation department to properly maintain the various reservations of the guests for future amendments or cancellation.
- ❖ Thus, a reservation agent should be efficient enough to organize and properly keep a track of the reservation records of the guests.
- ❖ Thus, if a person contacts the hotel to change a reservation, the reservations agent must be able to quickly trace the reservation record of the guest, verify its details and do the needful modification.

MODIFYING NON-GUARANTEED RESERVATIONS

- ❖ Guests often make non-guaranteed reservation for their stay, as they are mostly sure that they will reach the property before the stated cancellation hour of the hotel.
- ❖ Sometimes, it happens that the guests are not able to arrive on time at the hotel. In that case, most of the guests convert their non-guaranteed reservation into a guaranteed one.
- ❖ The following is the procedure to modify a non-guaranteed reservation: -
- ❖ Obtain the name of the guest and find out the correct non-guaranteed reservation record.
- ❖ Obtain the guest's credit card type, number and expiration date and the cardholder's name, and verify the validity of the credit card.
- ❖ Assign the guest, a new reservation confirmation number according to the policy of the hotel.
- ❖ Complete the change from non-guaranteed to guaranteed reservation status according to the procedures of the property.

RESERVATION CANCELLATION

- ❖ A reservation cancellation by the guests informs the reservation department that a particular room is again available on a particular date for the guest.

- It is extremely important for the hotels to properly process the reservation cancellation and the reservation agent should be very courteous to the guests while handling the reservation cancellation.

CANCELLING A NON-GUARANTEED RESERVATION

- To cancel a non-guaranteed reservation, the reservation agent should obtain the name and address of the guest, number of rooms reserved by the guest, scheduled date of arrival and departure.
- This information will make sure that the correct reservation record is found out and cancelled.
- After recording the cancellation, the reservations agent should assign a cancellation number to the guest.

CANCELLING A CREDIT CARD GUARANTEED RESERVATION

- To cancel a credit card guaranteed reservation, obtain the total information about the guest reservation related to the guest stay such as date of arrival and departure, name and address of the guest and reservation number.
- Mark the reservation as cancelled and add the cancellation number to the reservation record. If someone other than the guest makes the cancellation, the reservations agent should add the caller's name to the cancelled reservation record.

CANCELLING AN ADVANCE DEPOSIT GUARANTEED RESERVATION

- Cancelling an advanced deposit guaranteed reservation vary according to the policy of the hotel.
- The reservations agent should take extreme care while cancelling the advance deposit guaranteed reservation as this cancellation deals with cash deposit.

  Deposits are normally returned to guests who properly cancel the reservation.

CANCELLING OTHER GUARANTEED RESERVATION

- Generally it is the representative of the company or the travel agency who contacts the hotel to cancel a corporate account or travel agency guaranteed reservation.
- It is important to enter the name of the person cancelling the reservation on the reservation record.
- A reservation cancellation number should be issued in both the cases and should be recorded.

(For A Detailed Look of The Cancellation Form, Please See Topic -5 In The Practical Section).

OVERBOOKING

- "**Overbooking**" is a process of accepting more number of reservations than the actual number of guestrooms present in the hotel.
- This is not an error but is rather an action taken by the front office management in order to reduce losses to the hotel due to no-shows and cancellations.
- No-shows are guests who do not register in a hotel even after having a confirmed reservation and neither do they cancel their reservation. So, these guests cause a loss to the hotel and reduce the revenue for the hotel. Thus, overbooking is done in order to reduce the impact of the no-shows on the revenue of the hotel.
- Cancellations are guests who cancel their reservations either well before time or even at the last time and thus, the last minute cancellations also cause a lot of problem to the hotel management and reduce the overall revenue of the hotel. Thus, overbooking is done in order to reduce the impact of the cancellations on the revenue of the hotel.
- Thus, overbooking is a very complicated process and should be done in a cautious manner on the base of the history of reservation trends as improper overbooking can lead the hotel to a situation where the hotel has no choice but to bounce guests due to full house condition.

CHAPTER 9

JOB DESCRIPTION OF RESERVATION PERSONNEL

JOB DESCRIPTION OF RESERVATION MANAGER

Job Position Title	:	RESERVATION MANAGER
Job Category	:	Non-supervisory
Reports To	:	Lobby Manager or Front Office Manager
Position Summary	:	Supervises the functioning of the reservation staff and ensures maximization of revenue management by the selling of rooms of the hotel.
Hours of Operation	:	General shift of eight or nine hours from 0900 hrs to 1800 hrs

Duties and Responsibilities

- Participates in the recruitment and selection of the reservation staff of the hotel.
- Supervises the working of the reservation assistants of the section.
- Trains the reservation assistants in processing reservation requests.
- Possesses a thorough knowledge and information about the types and availability of rooms of the hotel property.
- Prepares the various rules and regulations of the hotel with the help of the rooms division and front office manager.
- Possesses total information about the various plans, packages and discounts to be offered to the guests during the process of reservation.
- Tracks and analyses the business generated by the reservation department from the sale of rooms to the individual guests and groups.
- Develops revenue management strategies to improve the sale of rooms of the hotel during the periods of low demand.

Educational Qualification	:	Four years Degree or Three years Diploma in Hotel Management and Catering Technology from a reputed and affiliated university or college. Command in reading, writing and speaking English and preferably knowledge of a foreign language.

Experience	:	Minimum two years of hotel experience with one year experience as a front office supervisor.

JOB DESCRIPTION OF RESERVATION ASSISTANT

Job Position Title	:	RESERVATION ASSISTANT
Job Category	:	Non-supervisory
Reports To	:	Reservation Manager or Front Office Manager
Position Summary	:	Processes the reservation of the guests through the central reservation system or any other sources of reservation and handles the various queries of the guests regarding reservation.
Hours of Operation	:	Eight hour shift each day or according to the policy of the hotel management.

Duties and Responsibilities

- ❖ Receives and handles the various reservation enquiries through telephone, telex, fax, e-mail and other modes of communication.
- ❖ Receive reservation from the sales and marketing division of the hotel property.
- ❖ Possesses a thorough knowledge and information about the types and availability of rooms of the hotel property.
- ❖ Possesses detailed information about the various rules and regulations of the hotel while processing the reservation requests of the guests.
- ❖ Possesses total information about the various plans, packages and discounts to be offered to the guests during the process of reservation.
- ❖ Creates and maintains the reservation record of the guests and assigns them a confirmation number as a proof of reservation.
- ❖ Makes guests understand about the types of reservation.
- ❖ Communicates the confirmed reservations to the front desk.

Educational Qualification	:	Four years Degree or Three years Diploma in Hotel Management and Catering Technology from a reputed and affiliated university or college.
Experience	:	Fresher can be accepted for the position.

USING PRACTICAL FORMATS IN RESERVATION

Topic 1: Reservations Booking Diary

HOTEL XYZ

DATE: April 16th 2010

Sr.No.	Date of Arrival	Date of Departure	Name of Guest	PAX	Address of The guest	Expected Time Of Arrival	Room Type Requested	Room Rate And Plan	Mode of Payment	Reservation Status	Reservation Number	Special Instructions	Reservation Requested By
1.	10/07/05	17/07/05	Gupta Mr. Rupesh	01	XYZ	1230 Hrs	HT	Rs. 2000 EP	Credit Card	Confirmed Guaranteed	XYZ – 23 – SG – 136 - 100	Airport Pick Up	Mr. Suresh
2.	10/08/05	15/08/05	Roy Mr. Vikas	02	ADG	1330 Hrs	DBL	Rs. 3000 EP	Cash	Confirmed Guaranteed *(Deposit Received)*	XYZ – 23 – SG – 136 - 101	Pool Facing Room	Mr. Vikas Roy

TOPIC 1

RESERVATIONS BOOKING DIARY

GENERAL DESCRIPTION

- The "**Reservations Booking Diary**" is found in hotels, which are small in size and thus, have limited number of guestrooms with them (15-20 rooms).
- This system consists of a booking diary which is maintained by the reservation office and is used for taking down the reservations for the coming or future period.
- The booking diary has got 365 to 366 pages, which mark the days of the year.
- Each page is for each day of the year for which guestrooms of the hotel will be reserved.
- Thus, the reservations are taken for the requested date in reservation and then transferred to the diary according to the date of arrival of the guest.

PHYSICAL DESCRIPTION

DATE OF ARRIVAL	:	The proposed date of arrival of the guest is written in this column.
DATE OF DEPARTURE	:	The proposed date of departure of the guest is writ ten in this column.
PAX	:	The total number of guests in the party is written in this column.
ADDRESS OF THE GUEST	:	The contact address of the guest is written in this column.
EXPECTED TIME OF ARRIVAL	:	The expected time of arrival of the guest in the hotel is written in this column.
ROOM TYPE REQUESTED	:	The room type requested by the guest at the time of reservation is written in this column.
ROOM RATE AND PLAN	:	The room rate decided between the hotel and the guest and the plan requested by the guest is written in this column.
MODE OF PAYMENT	:	The mode of payment of the bill by the guest is written in this column.

RESERVATION STATUS	:	The reservation status of the guest; whether guaranteed or non-guaranteed is mentioned in this column.
RESERVATION NUMBER	:	The reservation number assigned to the guest by the reservation agent at the time of reservation is written in this column.
SPECIAL INSTRUCTIONS	:	The special requests made by the guest at the time of reservation are written in this column.
RESERVATION REQUESTED BY	:	The name of the person requesting the reservation is written in this column.

Topic 2: Advance Letting Chart

HOTEL XYZ **APRIL 2010**

ROOM TYPE AND NUMBER	1	2	3	4	5	6	7	8	9	10	11	12	13	14	15	16	17	18	19	20	21	22	23	24	25	26	27	28	29	30	31
DBL 101		Roy	Mr.	Ram																											
DBL 102								Sen	Mr.	Sam																					
DBL 103																															
DBL 104																															
HT 105																															
HT 106																															
HT 107																															
SUITE 108																															
DBL 201																															
DBL 202																															
DBL 203																															
DBL 204																															
HT 205																															
HT 206																															
HT 207																															
SUITE 208																															

↔ Arrows indicate individual reservation of a guestroom in the name of the guest

☐ Boxes with colored letters indicate group reservation of guestrooms in the name of the company

TOPIC 2

ADVANCE LETTING CHART

GENERAL DESCRIPTION

- The Advance Letting Chart is maintained on a monthly basis and gives information about the availability of all the guestrooms of a hotel for a particular month.
- It is only after processing the reservation request in the advance-letting chart, the reservation agent notes down the other information of the reservation request of the guest in the reservation form or slip.
- But the advance-letting chart does not have space for doing overbooking and this limits the chart from being used in big hotels.

PHYSICAL DESCRIPTION

HOTEL	:	The name of the hotel is written in this space.
MONTH	:	The month for which the advance-letting chart is maintained is written in this space.
ROOM TYPE AND NUMBER	:	In this column, each of the room types of the hotel along with the room number is mentioned.
1 – 31	:	In these columns, the date of the month for which the chart is maintained is written in horizontal fashion.
	:	The arrow shown is used for drawing individual reservation from the box when the guest is going to arrive to the box when the guest is going to depart from the hotel. The arrow is always drawn against the room type requested by the guest.
	:	The box is used for drawing group reservations and is drawn covering the boxes denoting the dates of arrivals and departures to and from the hotel.

Topic 3: Density Control Chart

ROOM TYPE: TWIN ROOMS WITH ATTACHED BATHROOMS **HOTEL XYZ** **APRIL 2010**

NUMBER OF ROOMS	1	2	3	4	5	6	7	8	9	10	11	12	13	14	15	16	17	18	19	20	21	22	23	24	25	26	27	28	29	30	31	SP. INSTRUCTIONS
10	/	/	/	/	/	/	/	/		/	/	/				/	/															
09	/	/	/	/	/	/				/	/	/	/	/	/	/	/	/														
08																																
07																																
06																																
05																																
04																																
03																																
02																																
01																																

OVERBOOKING

NUMBER OF ROOMS	1	2	3	4	5	6	7	8	9	10	11	12	13	14	15	16	17	18	19	20	21	22	23	24	25	26	27	28	29	30	31	SP. INSTRUCTIONS
03																																
02																																
01																																

ROOM TYPE: DOUBLE ROOMS WITH ATTACHED BATHROOMS

NUMBER OF ROOMS	1	2	3	4	5	6	7	8	9	10	11	12	13	14	15	16	17	18	19	20	21	22	23	24	25	26	27	28	29	30	31	SP. INSTRUCTIONS
04	/	/	/	/	/	/	/		/	/	/	/	/	/			/	/	/	/	/	/	/	/				/	/	/	/	
03																																
02																																
01																																

OVERBOOKING

NUMBER OF ROOMS	1	2	3	4	5	6	7	8	9	10	11	12	13	14	15	16	17	18	19	20	21	22	23	24	25	26	27	28	29	30	31	SP. INSTRUCTIONS
02																																
01																																

ROOM TYPE: SUITE ROOMS WITH ATTACHED BATHROOMS

NUMBER OF ROOMS	1	2	3	4	5	6	7	8	9	10	11	12	13	14	15	16	17	18	19	20	21	22	23	24	25	26	27	28	29	30	31	SP. INSTRUCTIONS
02	/	/	/	/	/	/	/	/	/	/	/	/	/	/	/	/	/	/	/	/	/	/	/	/	/	/	/	/	/	/	/	
01	/	/	/	/	/	/	/	/	/	/	/	/	/	/	/	/	/	/	/	/	/	/	/	/	/	/	/	/	/	/	/	

OVERBOOKING

NUMBER OF ROOMS	1	2	3	4	5	6	7	8	9	10	11	12	13	14	15	16	17	18	19	20	21	22	23	24	25	26	27	28	29	30	31	SP. INSTRUCTIONS
01	/	/	/	/	/	/											/	/	/	/	/											

TOPIC 3

DENSITY CONTROL CHART

GENERAL DESCRIPTION

- ❖ The "**Density Control Chart**" is used for determining the availability of all the guestrooms of a hotel and is used for reservation application in medium and large hotel using non-automated system of reservation.
- ❖ The density control chart is also maintained on a monthly basis and gives information about the availability of all the guestrooms of a hotel for a particular month.
- ❖ The density control chart has got spaces for doing over bookings and is thus, more advantageous as compared to the advance-letting chart.
- ❖ In the chart, all the types of guestrooms of the hotel are grouped together separately and shown with separate table of over bookings for each of these categories.

PHYSICAL DESCRIPTION

ROOM TYPE	:	In this space, the inventory of each room type of the hotel is mentioned.
HOTEL	:	The name of the hotel is written in this space.
MONTH	:	The month for which the advance-letting chart is maintained is written in this space.
ROOM NUMBER	:	In this column, the total guestrooms of the particular type are arranged on an ascending order.
1 – 31	:	In these columns, the date of the month for which the chart is maintained is written in horizontal fashion.
OVERBOOKING	:	There is a separate table for over bookings to be carried on for each of the room category shown in the density control chart.
"/ "	:	The Density Control Chart is filled with strokes which are drawn in each box from the date of arrival to the date of departure of the guest.

Topic 4: Reservation Slip

HOTEL XYZ

RESERVATION SLIP

Name ______________________________.

______________________________.

Address ______________________________.

______________________________.

______________________________.

Arrival ____________________ Departure ______________.

Time of Arrival ____________________ FLT.______________.

	SINGLE	DOUBLE / TWIN	TRIPLE	SUITE
NO				
RATE				

Remarks / Special Instructions ______________________________.

Billing Instruction ______________________________.

______________________________.

Reservation Made By ____________________ Telephone No. __________.

Reservation taken By ______________________________.

______________________________.

Date______________.

TOPIC 4

RESERVATION SLIP

GENERAL DESCRIPTION

- ❖ The **"Reservation Slips"** are the most important formats used by the reservationists, the moment they receive any reservation requests through telephone, fax or mail.
- ❖ Although the reservations are immediately fed in the computers, but in case of computer failure, these are the only manual formats, which can be used for reference. Hence they are safely preserved in the month files for future reference.

PHYSICAL DESCRIPTION

NAME	:	The mane of the guest for whom the reservation is being made is written here.
ADDRESS	:	If the guest is a corporate guest, his company's address is written here. In other cases his residential address is written here.
ARRIVAL	:	The date of arrival of the guest is written here.
DEPARTURE	:	The date of departure of the guest is written here.
TIME OF ARRIVAL	:	The time of arrival of the guest is written here.
FLT.	:	The details of the flight is written in case the guest is arriving by flight for airport pick-up which is complementary for VIP guests.
TABLE	:	The table provides information about the various types of rooms available in the hotel. The reservationist puts the number of rooms requested under each type along with the tariff or room rates. The room rates negotiable as discounts are given to the corporate guests.
REMARKS AND SPECIAL INSTRUCTIONS	:	In this space, generally special requests of the guests are written here such as: 1) Room preference

		2) Garland welcome to VIP guests as requested by the person making the reservation.
RESERVATION MADE BY	:	In this space, the name of the person who has made the reservation for the guest is written here. If the guest has himself made the reservation, his name and telephone no. is written here. This helps the reservationist to contact the person concerned in case of cancellation or modification of the reservation made.
RESERVATION	:	In this space the reservationists who has taken the reservetion is written here.
DATE	:	The date when the reservation is taken is written here.
BILLING	:	The mode of settlement of the bill by the guest is written here.

Topic 5: Revision or Cancellation Slip

HOTEL XYZ

REVISION OR CANCELLATION SLIP

Name:

Address:

Original Reservation

Room	☐ Single	☐ Twin	☐ Suite

Arrival	**Departure**

REVISION

Room	☐ Single	☐ Twin	☐ Suite

Arrival	Departure

Remarks:

☐ Phone: ☐ Verbal:

Requested By:	**Received By:**	**Date**

TOPIC 5

REVISION OR CANCELLATION SLIP

GENERAL DESCRIPTION

- The "**Revision or Cancellation Slip**" is also a very important format frequently used by the reservationist in case cancellation or revision made by the reservation by the guest.
- It often is possible that the guest changes the date of arrival due to unavoidable reasons.
- Thus, it is the duties of the reservationist to do the needful i.e. modify the reservation or cancel the reservation as requested by the guest.

PHYSICAL DESCRIPTION

NAME	:	The name of the guest having the reservation is written here.
ADDRESS	:	The address of the guest having the reservation is written here.
ORIGINAL	:	In this space, the details about the original reservation is given such as a) Room Type b) Arrival details c) Departure Details.
REVISION	:	In this space, the details about the revision made by the guest is given. This may include a change in room type or arrival date or departure date.
REMARKS	:	This space is meant for writing whether the cancellation or revision is written here.
REQUESTED BY	:	The name of the person who had requested for cancellation or revision is written here.
RECEIVED BY	:	The name of the person who has received the cancellation or revision puts his or her name here.
DATE	:	The date when the cancellation or revision has been is written here.

UNIT – V
THE REGISTRATION AND INFORMATION SECTION

UNIT V

THE REGISTRATION AND INFORMATION SECTION

PART A (THEORY)

PART B (PRACTICAL FORMATS)

LEARNING OBJECTIVES

- ❖ To Understand The Concept of The Registration Activity and To Study The Functions And Roles of The Registration Section Of The Front Office Department.
- ❖ To Study The Various Systems of Registration Prevalent In Hotels.
- ❖ To Study The Importance of The Pre-registration Activity Performed By The Front Office Personnel.
- ❖ To Understand The Main Steps Involved Behind The Process of Registration.

- To Understand The Steps Involved In The Registration of VVIP, Foreigner and Groups Coming to The Hotel.
- To Study The Importance of The Information Section In The Hotel.
- To Study The Job Description of The Registration And Information Personnel of The Front Office Department.

CHAPTER 1

AN INTRODUCTION TO THE REGISTRATION SECTION

DEFINING REGISTRATION

- "**Registration**" is a term given to the entire procedure followed by the hotel authorities on the arrival of the guests to confirm the stay of the guest at the hotel and includes the process of signing of the guests on the registration card.
- The process of assigning a guestroom to a guest and checking him in after the completion of other legal formalities (establishing the method of payment and creating a registration record) on his arrival is also called "**registration**".

IMPORTANCE OF REGISTRATION

Registration satisfies legal requirements

- Registration process helps in satisfying the legal requirements for the guest coming to the hotel with or without reservation to stay in the hotel.
- It is only after the process of registration that a guest coming to the hotel with or without reservation becomes an in-house guest of the hotel.

Registration provides a record of actual arrival against bookings

- The process of registration gives the hotel actual information about the number of guests who have actually arrived in the hotel for staying in the hotel.
- Thus, the hotel is also able to know about the actual number of no-shows who are the guests who did not arrive even after having a confirmed reservation and neither did they cancel their reservation. Thus, the hotel charges retention charge from the all the guests who were no-shows and were having a confirmed guaranteed reservation with the hotel.
- The traditional justification for registration was that it provided some form of record in the case of a fire or any other natural disaster.

Registration confirms the acceptance of the guest regarding rules and regulation of stay in the hotel

- The process of registration also makes the guest agree to abide by the rules and regulations of accommodation to stay in the hotel.
- Thus, the signature of the guest on the registration card confirms the acceptance of the in-house rules and regulations by the guest to stay in the hotel.

DEFINING THE REGISTRATION SECTION

- The "**Registration Section**" is a very important part of the front office and is also popularly called the "**Reception**" of the hotel.
- The section is defined after the main function performed by it i.e. the registration of the guests coming with or without reservation to the hotel.
- In most of the hotel, the registration section has the information counter or the information section attached to it which performs the important duty of providing valuable information to the guests about the facilities and services of the hotel and the city at large.

ORGANISATION

- The **Shift Supervisor** or the **Front Office Supervisor** is the immediate chief of the registration section of front office.
- The entire registration section is ultimately under the **Lobby Manager**.
- The **Shift Supervisor** is assisted by the **front desk assistants** and **trainees** who work in the desk during the various shifts.

Shift or Front Office Supervisor

↓

Senior Receptionist

↓

Receptionist

↓

Trainee

LOCATION

- According to the traditional concept, the registration section or front desk is generally located on the left side of the lobby after the bell desk.
- But in modern hotels, a deviation from the traditional concept can be seen as the location registration section is seen as different in most of the hotels nowadays.

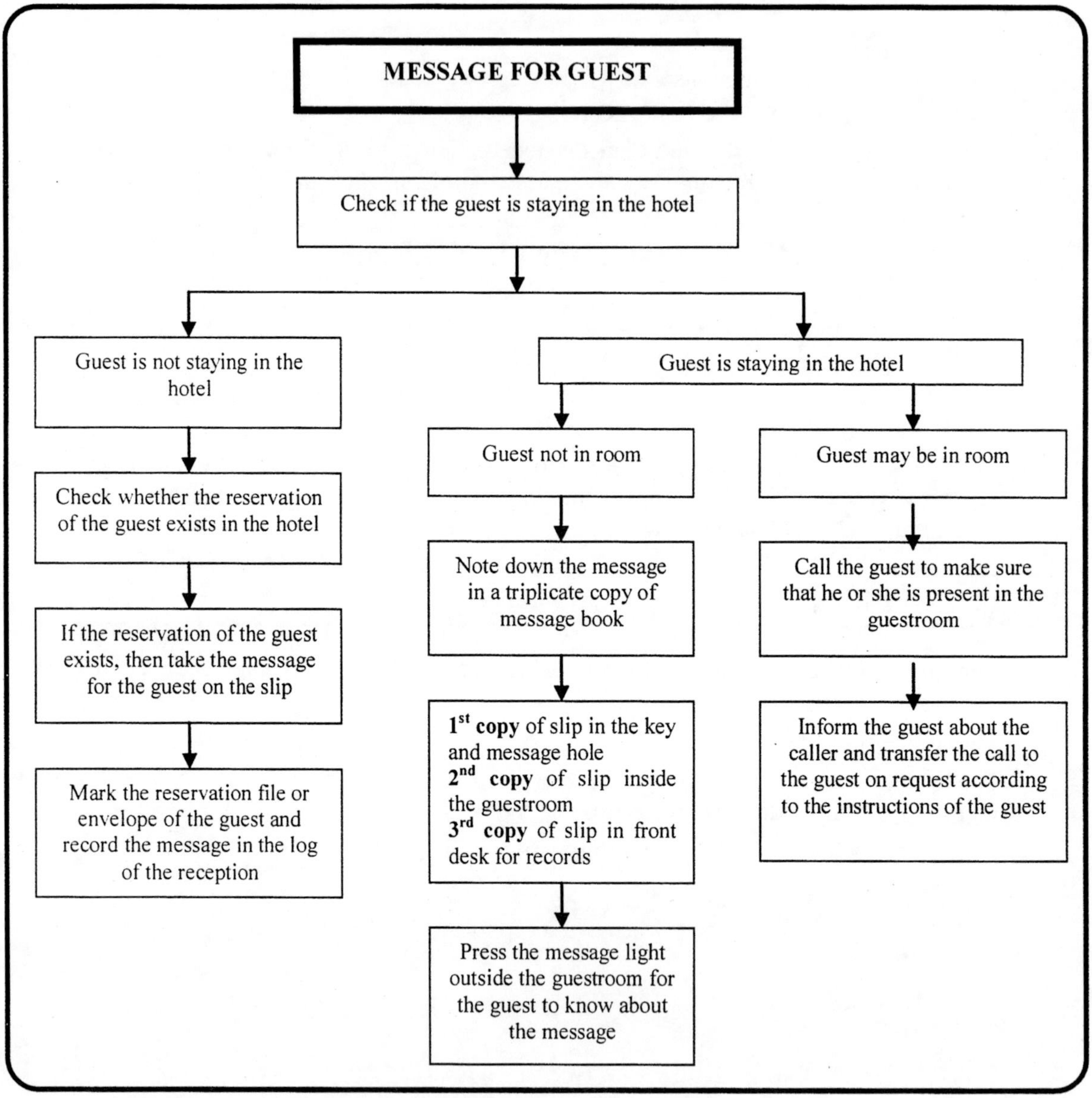

Fig. 5.1: Handling Incoming Messages of Guests (Verbal As Well As Telephone)

MAIN FUNCTIONS OF THE REGISTRATION SECTION OF FRONT OFFICE

Performing pre-registration activities

- The registration section performs the pre-registration activities of all the guests who have a confirmed reservation with the hotel and are arriving at the hotel the next day.

Greeting the guests on their arrival at the hotel

- The registration section also greets the guests on their arrival at the hotel and also offers them welcome drinks to refresh themselves.

Registering the guests with or without reservation on their arrival

- The registration section then completes the legal formalities associated with the registration of a guest with or without reservation.

(For A Detailed Look of The Arrival And Departure Register, Please Refer Topic – 4 In Practical Section).

Up-selling the accommodation product to the guest

- The registration section also negotiates the room rates with the guests and pursues them to purchase a more highly priced room that they had actually desired or requested for.

Completing the formalities associated with the registration of foreigner guest

- The registration section also takes care that all the formalities associated with the registration of a foreigner are duly completed such as filling up of **Form C** and dispatching the same to the concerned authorities.

Safekeeping the keys of the guestroom

- The registration section also performs the most important responsibility of safeguarding the keys of the guestrooms of the hotel and stores them in the mail, message and key rack.

Storing the mails and messages of the guests and delivering the same

- The registration section also receives and stores the mails and messages of the guests and delivers the mails and messages to the guests according to the instructions.

(For A Detailed Look of the Message Handling Process, Please Refer Figure 5.1).

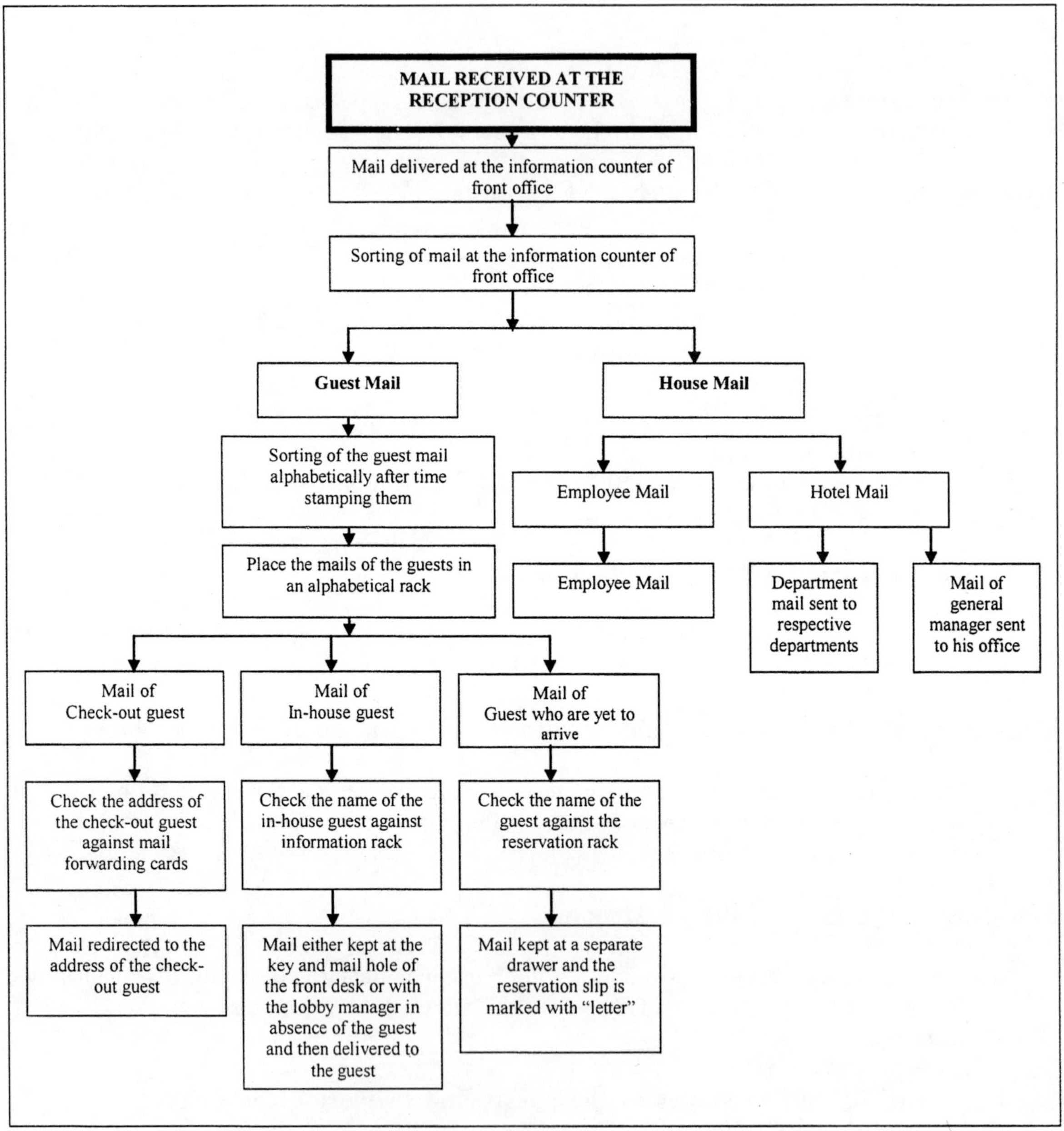

Fig. 5.2: Handling of Mails at the Information Counter of Front Office

(For A Detailed Look of The Mail Handling Process, Please Refer Figure 5.2).

(For A Detailed Look of The Message Slip, Please Refer Topic – 6 In Practical Section).

(For A Detailed Look of The Mail Register, Please Refer Topic – 7 In Practical Section).

Providing information to the guests about the hotel facilities

- Above all, the registration section also provides vital information to the guests about the services and facilities of the hotel.

(For A Detailed Look of The Work Of The Reception Section Of The Hotel, Please Refer Annexure 5.1).

Processing the check-out of the guests

- The registration section also performs the important function of processing the check-outs of the guest in conjunction with the cash section at the time of the departure of the guests from the hotel.

Preparing the guest history cards after the departure of the guests

- The registration section also prepares the history of the guests in conjunction with the reservation department. These history cards help the front office department to prepare a profile of the guest on the basis his personal and financial information.

(For A Detailed Look of The Guest History Card, Please Refer Topic – 5 In Practical Section).

CHAPTER 2

THE TOOLS OF REGISTRATION

The hotels around the world have been using a large number of **tools for the registration** of the guests according to their number of rooms, their system of operation and according to their budget and managing capacity.

The following are the tools of registration used in the hotel industry:

BOUND BOOK

- The "**bound book**" is a big register placed on the front desk and is used for the purpose of registration in the small hotels.
- Thus, all the arriving guests are required to fill in their details in the bound book as a step towards the completion of the registration formalities.

Advantage

- The bound book is very heavy; there are remote chances of the book getting lost.

Disadvantage

- The bound book being placed on the front desk gets spoiled easily due to frequent use and looks dirty.
- The information contained in the bound book cannot be kept confidential.
- The pre-registration activities cannot be preformed in the bound book method of registration.

LOOSE LEAF REGISTER

- The "**loose leaf register**" is a big register placed used for the purpose of registration in the medium-sized hotels.
- Thus, the only difference between the loose leaf register and bound book is that, in the loose leaf register, each of the sheets or the pages represent each day of the year.

Advantage

- The loose leaf register has more confidentiality than the bound book as the sheets of the previous days are removed as soon as the registration for that particular day is over.
- In case of the loose leaf register getting lost; only the information of one day is lost as the information of the previous day is already separated.

Disadvantage

- The sheets of the loose leaf register may not be fully filled on a particular day when there are few registration activities and so the remaining portion of the sheet may be wasted.
- In this method, only one guest can register at a time and so the registration process is very time-consuming.

INDIVIDUAL REGISTRATION CARDS (GUEST REGISTRATION CARDS)

- The individual system of registration is widely used in all the large hotels in the hospitality industry.
- This system details the use of individual registration cards which is used in duplicate or triplicate in order to enter all the required information for the guest during the process of registration.

Advantage

- The pre-registration activity is possible in this system.
- The registration cards can be systematically stored on the basis of alphabets.
- There is compete privacy of the information provided by the guest during the process of registration as separate registration cards are used for registering individual guests.
- During the peak hours, when there are large numbers of arrivals of the guests, many guests can be registered at the same time.

Disadvantage

- The individual registration cards are quite expensive for the management and hence, this system is prevalent in the large hotels only.
- If the registration cards are not stored properly, there are chances of the cards getting lost leading to the loss of valuable information related to the registration of the guests.

(For A Detailed Look of The Registration Card, Please Refer Topic – 1 In Practical Section).

SELF REGISTRATION TERMINAL

- The self-registration terminals are used in fully automated and world-class hotels in order to accelerate the process of registration due to a large number of guests arriving at the hotel.
- The self-registration terminal looks like an ATM machine and requires the guest to have a valid credit card to register in the hotel and also requires the guest to have an advance reservation with the hotel.
- The machine requests the guests to enter their reservation numbers and then their credit card number.
- As the self registration terminal is electronically linked to the reservation management and rooms' management system, the terminal is easily able to track the reservation information of the guest in the hotel.
- Then, the terminal dispenses the registration card to the guests to fill the same thereby completing the registration formalities.
- Finally, the registration terminal dispenses the guestroom keys to the guests on completion of the other formalities of the registration process.

CHAPTER 3

THE ESSENTIAL STEPS OF REGISTRATION

REGISTRATION OF A GUEST WITH RESERVATION

The following are the six main steps of the registration process of a guest coming with reservation:

PREREGISTRATION ACTIVITY

↓

CREATION OF THE REGISTRATION RECORD

↓

ASSIGNMENT OF THE ROOM AND RATE

↓

ESTABLISHMENT OF THE METHOD OF PAYMENT

↓

ISSUAL OF THE ROOM KEY

FULFILLMENT OF SPECIAL REQUESTS

Pre-registration Activity

- "**Pre-registration**" activities are the registration activities that occur before the guests arrive at the property (generally one day in advance) and are primarily aimed at saving their time during the registration process.
- Thus, the guest can be pre-registered using the information collected by reservations agents during the reservations process and so the pre-registered only need to verify information already entered on to a registration card and provide a valid signature in the appropriate place on the registration card.

- Pre-registration generally involves production of a registration card, room and rate assignment, creation of a guest folio and some other function in advance of the guest arrival.
- The pre-registration activities are only performed for guests having a confirmed reservation with the hotel and not for guests coming to the hotel without reservation (*walk-in*).

Creation of the Registration Record

- After the arrival of the guest in a hotel, the front office agent creates a registration record, which is a collection of important guest information.
- The registration cards facilitate the registration process in non-automated and semi-automated hotels.
- The registration card requires the guest to provide his or her name, address, telephone number, company affiliation and other personal data.
- The registration card usually contains a space for the guest's signature, which is a legal requirement in most of the hotels to establish a guest relationship with the hotel.
- Even in automated properties, guests are generally asked to sign a pre-printed registration card to verify the accuracy of the registration document.
- The registration cards, or their computer-generated equivalent, require the guests to indicate their intended method of settlement for rooms and other hotel goods and services and also require the guests to confirm their assigned room rate and their departure date.
- Many registration cards contain an acknowledgement on the part of the guest that he or she will abide by the rules of the hotel regarding payment and other aspects for a comfortable stay.

Assignment of Room and Rate

Assignment of guestroom to the guest

- "**Room assignment**" is an important part of the registration process and involves identifying and allocating an available room in a specific room rate category to a guest.
- On the basis of reservation information, specific rooms may be assigned before the arrival of the guest depending on the rooms' availability status and how appropriately the room meets the guest's needs.
- In smaller hotels, the allocation of rooms is normally done at the time of booking, by using the conventional chart. If when a guest arrives the room allocated is not ready, but a similar one is, then the chart has to be changed to show the re-allocation.
- VIPs and guests with special requirements are pre-allocated the rooms in order to save their valuable time.
- In allocating rooms the receptionist should aim to satisfy the guests as much as possible. Allocation should take place on the basis of putting the guests who are staying the longest

into the best rooms and guests who booked first in to rooms better than those who booked at the last moment.

Assignment of room rate to the guest

- A "**room rate**" is the price the hotel charges for overnight accommodations. The cost structure of the hotel sets the floor to the price for a room, and competition sets the ceiling to the price by establishing the maximum room rate.
- A hotel will usually designate a standard rate for each room. This rate is typically called the "**rack rate**" because traditionally the standard rate was the one posted on or near the room rack. The rack is considered the retail rate for the room. So, the discounts provided by the hotels are mostly on the rack rate.
- Room rates are generally assigned during the reservation process except for **walk-ins** who are assigned the room rates only during the registration process.
- Front desk agents are often allowed to offer discounts to the guests during reservation or registration and thus they can offer a room at a lower price than its standard rack rate when the management thinks it is appropriate.

Establishment of the Method Of Payment

- The establishment of the method of settlement of the bill by the guest during the stay is an important part of the registration process.
- The creation of the guest folio is an essential step of the registration process of the guest in a hotel.
- Regardless of whether the guest intends to pay by cash, cheque, credit card, or any other acceptable method, the hotel should take precautionary measures to ensure payment.
- Effective account settlement depends on the steps taken during registration to determine the guest's method of payment.
- Thus, the registration process plays an important part in front guest accounting since the front desk agents are responsible for collecting information on the intended method of payment during check-in.

Issual of the Room Key

- The front office agent completes the registration process by issuing the room key to the guest.
- Some hotels enclose the room key in a key card for the purpose of security. These key cards have the room numbers written or printed on them.
- Some hotels even hand over a copy of the hotel map and brochure for the sake of convenience of the guest.

- The guest is finally escorted with his luggage to his room by a bell-person, who also explains the special features of the hotel to the guest.

Fulfillment of Special Requests

- It is extremely important for the front office agents to pay attention to the special requests made by the guests during registration for acknowledgement.
- The front desk agent should mention the guest's special requests at check-in to make sure that the hotel has provided what the guest requested.
- If it appears that the special requests made by the guests during reservation have not been made, the front desk agent should try his or her best to meet these requests during the registration of the guests.
- The following are the some examples of special requests made by the guests:

Location : The guests may request for rooms close to the elevator or the emergency exit or far from the elevators.

View : The guests may request for rooms either facing the swimming or the lawns

Bed type : The guests may request for rooms with extra bed or a crib for children.

Amenities : The guests may even request for special amenities such as iron and ironing boards, additional pillows, audio-visual aids.

REGISTRATION OF A GUEST WITHOUT RESERVATION

The following are the six main steps of the registration process of a guest coming without reservation:

CREATION OF THE REGISTRATION RECORD

↓

ASSIGNMENT OF THE ROOM AND RATE

↓

ESTABLISHMENT OF THE METHOD OF PAYMENT

↓

ISSUAL OF THE ROOM KEY

↓

FULFILLMENT OF SPECIAL REQUESTS

CHAPTER 4

THE PRE-REGISTRATION PERFORMED AT FRONT DESK

DEFINING PRE-REGISTRATION

- "**Pre-registration**" can be defined as "**an activity performed by the front office 24 hours before the arrival of a guest in the hotel which includes making all the arrangements for his/her proper registration and accommodation in the hotel**".
- Pre-registration activity can be performed only for guest who have confirmed reservations with the hotel and is generally performed to accelerate the process of registration at the hotel.

NEEDS AND IMPORTANCE OF PREREGISTRATION

- The pre-registration process is an extremely important period of the front office operations and so the front office has to be extremely careful while handling the pre-registration activities.
- The various activities which are performed in the pre-registration process is: -
- Filling of the expected arrival list from the various reservation records.
- Assignment of the rooms and rate to the guest with his consent prior to his arrival.
- Preparation of the registration cards of the VIP guests.
- Since all the above activities are extremely important form the point of view of the front office operations, it is advisable that these activities should be performed in advance to reduce the time of the registration process at the time of arrival of the guests.
- Thus, the entire activities performed during the pre-registration process are totally based on the information collected from the reservation of the guest.
- The pre-registration activities not only accelerate the registration process but also help in the fulfillment of the various special requests made by the guests. E.g. requirement of a room with a good view or a room with special facilities for the disabled guest.
- The pre-registration can result in creation of unique registration options such registration of the guest in the vehicle itself that is sent for picking him up either from the airport or the railway station.

- Thus, it is clearly visible that the pre-registration activities are extremely important for an efficient registration process leading to the satisfaction of the guests.
- Thus, every front office department of every hotel should properly conduct the pre-registration activities so that the registration process is accelerated and the guest is satisfied so that he or she remains loyal to the hotel.

MAIN ACTIVITIES PERFORMED IN PRE-REGISTRATION

Preparation of the Expected Arrivals and Departures List

- The expected arrival list is prepared as a part of the pre-registration activities.
- The expected arrival list is prepared daily to indicate the number and names of the guests expected to arrive the next day.
- The expected arrival list contains names and addresses of the guests, time of arrival, date of departure, rooms requested, reservation status and other special instructions.
- In non-automated and semi-automated system, the front office department normally prepares this manually.
- Developing the expected arrival data is done from the reservation control book, wall chart, or reservation rack.
- Every afternoon, the reservation personnel review the data for the next day's arrival lists and arrange the reservations of the alphabetically and then bring them to the front desk.
- In a computerized system, a list of the expected arrivals is automatically displayed in the reservation department or at the front desk.
- The expected arrival list is of great use to the front office department as it helps the front desk agent to know about the details of the guests registering the next day.
- Thus, the front desk agent can accelerate the registration process during the arrival of the guest.
- Thus, the expected arrival list is an important report generated by the reservation department for the proper functioning of the front office department.

Calculation of the Room Position of the Property

- The front desk agent then calculates the room position or the room availability of the property for the next day after going through the expected arrivals and departures list and equating the other factors affecting the room position such as out of order rooms, overstays, under stays and no-shows.
- In all the cases the front office agent should make sure that the hotel should be in a position to allot rooms to the guests arriving at the hotel with reservation.

Preparation of the Amenities Voucher

- ❖ The front desk agent should then prepare the amenities vouchers for the arriving guests and send these vouchers to the concerned departments.
- ❖ These vouchers are documents, which are, generated in front office and instruct the food and beverage division and the housekeeping department to provide the various amenities in the guestrooms such as fruits and flowers prior to the arrival of the guest.

Review of the condition of the vacant guestrooms

- ❖ Finally the front desk agent reviews the condition of all the vacant and ready rooms of the hotel in order to make sure that the guests get the rooms in proper condition at the time of registration.

Preparation of the guest registration card

- ❖ The preparation of the guest registration card is a very important task performed during the pre-registration activity of the guest conducted by the registration section of the front office.

ADVANTAGES OF THE PRE-REGISTRATION PROCESS

- ❖ Pre-registration helps to plan for special requirements of guests as well as of the hotel such as requirement of special rooms for the disabled and sick guests.
- ❖ Pre-registration helps managers to know about the day when the hotel will be at full occupancy over the next several days.
- ❖ Pre-registration helps the guests to experience innovative registration options. E.g. Registration in the van sent for airport pickup.

CHAPTER 5

PROCESSING VVIP, FOREIGNER AND GROUP REGISTRATION

PROCESSING VVIP REGISTRATION

- The VVIP guests generally include the state guests, dignitaries, commercially important persons and well-known personalities from the field of entertainment, sports, and academics and so on and thus are huge source of revenue for the hotels besides publicity.
- Thus, it is extremely important that the registration process of the VVIP guests should be a highly efficient one and thus should consume minimum time of the guests.
- Thus, to ensure an efficient registration process, the front office has to perform the pre-registration activities of the VVIP guests who will be arriving the subsequent day.
- Hence, the reception will be preparing an expected arrivals list stating all the guests who will be arriving the next day highlighting the VVIP guests who will also be arriving.
- Then, the front desk staff will be blocking the guestrooms for the VVIP guests according to the special requests made by the guests at the time of reservation.
- Then, the front desk effectively communicates with the housekeeping department in order to inform the housekeeper to pay special attention to the guestroom by keeping it ready for the VVIP guests.
- The front desk prepares amenity vouchers in triplicate for the housekeeping and the room service department in order to make flower arrangements and place fruit and cookies basket in the guestroom prior to the arrival of the guest.
- The VVIP guests may be registered in the vehicle itself during airport pick-up or may be registered at the front desk or in the guestroom.
- When, the VVIP guest arrives, he or she is escorted by the lobby manager or the guest relation executive and bell boys to the reception or directly to the residential floor.
- The VVIP guests either signs the registration card either at the front desk or in the guestroom.
- It is the responsibility of the bell boys as well as the accompanying front desk personnel to provide information about the various facilities of the hotel including the salient features and facilities of the guestroom.

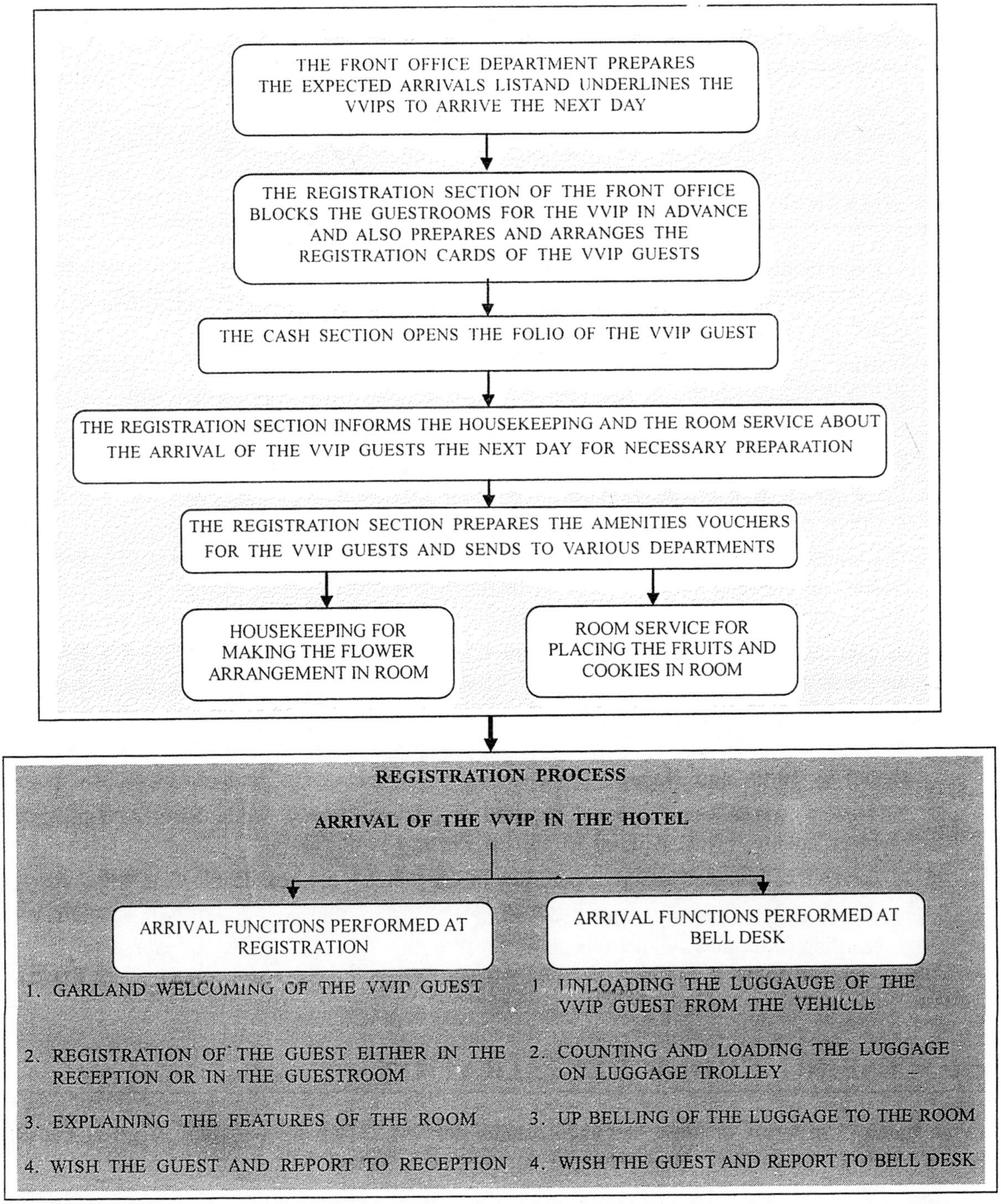

Fig. 5.3: Flow Chart of Vvip Registration in Hotels

- After, the assigned front desk assistant and the bell boy return to the front office after greeting the VVIP guests, it is the responsibility of the front office manager to contact the VVIP guest either personally or through the telephone and wish him a comfortable stay.

(For A Detailed Look of The VVIP Registration Chart, Please Refer Figure5.3).

PROCESSING FOREIGNER REGISTRATION

- A large number of foreigner guests visit the country every year and so it important for the government to have detailed knowledge about the total inflow of all foreigner guests under the foreigner rules and regulations act.
- Thus, it is extremely important for the hotel management to give detailed information about all the foreigner guests it has received on each and every day of the year.
- Thus, the registration procedure of the foreigner guests requires the filling up of the registration card as well as an important format called "**Form C**".
- The **Form C** is also called "**Hotel Arrival Report**" and is an important document giving passport, nationality details and stay of the foreigner guest in the hotel.
- The **Form C** has two copies: the first copy is sent to the "**Foreigners Regional Registration Office**" in the metropolitan cities or to the nearest local police station in case of small towns and cities; and the second copy is retained by the front office as records.
- In case of **Pakistani guests**, the **Form C** is sent within **12 hours** to the **FRRO** or to the nearest local police station and in case of **other foreigner guests**, the **Form C** is sent to the **FRRO** or to the nearest police station within **24 hours**.
- In case of **Nepalese guest**, no valid passport is required according to the **bilateral agreement** signed by **India and Nepal**.
- NRIs with "**green card**" are not required to fill up **Form C** while NRIs with passports of other countries are required to fill up **Form C**.
- In case of a foreigner group registering in the hotel, only one Form C is filled for the group leader and along with the rooming list of all the group members is filled along with the passport information and the signatures of the respected group members.

(For A Detailed Look of Form C or Hotel Arrival Report, Please Refer Topic – 2 In Practical Section).

PROCESSING GROUP REGISTRATION

A "**group**" in terms of hotel language can be defined as "**an aggregation of guest coming to a particular hospitality establishment for accommodation and food**".

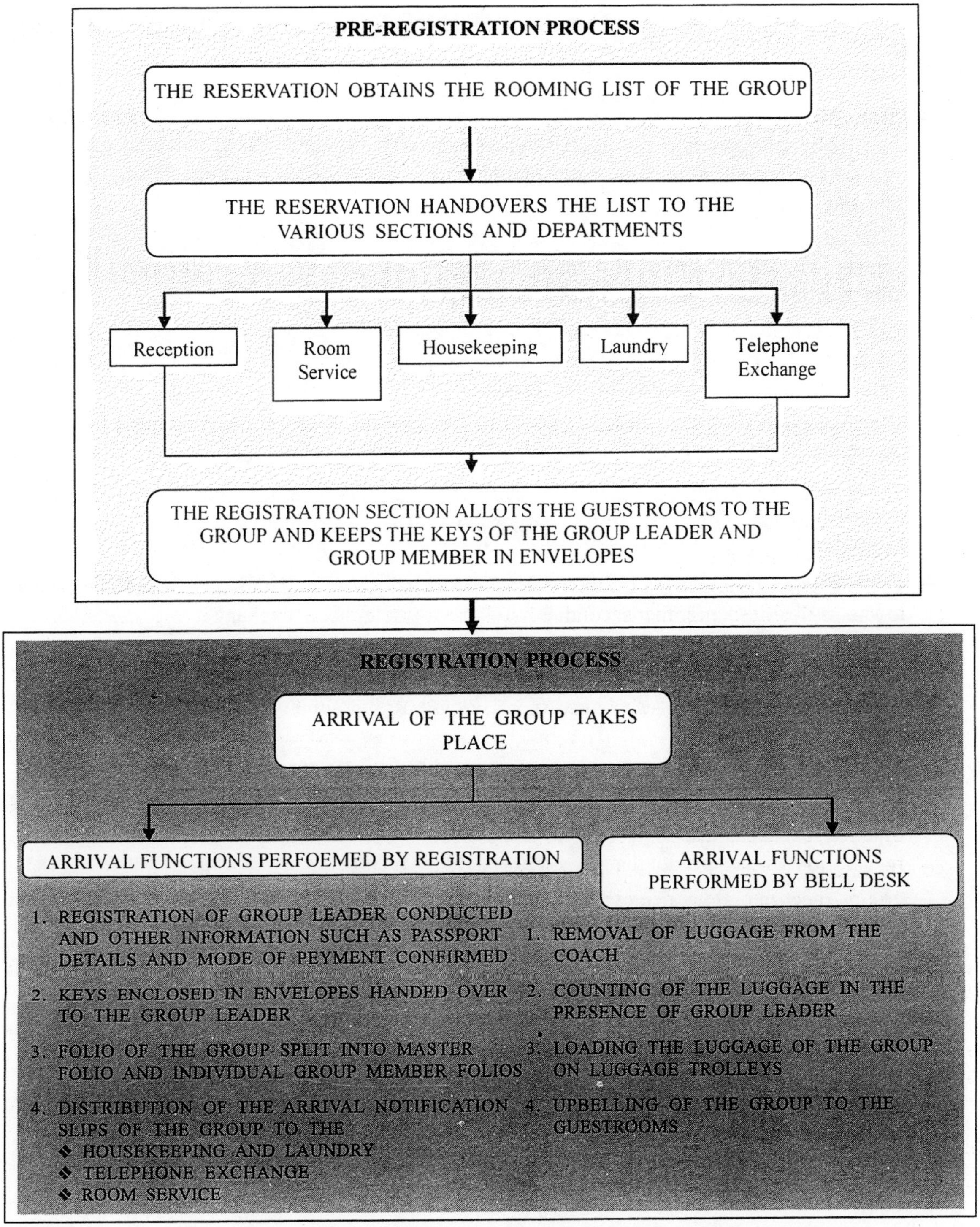

Fig. 5.4: Flow Chart of Group Registration In Hotels

REGISTRATION ACTIVITIES PERFORMED BY THE FRONT DESK

- The front desk staffs such as the receptionists and the front office executives such as the lobby manager and the guest relation executive welcome the group with garlands in traditional Indian style. The group members are also offered welcome drinks on arrival by the room service staffs.
- The reception desk then fills one registration card for the group in the name of the group leader. In case the group is a foreigner group, only one Form-C is filled and a copy of the rooming list is attached with the Form-C.
- At the cashier desk, the front office cashier prepares a **master folio** for the group and individual folios for each member of the group after the mode of payment of the bill is finally settled and decided by the group.
- The reception desk then finalizes the meal timings and venue of the group and then hands over the meal coupons to the group leader along with the final rooming list of the group.
- The front office receptionist then also hands over the guestroom keys enclosed in individual envelopes placed in the key tray to the group leader for distributing the same to the group members.
- The reception desk finally distributes the copies of the rooming list of the arrived group to the different departments of the hotel as the telephone exchange, the room service department, the housekeeping department in order to inform the concerned department about the arrival of the same.

(For A Detailed Look Of The Group Sheet, Please Refer Topic – 3 In Practical Section).

REGISTRATION ACTIVITIES PERFORMED BY THE BELL DESK

- The bell captain makes sure that he has sufficient bell personnel to assist him during the registration of the group that is supposed to arrive.
- The moment the group arrives in the hotel, the bell desk personnel help in the transportation of the baggage of the guest from the porch of the hotel to the lobby.
- Then the bell captain counts the total number of baggage of the members of the group and then fixes baggage tags on each of the baggage of the guest.
- Then the baggage are loaded in individual trolleys and transported to the guestrooms with proper care thus completing the process of registration.

(For A Detailed Look of The Group Registration Chart, Please Refer Figure5.4).

CHAPTER 6

THE INFORMATION SECTION

THE INFORMATION DESK

- The "**Information Desk**" of the front office is also an important section of the department and plays an important role in give the guests and visitors valuable information about the hotel and the city at large.
- The information desk is operated by a **Concierge** who is also known as the "**Information Assistant**".
- The concierge provides important information to the guests and the visitors about the various facilities and services of the hotel and also gives important information about the city such as the routes to the nearest airport or railway station or hospitals and banks.
- The concierge also plays an important role in arranging tickets for the guests in various concerts taking place in the city.

TOOLS OF INFORMATION SERVICES

Information Directory

- The front office staff must be able to respond in a knowledgeable way when guests contact the front desk for information.
- Some front offices accumulate such data in a bound guide called an "**information directory**".
- The following are the main information provided by the information directory: -
  - Local restaurant recommendations.
  - Contacting a taxi company.
  - Directions to the local companies.
  - Directions to the nearest shopping center, drug store, etc.
  - Directions to the nearest places of worship.
  - Directions to the nearest bank or the automated teller machine.
  - Direction to the theater, stadium, or ticket agency.
  - Directions to the universities, libraries, museums, or other points of local interest.

- ❑ Directions to the local courts or the city hall.
- ❑ Information about the hotel policies and recreational facilities or those near the hotel.

Reader's Board

- ❖ The "**Reader's Board**" is a very important tool of providing information to the guests, visitors and patrons of the hotel.
- ❖ The Reader's Board is located in the lobby of the hotel and consists of a velvet board with a golden metallic boarder and the board is fixed with the help of a stand.
- ❖ The board shows all the current events which are presently taking place in the hotel such as wedding ceremonies in the banquets, meetings, conferences and other important official events, festivals and exhibitions taking place in the hotel.
- ❖ The events are shown on the board with golden alphabets on a red velvet background and thus, are clearly visible to the guests, patrons and visitors to the hotel.

Tent Card

- ❖ The "**Tent Card**" is also a very important tool of promoting the hotel to the in-house guests of the hotel and displays important features and events of the hotel.
- ❖ The tent card is a card made of glossy paper and looks like a tent and is kept on the reading table of the guest in the guestroom.

The card elicits important information about the hotel to the in-house regarding the facilities and services of the hotel and the events taking place in the property.

CHAPTER 7

JOB DESCRIPTION OF REGISTRATION AND INFORMATION STAFF

JOB DESCRIPTION OF FRONT DESK ASSISTANT / RECEPTIONIST

Job Position Title	:	FRONT DESK ASSISTANT / RECEPTIONIST
Job Category	:	Non-supervisory
Reports To	:	Lobby Manager or Front Office Manager
Position Summary	:	Registers and assigns rooms to the guests on their arrival, represents the front office and remains in direct contact with the guests throughout the guest cycle.
Hours of Operation	:	Eight hour shift each day or according to the policy of the hotel management.

Duties and Responsibilities

- ❖ Possesses a thorough knowledge about handling guests and should have all the basic etiquettes while handling the guests especially through telephones.
- ❖ Possesses a thorough knowledge about the various front desk procedures regarding normal and walk-in registration of free individual traveller as well as groups and should be well skilled in various marketing skills.
- ❖ Possesses a thorough knowledge about the rooms of the hotel that includes the room location, types, plans and rates applicable.
- ❖ Maintains update room status information which includes the number of occupied rooms in the hotel, number of out of order rooms in the hotel, number of vacant rooms in the hotel and so on.
- ❖ Possess thorough knowledge about the various rules and regulations to be followed while registering a foreigner guest.
- ❖ Possess a thorough knowledge about handling various front office equipments such as telephone and computers.

❖ Processes guest check-out during the last stage of the guest cycle which is departure.

Educational Qualification : Three years Diploma in Hotel Management and Catering Technology from a reputed university or college with command in reading and writing English.

Experience : Previous hotel experience desired but not compulsory.

JOB DESCRIPTION OF INFORMATION ASSISTANT CONCIERGE

Job Position Title : INFORMATION ASSISTANT / CONCIERGE

Job Category : Non-supervisory

Reports To : Lobby Manager or Front Office Manager

Position Summary : Provides various information services to the guest and helps him in arranging travel tickets

Hours of Operation : Eight hour shift each day or according to the policy of the hotel management.

Duties and Responsibilities

❖ Possesses a thorough knowledge about handling guests and should have all the basic etiquettes while handling the guests especially through telephones.

❖ Possesses a thorough knowledge about the facilities and services of the hotel.

❖ Possesses a thorough knowledge about the city and state in which the hotel is located and should possess knowledge about the road maps of the city.

❖ Possesses a sound public relationship and social contacts with the various suppliers of the hospitality sector and entertainment providers.

❖ Assists the guest in securing tickets for traveling in various means of transportation.

❖ Assists the guest in securing the tickets for the various shows and entertainment programs going around in the city.

❖ Arranges car rentals for the guest on the request of the guest.

Educational Qualification : Graduate from a reputed university or college with command in reading and writing English.

Experience : Previous hotel experience desired but not compulsory.

USING PRACTICAL FORMATS IN REGISTRATION

TOPIC 1: GUEST REGISTRATION CARD

NAME ____________________
Surname first Name

DESIGNATION ____________________
ORGANISATION ____________________
ADRESS ____________________
____
____
CITY COUNTRY

ARRIVAL DATE DEPARTURE DATE

ARRIVAL TIME

ROOM TYPE	ROOM NO.	ROOM RATE	NO.OF GUESTS	DEPOSIT RECEIVED

MODE OF PAYMENT

CASH CREDIT CARD CO TA OTHERS

VOUCHER NO. ____________________
CREDIT CARD ____________________
CREDIT CARD NO. ____________________
EXPIRY DATE ____________________
BILLING ____________________
____
____
____
____

ROOM TO BE CHARGED FROM ____________________

LOBY MANAGER F. O. ASST.

DATE OF ARRIVAL IN INDIA ____________________
DURATION OF STAY IN INDIA ____________________
ARRIVAL FROM ____________________
NEXT DESTINATION ____________________
PURPOSE OF VISIT ____________________
DATE OF BIRTH ____________________
DAY MONTH YEAR

PASSPORT DETAILS

NATIONALITY ____________________
NUMBER ____________________
DATE OF ISSUE ____________________
PLACE OF ISSUE ____________________

CERTIFICATE OF REGISTRATION

NO. ____________________
DATE ____________________
ISSUED AT ____________________

The hotel shall not bear any liability for any loss incurred during the tenure of patron's stay.

The holds the privilege to exercise its right of admission without assigning any reasons.

I hereby declare that I understand & agree to the above stated & that the facts stated in this card are correct.

GUEST'S SIGNATURE ____________________

TOPIC 1

GUEST REGISTRATION CARD

GENERAL DESCRIPTION

- The "**registration card**" is a format used by the front office assistant when a guest checks-in. In fact the filling of the registration card is a prerequisite for registration and completes the entire registration process.
- The front office assistant fills the registration card in advance, if the guest has a reservation. The guest only has to sign the card on registration.
- If the guest has no reservation and is a walk-in, then the guest fills his name and the front office assistant completes address and the rest of the details.

PHYSICAL DESCRIPTION

(Arrival Details For All Guests)

NAME	:	The name of the guest is written here with the sur name first and the first name second.
DESIGNATION	:	The designation of the guest in the company in which he works is written here.
ORGANISATION	:	The name of the organization or company in which the guest is working is written here.
ADDRESS	:	The address of the company in which the guest is working is written here.
ARRIVAL DATE	:	The date of the arrival of the guest in the hotel is written here.
DEPARTURE DATE	:	The date of departure of the guest from the hotel is written here.
ROOM TYPE	:	The type of the room reserved by the guest is written by the guest.
ROOM RATE	:	The rate of the room charged by the guest is written here.

NO. OF GUESTS	:	The number of guests in the visiting party registered is written here.
DEPOSIT RECEIVED	:	The advance deposit if any, given by the guest is written here.
MODE OF PAYMENT	:	The mode of payment by the guest is selected by the guest out of the available options.
VOUCHER NO.	:	The travel agent voucher number is written here if the guest decides to pay through travel agent voucher.
CREDIT CARD	:	If the guest pays through credit card, the name of the credit card is written here.
CREDIT CARD NO.	:	The credit card number is written here.
EXPIRY DATE	:	The expiry date of the credit card is written here.

(In Case Of A Foreigner Guest)

DATE OF ARRIVAL IN INDIA	:	The date of arrival of the foreigner guest is written here.
DURATION OF STAY IN INDIA	:	The duration of stay of the foreigner guest in India is written here.
NEXT DESTINATION	:	The next destination of the foreigner guest is asked and written.
PURPOSE OF VISIT	:	The purpose of visit of the foreigner guest is asked and asked and written.
DATE OF BIRTH	:	The date of birth of the foreigner guest is written here.

Passport Details

NATIONALITY	:	The nationality of the foreigner guest is written.
NUMBER	:	The passport number of the foreigner guest is writ ten here.
DATE OF ISSUE	:	The date of issue of the passport is written here.
PLACE OF ISSUE	:	The place of issue of the passport is written.

Certificate of Registration/Visa

NO., DATE, ISSUED AT	:	The details about the registration certificate or Visa is written along with the certificate number, date and place of issue.

(Final Formalities)

FRONT OFFICE ASSITANT	:	In this space, the front desk assistant puts his or her signature after filling up the details of the registration card.
GUEST'S SIGNATURE	:	In this space, the guest puts his or her signature after verifying the details of the registration card and thus completing the process of registration.
LOBBY MANAGER	:	Finally, the lobby manager puts his or her signature on the registration card and handovers the card to the front office cashier who opens the folio of the guest for carrying over the various postings and other transactions.

Topic 2: Hotel Arrival Report

Form C (Hotel Arrival Report) Under Rule 14 of the Registration of Foreigners Rules, 1939

FORM C
HOTEL ARRIVAL REPORT
(To be completed in Duplicate)

1. **Name of Hotel** :- Hotel XYZ, New Delhi.
2. **Name of Foreign visitor in full** :- ____________________.
   (in block capitals, surname first)
3. **Nationality** :- ____________________.
4. **Number, Date and Place of issue of passport** :- ____________________.
5. **Address in India**
   (other than Tourists) :- ____________________.
6. **Date of arrival in India** :- ____________________.
7. **Arrival from** :- ____________________.
8. **Whether employed in India** :- ________**Yes / No**________.
9. **Proposed duration of stay in India** :- ____________________.
10. **Number, date and office of issue of Certificate of Registration, if any** :- ____________________.
11. **Date and time of arrival in hotel** :- ____________________.

Prepared by **Manager's Signature**

TOPIC 2

THE HOTEL ARRIVAL REPORT

GENERAL DESCRIPTION

- The "**Hotel Arrival Report**" or "**Form C**" is filled by the front office for the registration of a foreigner guest.
- The form contains the details of the foreigner visitor in full is filled up in duplicate.
- The first copy of the form is submitted to the "**Foreign Regional Registration Office**" in a metropolitan city or to the local police station in small towns and districts.
- In case of a **Pakistani guest**, the forms are submitted within **12 hours** after the registration of the guest.
- In case of any **other foreigner guests**, the reports are submitted within **24 hours** after their arrival.
- The second copy of the "**Hotel Arrival Report**" is retained in the front office for records.

PHYSICAL DESCRIPTION

NAME OF HOTEL	:	The name and address of the hotel is already printed in the C-Form.
NAME OF FOREIGN VISITOR IN FULL	:	The full name of the foreigner guest is written in block letters with the surname first and the first name second.
NATIONALITY	:	The details of the passport are written which includes the Passport no., date and place of issue of the Passport.
ADDRESS IN INDIA	:	If the guest is not a tourist and he is staying in India, his address in India is written here.
DATE OF ARRIVAL	:	The date of arrival of the foreign guest in India is written here.
ARRIVAL FROM	:	The country from which the guest has arrived is written here.
WHETHER EMPLOYED IN INDIA	:	If the guest is employed in India, the details about his employment is written here.

PROPOSED DURATION IN INDIA :	The period or the duration for which the guest will be staying in India is written.
DETAILS ABOUT CERTIFICATE OF REGISTRATION :	The registration certificate number of the guest along with the date and place of issue of the same is written.
DATE AND TIME OF ARRIVAL :	The date and time of arrival of the guest in the hotel is written.

(Final Formalities)

PREPARED BY :	The front office assistant who has prepared the Form - C writes his name here and puts his signature.
MANAGER'S INITIALS :	The lobby manager of the particular shift puts his signature in this space after verifying the details of the form.

Topic 3: Group / Crew Sheet

GROUP – CREW SHEET

FLIGHT ________________.

ARRIVAL DATE ________________. **DEPARTURE DATE** ________________.

E.T.A ________________. **E.T.D** ________________.

S.No.	Code	Room No.	Name	Nationality	Passport No.	Date of Issue	Place of Issue	Signature

TOPIC 3

GROUP/CREW SHEET

GENERAL DESCRIPTION

- The "**Group Crew Sheet**" is also a very important format maintained by the front office department used in the registration process of a foreigner group and is thus a sheet on which the passport details of all the members of the group can be summarized.
- If a flight crew of many members or if a group of a number of guests arrives in the hotel, only one Form – C is prepared and the group / crew sheet is filled in duplicate.
- The first copy is attached to the Form – C prepared for the entire crew or group and sent to the Foreigners Regional Registration Office, while the second copy of the sheet is filled and attached to the registration card.

PHYSICAL DESCRIPTION

(Arrival Details)

NAME OF HOTEL	:	The flight number by which the group of guests has arrived is written here.
ARRIVAL DATE	:	The date of arrival of the group is written here.
DEPARTURE DATE	:	The date of the departure of the group is written.
E.T.A / E.T.D	:	The expected time of arrival of the group to the hotel and the expected time of departure of the group from the hotel is mentioned in this space.
CODE	:	In this column, the alphabetical code numbers allotted to the group leader and to each of the group member is mentioned.
ROOM NUMBER	:	The room numbers of the guests are written under this column.
NAME	:	The names of the guests are written under this column.
NATIONALITY	:	The nationality of the guests is written here.
PASSPORT NUMBER	:	The passport numbers of the guests are written under this column.

DATE OF ISSUE	:	The date of issue of the passports is written under this column.
PLACE OF ISSUE	:	The place of issue of the passports is written under this column.
SIGNATURES	:	The signatures of the guests are taken under this column.
REMARKS	:	The remarks if any such as VIP, VVIP, CIP are written by the Front office assistant.

Topic 4: Arrival and Departure Register

HOTEL XYZ

INDIA

ARRIVAL AND DEPARTURE REGISTER

S.N	Date	Reg. Card No	Name Of The Guest Registered in The Hotel.	C/O	Date & Airport/ Port/ Station of Arrival in India.	P lace From Where the Guest Had arrived.	Time of Arrival	Reason in Detail For Visit	Probable Duration of Stay in India	Room No.	PAX	Rates	Prob able Date Of Dep- artur -e	Passp ort No. & Place of Issue	Name of the Departing Guest	Reg. Card No.	Natio- nality	Room No.	PAX	Tim- e of Dep- artur -e	Departure Given to Person	
																					HK	Room service

TOPIC 4

ARRIVAL AND DEPARTURE REGISTER

GENERAL DESCRIPTION

- The "**arrival and departure register**" is the most important register maintained in the front desk.
- It gives details about all the arrivals and departures for the day.
- Immediately after a guest checks in, the front office assistant fills the details in the register and then in the computer.
- Similarly when the guest checks-out, the front office assistant enters the same in the register.
- Thus, it is very easy to trace the details of the guests who had departed many days ago.

PHYSICAL DESCRIPTION

(Arrival Details)

DATE	:	The date of the arrival of the guest is written in this column.
REG. CARD NO.	:	The registration card number of the guest is written in this column.
NAME OF GUEST	:	The name of the guest is written in this column.
NATIONALITY	:	The nationality of the guest is written in this column.
C/O	:	The company to which the guest belongs if the guest is a corporate client or the travel agent company through which the guest had done the reservation is written in this column.
DATE OF ARRIVAL IN INDIA	:	The details about the arrival of the guest are written here which includes the date of his arrival in India. This column is filled only in case the guest is a foreigner.
PLACE FROM WHERE	:	The country or the city from which the guest has arrived is written in this column.

TIME OF ARRIVAL	:	The time of arrival of the guest is written in this column.
REASON OF VISIT	:	The purpose of the visit of the guest is written under this column.
PROBABLE DURATION OF STAY	:	The duration for which the guest will be staying in the hotel is written under this column.
ROOM NO.	:	The room no. allotted to the guest is written under this column.
PAX	:	The number of guests arriving in the party is written here.
RATES	:	The room rate charged from the guest is written in this column
PROBABLE DATE OF DEPARTURE	:	The date of departure of the guest is written under this column.
PASSPORT NUMBER	:	The passport details of the foreigner guests are written here.

(Departure Details)

NAME OF THE DEPARTING GUESTS	:	The name of the guest who is departing, is written here at the time of departure.
REG. CARD NO.	:	The registration card of the departing guest is written here.
NATIONALITY	:	The nationality of the departing guest is written here.
DEPARTURE TIME	:	The time of the departure of the guest is written here.
DEPARTURE GIVEN	:	After the guest has departed the guestroom becomes vacated. i.e. (not cleaned though departure has taken place). Hence the front office assistant immediately informs the Housekeeping department to get the room cleaned and also informs the Room Service department for replenishing the supplies of the guestroom.

Topic 5: Guest History Card

GUEST HISTORY CARD

NAME -- POSITION --------------------------------------

OFFICIAL ADDRESS: NATIONALITY: PASSPORT NO.

RESIDENTIAL ADDRESS: DATE OF BIRTH:

VISIT NO.	ROOM NO.	ROOM RATE	DATES OF		EXPRESSION	BILLING	REMARKS
			ARRIVAL	DEPARTURE			
1.							
2.							
3.							
4.							
5.							
6.							
7.							
8.							
9.							

TOPIC 5

GUEST HISTORY CARD

GENERAL DESCRIPTION

- The "**Guest History Card**" is a very important report prepared by the registration section of the front office in conjunction with the cash and the reservation section and is a collection of the personal and financial information of the guest recorded by the hotel during his or her stay at the hotel.
- The guest history cards serve as important tools of information for the front office management and help the front office to draft a profile of the guest based on his or her previous stay.
- The information in the guest history card is taken by the front office assistant at the time of reservation, registration and also at the time of the departure of the guests from the hotel.
- Thus, guest history management helps the hotel to maintain a good relationship with the guests and also helps the hotel management to get rid of unwanted guests by refusing them guestrooms.

PHYSICAL DESCRIPTION

NAME	:	In this space, the name of the guest for whom the guest card is filled is written.
POSITION:	:	In this space, the designation of the guest for whom the guest card is filled is mentioned.
OFFICIAL ADDRESS	:	In this space, the official address of the guest is written.
RESIDENTIAL ADDRESS	:	In this space, the residential address of the guest is written.
NATIONALITY	:	In this space, the country of origin of the guest is mentioned.
PASSPORT NUMBER	:	In this column, the passport number of the foreigner guest is written.
DATE OF BIRTH	:	In this space, the date of birth of the guest is mentioned so that the hotel management can greet

the guest if he or she stays at the hotel during his birthday.

ROOM NUMBER	:	In this column, the room numbers allotted to the guest during each of his or her stays at the hotel is mentioned.
ROOM RATE	:	In this column, the room rate charged from the guest during each of his or her stays at the hotel is mentioned.
DATES OF ARR / DEP	:	In these columns, the dates of arrival and departure of the guest from the hotel during each of his her stays at the hotel is mentioned.
EXPRESSION	:	In this column, the personal information about the guest such as his conduct in the hotel with the staff during each of his or her stays at the hotel is mentioned.
BILLING	:	In this column, the mode of payment of bill by the guest during each of his or her stays at the hotel is mentioned.
REMARKS	:	In this column, the financial information about the guest such as promptness of paying the bill during each of his or her stays at the hotel is mentioned.

Topic 6: Message Slip

HOTEL XYZ
INDIA

Date ______________________ Time ______________________

To ____

Room No. ____

WHILE YOU WERE OUT

MR. / MRS. / MISS ______________________________________

OF ____

TELEPHONED	☐	PLEASE CALL BACK	☐
CALLED IN PERSON	☐	WILL CALL AGAIN	☐
		WAITING TO SEE YOU	☐

____

____

____

____

(ACCOMMODATION / FRONT OFFICE ASSISTANT)

TOPIC 6

MESSAGE SLIP

GENERAL DESCRIPTION

- The "**Message Slip**" is a very important format maintained by the front desk and is used for recording messages for the guests *(by a visitor or a by a caller)* when the guest is not in his or her room or is out of the hotel.
- The message slip is maintained in triplicate: the first copy is kept in the mail and message rack, the second copy is put in the guestroom under the door of the guestroom and the third copy is maintained by the front desk assistant for records.

PHYSICAL DESCRIPTION

DATE	:	In this space, the date of filling of the message slip is mentioned.
TYPE OF MAIL RECEIVED	:	In this space, the time of filling of the message slip is mentioned.
TO	:	In this space, the name of the guest for whom the message is being written is mentioned.
ROOM NUMBER	:	In this space, the room number of the guest for whom the message is being received by the front office is mentioned.
MR/MRS/MISS	:	In this space, the name of the visitor or the caller who has left the message for the guest is mentioned.
OF	:	In this space, the contact address of the visitor or the caller who has left the message for the guest is mentioned.
TELEPHONED	:	In this space, the front office assistant puts a tick mark if the message giver has called the guest.
CALLED IN PERSON	:	In this space, the front office assistant puts a tick mark if the message giver had come to meet the guest.

PLEASE CALL BACK	:	If the visitor or the caller has requested the guest to call him or her back, a tick mark is put in this space.
WILL CALL AGAIN	:	If the caller has left the left the message that he or she will call the guest again after sometime, a tick mark is put in this space.
WAITING TO SEE YOU	:	If the visitor who had come to see the guest is still waiting in the hotel to see him, a tick mark is put in this space.
BLANK LINES	:	In the blank lines provided in the message slip, any other message left by the caller or the visitor for the guest is mentioned.
ACCOMMODATION ASSIST	:	In this space, the front desk assistant puts his or her signature after the message for the guest has been recorded by him or her in the message slip.

Topic 7: Mail Register

HOTEL XYZ

INDIA

MAIL SIGNATURE REGISTER

Sr. No.	Date	Type of Mail Received	Name of Guest	Room No.	Registry No.	From Where Arrived	Name of the Clerk Who Received	Forwarded To Address	Remarks

TOPIC 7

MAIL REGISTER

GENERAL DESCRIPTION

- The "**Mail Register**" is a vital record document which keeps a track of all the mails received by the front office for the future guests, present in-house guests as well as for the past guests of the hotel property.
- It is important for the front office employees to write all the important information about a mail of a guest when the same is received by them.
- Thus, immediately the front desk assistants receive mails of the guests, they punch the time of receipt of the mail on the mail and record all the information of the mail in the mail register and then keep the mail in the mail and message rack and inform the guest about the receipt of the same.

PHYSICAL DESCRIPTION

DATE	:	In this column, the date of receipt of the guest mail by the front office is mentioned.
TYPE OF MAIL RECEIVED	:	In this column, the nature of the guest mail received by the front office is mentioned such as courier, registered mail etc.
NAME OF GUEST	:	In this column, the name of the guest for whom the mail has been received by the front office is men tioned.
ROOM NUMBER	:	In this column, the room number of the guest for whom the mail has been received by the front office is mentioned.
REGISTRY NUMBER	:	If the front office has received a registered mail for the guest, the number of the same is written in this column.
FROM WHERE ARRIVED	:	In this column, the dispatch address of the mail is mentioned.

NAME OF THE CLERK WHO RECEIVED	:	In this column, the name of the front desk assistant who has the mail for the guest is mentioned.
FORWARDED TO ADDRESS	:	If the mail of any previous guest has been received by the hotel, the mail forwarding address is mentioned in this column.
REMARKS	:	In this column, any special instructions from the sender regarding the mail received are written.

TOPIC 8: FRONT DESK LOG BOOK

Hotel X.Y.Z

INDIA

LOG BOOK
(RECEPTION)

Date ____________

Day ____________

Shift ____________

Lobby Mgr./ GRE ____________

S.NO.	DETAILS	REMARKS

TOPIC 8

FRONT DESK LOG BOOK

GENERAL DESCRIPTION

- The "**Front Desk Log Book**" is a very important register maintained by the front desk personnel and serves as an important mode of written communication between two consecutive shifts of the bell desk.
- The book is used by the front desk personnel for leaving any important instructions and important piece of information for the staff of the next shift.

PHYSICAL DESCRIPTION

DATE	:	In this space, the date when the log book is filled is written.
SHIFT	:	In this space, the shift when the when the log book is filled is written.
LOBBY MANAGER	:	In this column, the name of the lobby manager who is on duty during the particular shift is mentioned.
DETAILS	:	In this column, the details of the instructions and information left for the next shift is mentioned.
REMARKS	:	In this column, the follow up action taken by the bell personnel for any instructions left by the previous shift is mentioned.

ANNEXURES

ANNEXURE I

CHECK LIST OF RECEPTION FUNCTIONS OF A FIVE STAR HOTEL

CHECK LIST FOR THE MORNING SHIFT

- Read the Log Book for any instructions left by the previous shift
- Call the other competitor hotel properties to know about their occupancy figures and room position.
- Read the Arrivals and Departures Register for knowing the expected arrivals and departures in the particular shift.
- Check the VIPs list for knowing all the VIPs staying with the hotel.
- Check whether the requisition or the order for the welcome drinks have been executed.
- Check for all the guestrooms which are out of order or are under repair and confirm their present status.
- Check for the room changes for the particular shift and inform the housekeeping department about the same.
- Inform the housekeeping department in order to confirm about the total expected departures for the particular shift and follow up with the housekeeping department to make sure that the rooms are ready for the expected arrivals.
- Respond to all the incoming queries about reservations and accommodation in the hotel.
- Make sure that all the coaches depart in proper time to the airport carrying the luggage.
- Manage the guest messages and mails carefully by delivering them to the guestrooms promptly.
- Handling the registration procedures of the individuals, groups and foreign guests.
- Fill up all the registration cards for all the registration conducted during the particular shift.
- Fill up the hotel arrival reports and C-forms of all the foreign guests.
- Update and maintain the arrivals and departures register.
- Properly handle all the complaints lodged by the guests
- Fill up the log book for sending instructions to the next shift

CHECK LIST FOR THE AFTERNOON / EVENING SHIFT

- Read the Log Book for any instructions left by the previous shift
- Check the Arrivals and Departures Register for all the VIPs who are expected to arrive at the hotel in the particular shift
- Handle all the check-ins for the particular shift
- Fill up all the registration cards for all the registrations conducted during the particular shift
- Fill up the hotel arrival reports and C-forms of all knowing the expected arrivals and departures in the particular shift
- Check for all the VIP guests staying in the hotel and the foreign guests
- Check for the room changes for the particular shift and inform the housekeeping department about the same
- Handle all the reservation and other information queries reaching the front desk
- Manage all the messages and mails of the guests properly and promptly deliver them to the guestrooms
- Send welcome drinks requisition for the next day to the food and beverage service department
- Check the housekeeper's report with the room rack and take action in case of any discrepancies in the occupancy status of the guestrooms
- Release all the guestrooms which were blocked for no-shows who had confirmed non-guaranteed reservations with the hotel
- Give rooms on out of service as per formula by 6pm to the housekeeping department daily
- Fill up the log book for sending instructions to the next shift

CHECK LIST FOR THE NIGHT SHIFT

1. Read the Log Book for any instructions left by the previous shift
2. Sort and arrange all the registration cards of the guests who had checked in during the day
3. Prepare and pack all the C-forms to be sent to the Foreigners Regional Registration Office or to the nearest police station
4. Check for all the guests who are expected to arrive at the hotel the next day
5. Check whether the welcome drinks have been ordered for the next day

6. Complete the pre-registration process for all the guests expected to arrive at the hotel the next day
7. Complete the pre-registration process for all the VIP guests expected to arrive at the hotel the next day
8. Print the Expected Arrivals List for the next day and file the same
9. Print and file the No-Show Report
10. Print and file the In-House Guests, Foreigner's and VIPs Report

UNIT – VI
THE FRONT OFFICE CASH SECTION

UNIT VI

THE FRONT OFFICE CASH SECTION

PART A (THEORY)

Chapter 1	An Introduction to the Cash Section
Chapter 2	The Main Functions of Cash Section
Chapter 3	Night Audit in Cash Section
Chapter 4	Job Description of Cash Section Personnel

Part B (Practical Formats)

Topic 1	Guest Account Sheet
Topic 2	Paid Out Voucher
Topic 3	Guest Receipt
Topic 4	Front Office Cash Sheet
Topic 5	Encashment Certificate
Topic 6	Summary of Foreign Currency Exchanged
Topic 7	Safe Deposit Locker's Card

LEARNING OBJECTIVES

- To Study the Organization and Location of The Cash Section of Front Office Departmen
- To Study the Main Functions of The Cash Section During The Various Stages of The Gue: Cycle Which Includes The Functions of The Section During The Reservation, Registratioı Occupancy of The Guest And During Check-out And Settlement Of The Guest..
- To Study The Night Auditing Process Conducted In The Cash Section of The Front Offic
- To Study The Formats Used In The Cash Section of the Front Office.

CHAPTER 1

AN INTRODUCTION TO THE CASH SECTION

DEFINITION

The Cash Section of the front office department is "an integral part of the front office which records the various transactions between the guest and the hotel and verifies the guest and non-guest account of front office for their accuracy and completeness".

ORGANISATION

- It is important to consider and know that the staffs of the cash section are actually under the accounts division of the hotel but they report to the front office manager. This proves that there is an indirect control of the front office manager over the staff of the cash section of the front office department.
- The **Night Auditor** is the head of the cash section of the front office department of a hotel.
- The **Night Auditor** is assisted by the senior cashier and cashier for carrying out the operations and management of the cash.

Night Auditor

↓

Senior Cashier

↓

Cashier

LOCATION

- The cash section is an integral part of the front desk or the reception of a hotel.
- The cash section is generally located in the lobby of the hotel and is seen in the left hand side of the entrance after the bell desk.

IMPORTANCE OF THE CASH SECTION

- The cash section is important for maintaining the folios of the guests in the hotel.
- This section also records the various financial transactions between the guest and the hotel from time to time in the guest folios.
- This section also conducts periodic reviews of the various accounts of the guests and the front office in order to make sure that departmental accounts are balanced against the guest accounts.
- The section is important for profiling the guest on the basis of settlement of bill which is extremely important for the creation of guest history by the front office department.

CHAPTER 2

THE MAIN FUNCTIONS OF CASH SECTION

- The Cash Section of the front office department of a hotel is the nerve centre of the hotel and controls all the financial operations related to the front office department.
- The Cash Section performs a large number of important roles and functions that is important from the point of view of the operations and management of the entire front office department.

RECORDING THE ADVANCE DEPOSIT PAID BY GUESTS AT THE TIME OF RESERVATION

- The cash section of the front office department receives and records the advance payment made by the guest at the time his/her reservation at the hotel.
- Many guests guarantee their reservation by making advance payment to the hotel that is recorded by the cash section.

ESTABLISHING THE METHOD OF SETTLEMENT OF BILL BY THE GUEST ON HIS ARRIVAL AT THE HOTEL AND PROCESSING THE MODE OF PAYMENT

- The cash section of the front office department establishes the method of payment by the guest at the time of his arrival at the hotel.
- The cash section asks the guest to mention his mode of settlement of bill that can be cash, credit card, traveller's cheque, travel agent voucher, letter from the company etc.
- After confirming the mode of settlement of bill by the guest, the cash section performs various official procedures to process the settlement of bill.

(For A Detailed Look of Processing The Various Mode of Payment By The Guest, Please Refer Annexure 6.1 and 6.2).

OPENING THE FOLIO OF THE GUEST ON HIS ARRIVAL AT THE HOTEL

- ❖ The cash section of the front office department opens the folio or account of the guest as soon as the guest has registered himself in the hotel.
- ❖ The main reason behind the opening the folio of the guest is to record the various financial transactions between the guest and the hotel during his or her stay in the property.

RECORDING THE VARIOUS TRANSACTIONS BETWEEN THE GUEST AND THE HOTEL DURING OCCUPANCY

- ❖ The cash section of the front office department of the hotel records all the financial figures related to the financial transactions between the guest and the hotel during the entire guest cycle.
- ❖ The cash section posts the various charges incurred by the guest in the various revenue centres of the hotel such as the restaurants, coffee shops, beauty parlours etc.
- ❖ The cash section completes all the postings in the accounts of the guests on the basis of various source documents that are also called "vouchers".

DISBURSEMENT OF PAID-OUTS TO GUEST

- ❖ The cash section also disburses various petty amounts to the guests on the request of the guests to clear or pay the taxi bill and other small transactions. *(Paid Out)*
- ❖ The cash section prepares vouchers to support such transactions between the guest and front office.

(For A Detailed Look Of The Paid Out Voucher, Please Refer Topic -2).

PREPARATION OF ACCOUNT ALLOWANCE AND ACCOUNT CORRECTION VOUCHERS

- ❖ The cash section prepares account allowance vouchers in order to give discounts and concessions to the guests due to poor services and products offered to the guests during their stay at the hotel.
- ❖ The cash section also prepares various account correction vouchers in order to rectify any posting errors in the folios of the guests, which may increase or decrease the overall account balance of the guest.

THE GUEST DEPARTURE PROCESS

DEPARTURE FUNCITONS PERFORMED AT REGISTRATION

1. Confirming the Date and Time of Departure of the guest from the hotel.
2. Securing the guestroom keys from the guest at the time of departure
3. Updating the room status of the guestroom from occupied to not-cleaned.
4. Informing the housekeeping department about for cleaning the guestroom.
5. Send guest departure notification slips to the other concerned departments and section of the hotel such as room service and telephone exchange.

DEPARTURE FUNCITONS PERFORMED AT REGISTRATION

1. Confirming all the charges incurred by the guest have been posted in the guest folio.
2. Look out for any late charges that require posting into the account of the guest.
3. Prepare and print the folio of the guest with all the vouchers of transactions.
4. Present the folio to the guest for settlement And give clearance to the bell personnel.

DEPARTURE FUNCTIONS PERFORMED AT BELL DESK

1. Confirming the baggage brought down from the guest.
2. Down-belling of the guest luggage from the guestroom to the lobby.
3. Waiting for the check-out process of the guest and clearance from cash.
4. Load the luggage of the guest from the luggage trolley to the vehicle.

Fig. 6.1: The Guest Departure Flow Chart

ENCASHING THE FOREIGN CURRENCY OF THE GUEST

- The cash section of the front office department also exchanges the foreign currencies given by the guest during their occupancy at the front hotel or at the time of their departure from the hotel.
- The cash section gives an encashment certificate to the guest as a proof of foreign currency exchanged by the guest.

(For A Detailed Look of The Encashment Certificate, Please Refer Topic -5).

PROCESSING CHECKOUT AND SETTLEMENT OF GUESTS

- The cash section of the front office department also performs the important function of processing the checkouts and settlement of the guests at the time of the departure of the guest from the hotel.
- The cash section confirms the proper settlement of bill by the guest at the time of his departure from the hotel.

(For A Detailed Look of The Guest Departure Flow Chart, Please Refer Figure 6.1).

(For A Detailed Look of The Account Sheet, Please Refer Topic -1).

(For A Detailed Look of The Guest Receipt, Please Refer Topic -3).

PROCESSING REGULAR NIGHT AUDITS OF FRONT OFFICE AND GUEST ACCOUNTS

- The cash section also performs the important function of performing routine night audits to verify the accuracy of the accounts of the guests and to resolve any sort of discrepancies.
- The cash section prepares various important management reports as an integral step of the night audit process.

PROVIDING SAFE DEPOSIT LOCKER FACILITIES TO THE GUEST ON REQUEST

- The cash section also provides safe deposit locker facilities to the guests on the request of the guests in order to keep their valuable items and belongings in the safe custody of the hotel.
- These lockers are located in the back of the front office in the lobby and are managed by the front office cashiers.

(For A Detailed Look of The Safe Deposit Locker Card, Please Refer Topic -7).

PREPARING THE SUMMARY OF FRONT OFFICE CASH TRANSACTIONS AND FOREIGN CURRENCY EXCHANGED

- The front office cash section also prepares the summary of the total financial transactions taking place in the front office in each shift of the hotel.
- The cash section also prepares a separate report summarizing the total foreign currency exchanged in each of the shifts.

(For A Detailed Look of The Summary of Foreign Currency Exchanged Report, Please Refer Topic -6).

CHAPTER 3

NIGHT AUDIT IN CASH SECTION

BRIEF DESCRIPTION OF THE TEN STEPS OF THE NIGHT AUDIT PROCESS

Post all Departmental Charges in Guest Accounts and Also Complete the Postings of Non-guest Accounts

- This is the first step in the Night Audit process in which the night auditor makes sure that all the postings of the guest accounts are properly completed to begin the night audit process.
- The night auditor should therefore confirm that all transactions have been posted to the proper accounts as they are received at the front desk before starting the audit routine.
- In addition to completing the posting function, the auditor verifies that all vouchers for revenue center transactions are posted and have reached the front office.

Solving Room Status Discrepancies:

- This is the second step in the Night Audit process in which the room status of all the guestrooms are checked in order to find out the rooms which have errors in their room status according to the reports of the front office and housekeeping departments.
- Errors in room status can lead to lost and uncollectible room revenue and omissions in postings.
- The front office should maintain accurate room status information to effectively determine the number and types of rooms available for sale and at the same time to make sure that room rates are properly posted in the occupied rooms only.
- At the end of the day, the room status report is compared with the housekeeper's report and the bucket where the registration cards for in-house guests are kept in order to make sure that the occupancy status of the guestroom is correct. ***(Bucket Check)***

Conduct Trial Balance To Balance All Departmental Accounts Against Front Office Accounts

- This is the third step in the Night Audit Process in which the night auditor balances all the departmental postings against the front office accounts.
- It is generally considered easier for the front office staffs to balance all the departments first and then look for posting errors that has been committed in the front office department.
- The night auditor typically balances all the revenue center departments using the source documents that originated in the revenue center.
- The process used to balance the revenue center departments is often called the "**trial balance**".
- It is only after performing the trial balance; the front office posts room rates and taxes in the accounts of the guests.

Advantages of Trial Balance

- The trial balance usually uncovers any corrections or adjustments that need to be made during the night audit process.
- The trial balance is performed before posting the room rates and thus, if the trial balance is correct but the final balance is wrong, then the auditor can find that the error has been made in the posting of the room rates and taxes.
- Thus, performing the trial balance before the room rates posting avoids the creation of confusion during the night audit process due to the errors.

Verifying the No-show Reservations:

- This is the fourth step in the Night Audit process in which the night auditor verifies all the guests who had a confirmed guaranteed reservation with the hotel but did not register in the hotel.
- Thus, verification of the no-show reservation will enable the night auditor to post retention charges in to the account of the no-show guests who had a confirmed guaranteed reservation with the hotel.

Posting of Room Rates and Taxes

- This is the fifth step in the Night Audit process in which the night auditor verifies the various room rates and taxes that are going to be posted into the accounts of the guests in order to make sure that the right room rates are posted in to the accounts of the guests.
- The posting of room rates and taxes takes place at the end of the business day.
- Once the room rates are posted, a room rate and tax report is generated for the front office management review.

Preparation of Reports

- ❖ This is the sixth step in the Night Audit process in which the night auditor prepares various operational and management reports as an integral part of the night audit process.
- ❖ The following are the important reports generated by the night auditor during the night audit:

Daily Operations Report

- ❖ The daily operations report summarizes the day's business and provides insight into revenues, operating statistics and cash transactions related to the front office.
- ❖ This report is considered the most important outcome of the front office audit.

High Balance Report

- ❖ The high balance report identifies guests whose charges are approaching an account credit limit designated by the hotel.
- ❖ In automated hotels, the high balance report may be produced at any time during the day.

Groups Report

- ❖ The group summary report generally details the various activities of the groups registered in the hotel.
- ❖ It generally shows the number of rooms occupied by each group in the hotel, the number of guests for each group, and the revenue generated by each group.

VIPs Report

- ❖ The VIPs report gives information about the total number of VIP guests registered in the hotel.
- ❖ This report is useful for providing various special services to these guests and also for the hotel in its ability to draw such type of elite guests.

Flash Sales Summary Report

- ❖ The Flash Sales Summary report gives information about the total income generated from the hotel from its food and beverage division as well as from the other revenue centers and also gives information about the occupancy of the rooms of the hotel for the particular day.

Manager's Report

- The Manager's report is also a very important report generated in the night audit process.
- This report gives information about the occupancy percentage of the hotel, total rooms revenue, average room revenue, room count and house count.

Deposition of Cash

- This is the seventh step of the Night Audit process in which the night auditor collects all the cash from the section depositing them to the accounts division in the morning.
- The night auditor counts all the cash collected in the cashier's drawer and separates the cash bank or the "**float**", which had been allotted to him at the beginning of his shift for carrying out the departmental transactions between the guests and him.
- After removing the cash bank from the total amount collected, the night auditor keeps the money in a front office cash deposit envelope and mentions the details of all the money kept in the envelope by stating their denominations and numbers and also mentions if there is any shortage or overage in the amount to be deposited.

Ending the Day's Balance

- This is the eighth step in the Night Audit Process in which all the balances of each of the guest accounts are totaled less the settlements if any made by the guest.
- After totaling the day's balance, the balance is zeroed out or closed for the particular day and is moved as the opening balance of the next day.
- Thus, the night auditor finally begins a fresh business day for the hotel to carry on its business for the next day.

Distribution of Reports

- The distribution of the reports prepared is the final step of the night audit routine.
- It is an essential responsibility of the night auditor to properly hand over the various reports of the night audit to the authorized and designated individuals due to the confidential nature of the reports.
- The reports prepared during the night audit process are generally distributed by the bell boys in the morning to the relevant departments.

CHAPTER 4

JOB DESCRIPTION OF CASH SECTION PERSONNEL

JOB DESCRIPTION OF NIGHT AUDITOR

Job Position Title	:	NIGHT AUDITOR
Job Category	:	Supervisory
Reports To	:	Rooms Division Manager / Front Office Manager
Responsible To	:	Chief Accountant
Position Summary	:	Compile and audit all revenue transactions and reconcile the revenue statements of outlets with the front office accounting machine with a view to prepare a daily report of the day's business.
Hours of Operation	:	Night shift of nine hours from 2100 hrs to 0600 hrs

Duties and Responsibilities

- ❖ Trains the front office cashiers in the Night Auditing.
- ❖ Supervises the working of the front office cash section.
- ❖ Posts room rates and taxes in the guest accounts.
- ❖ Verifies all postings and balances.
- ❖ Tracks rooms revenue collected with the occupancy percentage and other front office statistics.
- ❖ Check guest folios and verify the front office cashier's report.
- ❖ Monitor the credit limit of the guests and prepare various important night audit reports.
- ❖ Prepares a summary of all the cash and credit card settlements from the front office section on a particular day.
- ❖ Prepares important management report which details the results of operations for the management of the department and the hotel at large.

Educational Qualification : Four years Degree or Three years Diploma in Hotel Management and Catering Technology from a reputed and affiliated university or college. A Degree or a Diploma in management accounting is preferred.

Experience : Minimum five years of hotel experience as a front office cashier

JOB DESCRIPTION OF CASHIER

Job Position Title : CASHIER

Job Category : Non-supervisory

Reports To : Front Office Manager

Position Summary : Processes the various transactions between the guests and the hotel during the entire guest cycle. Process the billing arrangements of the guests during the time of check-in and check out.

Hours of Operation : Eight hour shift each day or according to the policy of the hotel management.

Duties and Responsibilities

- Has total knowledge of the various equipments used in the cash section of the front office such as credit card validator and computers.
- Has total knowledge of the various cash handling and credit policies of the hotels.
- Completes the check-in procedure of the guest by opening the folio of the guests.
- Receives cash, drafts and cheques and other mode of payments from the guests during the check-in of the guest.
- Manages the various non-guest accounts related to the guests.
- Post the various charges incurred by the guests in the individual guest folio.
- Process the various paid-outs in the individual accounts of the guests.
- Settles the accounts of the guests during the time of the departure of the guests.
- Balances the department totals at the end of each shift.
- Takes care and manages the operation of the safety deposit boxes.

Educational Qualification : Graduation from commerce stream from a recognized college or university with proficiency in handling cash and processing the various hotel related transactions. Command in reading, writing and speaking English.

Experience : Minimum two years experience as a cashier in any reputed firm or organization.

USING PRACTICAL FORMATS IN REGISTRATION

Topic 1: Guest Account Sheet

Hotel X.Y.Z

GUEST ACCOUNT SHEET

(*ORIGINAL COPY*)

GUEST'S NAME: - ____________ **ARRIVAL DATE: -** ____________

ROOM NUMBER: - ____________ **DEPARTURE DATE: -** ____________

DATE	DESCRIPTION	CHARGE	CREDIT

I agree that I am liable for the above statement and if the person, company or Association by me as being responsible for the payment of the same does not do so, that my liability for such payment shall be joined and several with such person, company or association.

____

GUEST SIGNATURE

ABC, New Delhi– 110001
Tel: 011-26215153
Amadeus access code-IHDELVO34

TOPIC 1

GUEST ACCOUNT SHEET

GENERAL DESCRIPTION

- The **Guest Account Sheet** may be defined "**as a statement detailing the financial transactions between the guest and the hotel**".
- In this sheet, the charges posted into the account of the guest get printed at the time of settlement of bill by the guest during his departure from the hotel.
- The guest account has three copies, out of which the first copy of the account sheet is given to the guest as the guest copy, the second copy is sent to the accounts division for auditing and third copy remains with the front office cashier for records.

PHYSICAL DESCRIPTION

NAME	:	In this space, the name of the guest is mentioned.
ROOM NO.	:	In this space, the room number allotted to the guest is mentioned.
ARRIVAL DATE	:	In this space, the date of arrival of the guest in the hotel is mentioned.
DEPARTURE DATE	:	In this space, the date of departure of the guest from the hotel is mentioned.
DATE	:	In this column, the dates when the different charges have been posted in the account of the guest is mentioned.
DESCRIPTION	:	In this column, the details about the various charges posted in the account of the guest are mentioned and this includes the taxes also.
CHARGE	:	In this column, the amount of the various charges posted in the account of the guest is mentioned.
CREDIT	:	In this column, the amount of charges paid or settled by the guest at the time of arrival, occupancy or departure is mentioned.
GUEST SIGNATURE	:	The guest puts his signature in this space after going through the account sheet at the time of his or her departure from the hotel.

Topic 2: Paid-out Voucher

HOTEL XYZ **PAID OUT** NO. ....

DATE ....

NAME OF GUEST: ____________________

ROOM ACCOUNT NO: ____________________

DETAILED EXPLANATION		

Rupees (in words)

PREPARED BY	AUTHORISED BY		AUDITED BY	
				SIGNATURE OF RECEPIENT

TOPIC 2

PAID-OUT VOUCHER

GENERAL DESCRIPTION

- ❖ The **Paid-out Voucher** is a very important source document used for tracking paid-outs disbursed by the front office on behalf of the guest to settle petty taxi bills.
- ❖ The voucher has three copies out of which the first copy is sent to the accounts division for verification, the second copy is attached to the folio of the guest and given to the guest at the time of his/her departure from the hotel and the third copy is retained in front office for records.

PHYSICAL DESCRIPTION

DATE	:	In this space, the date when the paid-out is made for the guest is written.
NAME	:	In this space, the name of the guest is written.
ROOM ACCOUNT NO.	:	In this space, the room account number of the guest is written.
DETAILED EXPLANATION	:	In this space, the detailed explanation about the reason behind the preparation of the paid-out for the guest is written.
AMOUNT (IN WORDS)	:	In this space, the amount of money disbursed frcm the cash section on behalf of the guest is mentioned in words.
PREPARED BY	:	The cashier who has prepared the paid-out puts his name and signature in this space.
AUTHORISED BY	:	The lobby manager authorizes the transaction by putting his name and signature in this space.
AUDITED BY	:	The night auditor puts his signature in this space after verifying the transaction.
SIGNATURE OF RECEPIENT	:	The person to whom, the front office cashier gives the money on behalf of the guest puts his signature in this space.

HOURS	:	The time when the guest uses the safe deposit locker each time is written in this space.
SIGNATURE	:	The guest signs in this column each time he or she uses the safe deposit locker.
CASHIER	:	The cashier puts his signature in this column each time the guest uses the safe deposit locker.

Topic 3: Guest Receipt

HOTEL XYZ

RECEIPT

SL. NO. / GL Date ______________

RECEIVED WITH THANKS FROM ____

ADDRESS ____

____

THE SUM OF RUPEES ____

____

CASH / CHEQUE NO. ____________________ Date ______________ Bank ______________

Stn. ____________________ ON ACCOUNT OF ________________________________

Rs. A/C Code ______________ CASHIER ____________________

Receipt valid subject to encashment of cheque

HOTEL XYZ

ABC STREET DELHI, INDIA

TOPIC 3

GUEST RECEIPT

GENERAL DESCRIPTION

- The **Guest Receipt** is also a very important format used in the cash section of the front office department.
- The front office cashier normally gives the receipt to the guest when the guest decides to settle his account through cash or cheque on his arrival at the hotel, during his occupancy and at the time of his/her departure from the hotel.
- The front office cashier also issues receipt to the guest when he or she exchanges his or her foreign currency from the front office and thus, the receipt acts as proof that the front office cashier has received the money from the guest.

PHYSICAL DESCRIPTION

DATE	:	In this space, the date when the receipt is made is written.
RECEIVED FROM	:	In this space, the name of the guest to whom the receipt is given is written.
THE SUM OF RUPEES	:	In this space, the amount of money received by the front office cashier from the guest is written in words.
CHEQUE NO.	:	In case he pays through cheque, the cheque number is written in this space.
BANK	:	In this space, the name of the bank of which the cheque has been made and given to the cashier is written here.
A/C CODE	:	The account number of the guest is written in this space.
Rs	:	The amount of money received by the front office cashier from the guest is written here in numerical.
CASHIER	:	The front office cashier puts his signature in this space.

Topic 4: Front Office Cash Sheet

HOTEL XYZ

FRONT OFFICE CASH SHEET OR CASHIER'S REPORT

DATE: ____________

NAME OF THE SHIFT: ____________

NAME OF THE CASHIER: ____________

CASH RECEIPTS					INDIAN RESIDENTS	Foreign Nationals And Non-Residents			Exemption Under Clause No.	Room No.	Name	Explanation	CASH DISBURSMENTS		
Bill No.	Room					Received In Indian Currency	Received In Foreign Currency	Received In Indian Currency Under Exempted Category					Guest Ledger	City or Misc. Ledger	Paid out No.
	In Advance	On Account	On Departure	NAME											

TOPIC 4

FRONT OFFICE CASH SHEET

GENERAL DESCRIPTION

- The **Front Office Cash Sheet** is a very important report generated by the front office cash section in each of the shifts of the hotel.
- The front office cash sheet summarizes the transactions of the front office during a particular shift of hotel.
- The front office cash sheet has got separate columns for stating the receipt and disbursement of cash to and from the front office cash section.

PHYSICAL DESCRIPTION

DATE	:	In this space, the date when the front office cash sheet is maintained is written.
NAME OF THE SHIFT	:	In this space, the name of the shift in which, the cash sheet is maintained is written.
NAME OF THE CASHIER	:	In this space, the name of cashier who has maintained the cash sheet is mentioned.
CASH RECEIPT	:	In this column, the details of the payment made by the guest at the time of reservation / registration, at the time of occupancy of the guest or at the time of departure of the guest from the hotel are written. In the columns provided, the room numbers of the guest who had made any settlement is written along with the name and bill number of the guest.
INDIAN RESIDENTS	:	In this column, the amount paid by all the domestic Indian guests is mentioned.
FOREIGN NATIONALS AND NON-RESIDENTS	:	In this column, the amount paid by all the foreign guests and all the Indian guests in Indian or foreign is mentioned.
EXPLANATION	:	In this column, the detailed explanation of the settlement made by the guest is mentioned.

CASH DISBURSEMENT : In this column, the details of the cash disbursed from the front office cash section are mentioned which includes the details of the guest or non-guest ledger and paid-out number if the front office has issued a paid-out on behalf of the guest.

Topic 5: Encashment Certificate

Hotel XYZ
ABC Road
New Delhi: -110001.
Telephone: - 26215152

ECR

(To be issued by Restricted money Changer on official letter head indicating name and address)

(Valid for three months from the date of purchase of foreign currency)
RBI License No: -ACDH711/8245

Encashment Certificate

Serial No: - ____________________ Date: - ____________________

We hereby certify that we have purchased today foreign currency from .... holder of Passport no. .... Nationality ....
(Name of the person)
and paid net amount in rupees after adjusting the amount towards the settlement of bills for goods supplied / services rendered as per details given below:

A. Details of foreign currency notes/coins/traveler cheques purchased

Currency purchased (Indicating clearly notes and travelers cheques separately)	Amount	Rate	Rupees Equivalent
(1)	(2)	(3)	()4

B. Details of adjustments made towards settlement of bills for goods supplied/services rendered

Bill No./s	Date	Amount
(1)	(2)	(3)

Total ____________________

C. Net amount paid in rupees: .... Amount in words ....
(Total under A minus total under B)

....
(Signature of authorized official)

TOPIC 5

ENCASHMENT CERTIFICATE

GENERAL DESCRIPTION

- The **Encashment Certificate** is a very important format used by the hotel front office to exchange the foreign currencies given by the guests during settlement of the bill by the guest during the occupancy or at the time of the departure of the guest from the hotel.
- The certificate is a license given from the **Reserve Bank Of India** which all standardized hotels hold by them for exchanging the foreign currencies given by the guest.
- The encashment certificate is maintained in triplicate out of which the first copy is given to the guest as a proof of foreign currency exchange, the second copy is sent to the Reserve Bank Of India along with the foreign currency notes and the third copy remains with the front office cashier for hotel records.
- The format has three sections out of which all the three sections are filled only when the guest pays his bill in foreign currency and owes some money in Indian currency from the front office cash section.

PHYSICAL DESCRIPTION

SERIAL NO.	:	In this space, the serial number is printed on the encashment certificate.
FROM	:	In this space, the name of the guest who has exchanged his foreign currency is written.
PASSPORT NO.	:	In this space, the passport number of the guest is written.
NATIONALITY	:	In this space, the country of origin of the foreign guest is mentioned.

A. DETAILS OF FOREIGN CURRENCY NOTES / COINS / TRAVELER / CHEQUES PURCHASED

CURRENCY PURCHASED	:	The details of the foreign currency in which the foreign guest is paying either in cash or in traveler's cheques is written in this space. If the guest is paying

in cash, the numbers of the notes along with the number imprinted on the notes are written. If the guest is paying through traveler's cheques, the cheques numbers are written.

AMOUNT	:	In this column, the amount paid by the guest in foreign currency is written.
RATE	:	In this column, the exchange rate or value of the foreign currency is mentioned.
RUPEES EQUIVALENT	:	In this column, the entire amount in foreign currency multiplied by the Indian equivalent to generate the total amount in Indian rupees.

B. DETAILS OF ADJUSTMENTS MADE TOWARDS SETTLEMENT OF BILLS FOR GOODS SUPPLIED / SERVICES RENDERED

BILL NO.	:	In this column, the bill number of the guest is written.
DATE	:	In this column, the date when the bill is prepared is written.
AMOUNT & TOTAL	:	In this column, the total amount that the guest requires to pay to the front office cashier is written.

C. (A-B) NET AMOUNT PAID IN RUPEES

AMOUNT IN WORDS	:	In this space, the balance amount that the hotel returns to the guest is written in words.
SIGNATURE OF AUTHORISED OFFICIAL	:	In this space, the front office cashier puts his or her signature
NAME	:	In this space, the front office writes his name after the transaction is over.
DESIGNATION	:	In this space, the front office cashier writes his designation.

Topic 6: Summary of Foreign Currency Exchanged

SUMMARY OF FOREIGN CURRENCY EXCHANGED

DATE .... SHIFT FROM .... TO .... CASHIER'S NAME ....

FOREIGN EXCHANGE CERTIFICATE NUMBER	TYPE OF CURRENCY	AMOUNT	@ TC	CN	INDIAN CURRENCY
123567	U.S. Dollar	100.00		1675688 (46.20)	Rs.4, 620

TOPIC 6

SUMMARY OF FOREIGN CURRENCY EXCHANGED

GENERAL DESCRIPTION

- The **foreign currency encashment summary sheet** is a very important format maintained by the front office cash section.
- This format gives a detailed report of all the foreign currency exchanged in a hotel in a particular shift of the day.
- Thus, the front office cashier in each shift of the hotel prepares this report and the same is submitted to the accounts division everyday between 0900hrs and 1800hrs.

PHYSICAL DESCRIPTION

DATE	:	The date when the report is prepared is written in this space.
SHIFT FROM	:	The shift for which the report has been generated is written in this space.
CASHIER'S NAME	:	The name of the cashier who has prepared the report is written in this space.
FOREIGN EXCHANGE CERTIFICATE NUMBER	:	The foreign currency encashment certificate number is written in this column.
TYPE OF CURRENCY	:	The details about the type of currency exchanged are written in this column.
AMOUNT	:	The amount given by the guest in foreign currency is written in this column.
@TC	:	The value of the traveler's cheques is written under this column and the traveler's cheques number is also men tioned.
CN	:	The value of the foreign currency in Indian rupees is written along with the currency note number.
INDIAN CURRENCY	:	The total value of the foreign currency encashed or exchanged in Indian rupees is written.

Topic 7: Safe Deposit Locker's Card

SAFE DEPOSIT LOCKER CARD

(FRONT SIDE OF THE CARD)

HOTEL XYZ	LOCKER NO.	ROOM NO.

NAME ____________________

PERMANENT ADDRESS ____________________

____

AUTHORISED SIGNATURE	

DATE ______________200_____ KEY DELIVERED BY ______________

NOTE: I / We shall not hold the management of hotel liable for any loss of, theft of or shortage in the contents of the Safe Deposit Box Locker which is being used by me / us exclusively.

SIGNATURE / S OF THE GUEST

(BACK SIDE OF THE CARD)

DATE	TIME	SIGNAUTRE	CASHIER

NOTE: - A charge of Rs. ____/- will be leveled for the loss of the Safe Deposit Key.

TOPIC 7

SAFE DEPOSIT LOCKER'S CARD

GENERAL DESCRIPTION

- **Safe Deposit Locker's Card** is a very important format maintained by the cash section of the front office department.
- The safe deposit locker's card is issued to guests wishing to use the safe deposit lockers of the hotel.
- The guests registered in the hotel are required to fill up this card in order to gain access to the safe deposit lockers of the hotel.
- The guest has to sign the safe deposit locker card each time he or she wishes to open the safe deposit locker for keeping his or her valuables.

PHYSICAL DESCRIPTION

LOCKER NO.	:	In this space, the locker number allotted to the guest is written.
ROOM NO.	:	In this space, the room number of the guest is written.
NAME	:	In this space, the name of the guest is written.
PERMANENT ADDRESS	:	In this space, the permanent residential address of the guest is written.
AUTHORISED SIGNATURE	:	In this box, the guest puts his specimen signature.
DATE	:	The date when the safe deposit locker card is prepared is mentioned in this space.
KEY DELIVERED BY	:	The front office cashier who delivers the key to the guest writes his name.
SIGNATURES	:	The guest puts his or her signature finally after reading the above instructions.
DATE	:	The dates when the guest uses the safe deposit locker each time is written in this space.
HOURS	:	The time when the guest uses the safe deposit locker each time is written in this space.

SIGNATURE	:	The guest signs in this column each time he or she uses the safe deposit locker.
CASHIER	:	The cashier puts his signature in this column each time the guest uses the safe deposit locker.

ANNEXURES

ANNEXURE 6.1

PROCESSING THE VARIOUS MODES OF PAYMENT BY THE GUEST IN HOTEL

PAYMENT THROUGH CASH

- Many guests around the world prefer to settle their bill through cash at the time of registering in the hotel.
- Thus, if a guest decides to pay through cash, the front office cashier will request the guest to pay the entire amount of his stay (room charges) in advance during the time of registration.
- Thus, these guests are called **PIA** guests or **Paid In Advance** guests and the hotel does not extend any type credit facilities to these guests as these guests may depart from the hotel without settling the various charges incurred by them other than the room charges in the hotel.
- Thus, when a guest pays through cash, the front office cashier counts the notes and then gives a receipt to the guest as a proof of receipt of payment from the guest and at the time of departure of the guest, marks his folio with "**PAID**" stamp.
- The duplicate copy of the receipt is retained by the front office cash for record purpose.

PAYMENT THROUGH CHEQUE

- Most of the hotels do not consider personal cheques as a very acceptable method of payment.
- Although a hotel has no legal obligation to accept cheques, they cannot refuse the payment through cheques on the basis of illegal reasons.
- Nowadays most of the hotels require cheque guarantee cards for accepting the personal cheques.

The Cheque Guarantee Cards

- The cheque guarantee cards guarantee payments up to the agreed amount (usually between 50 pounds and 100 pounds) provided certain rules are followed.
- Only one cheque is issued per transaction.

- It is signed in the presence of cashier.
- The bank code of the cheque and the guarantee card agree.
- The card number is written on the reverse side of the cheque.
- The card has not expired.

Second- and Third- Party Cheques

- In general, hotels do not accept a second- or a third-party cheque.
- A second-party cheque is one made out to the guest presenting the cheque.
- A third-party cheque is a cheque made out to someone who has in turn signed the cheque over to the guest presenting it.

PAYMENT THROUGH CREDIT CARD

- Credit cards are the most acceptable mode of settlement of bill by the guests all around in the accommodation industry.
- The customer has to pay an annual subscription for the cards and has to settle each month's settlement in full.
- There are no facilities for extending repayment. Generally, the credit limit on charge cards will be higher, and they are likely to be used for the purchase of airline tickets, hotel bills and restaurant bills, and also as company charge cards.
- The procedure for accepting payment by each type of card is broadly the same.
- The card company offers a franchise to the hotel which enables the hotel to accept the cards in payment.
- The hotel is given a "**floor limit**" which sets the maximum amount that can be paid by the card without telephoning or authorization.
- All major card companies operate a 24-hour authorization centre where a cashier may make a reverse charge call to check on the validity of the card or obtain clearance to accept payment of bill above the "**floor limit**'.
- Many front office departments of hotels keep "stop list' of lost or stolen cards.

Procedure Of Payment By Credit Card

- Check that the bill is inside the "floor limit".
- Obtain the card from the client.
- Swipe the card through the machine.
- Ask the client to sign the audit roll (retain the card).
- Check that the signatures on the card and the voucher agree.
- Return the card and the top copy to the guest.

- At the time of departure of the guest from the hotel mark his folio as "**PAID**".

PAYMENT THROUGH DEBIT CARD

- Debit cards have now become a common alternative to cheques and are used by guests to settle their bill in hotels.
- The outstanding sum is taken directly from the account of the guest, in the same way that a cheque payment would be, but the transfer is through an electronic point-of-sale system, and no cheque is necessary.
- The parties, the guest and the hotel instead, receive a slip notifying them of the details of the payment.
- The card used for this purpose is frequently the same card that is used to guarantee a cheque, or withdraw money from a cash point.
- At the time of departure of the guest, marks his folio with "**PAID**" stamp after the transaction is over.

PAYMENT THROUGH TRAVEL AGENT VOUCHER

- This is a very important mode of settlement of bill by guests who come to the hotels for vacation and tourism purposes.
- In this type of settlement, the guest purchases a package from the travel agent by paying him an amount.
- The travel agent in return issues the guest a voucher in original copy for producing the same to the hotel front office at the time of registration in the hotel. This voucher is a promise of payment to the hotel by the travel agent.
- The travel agent already the sends the duplicate copy of the travel agent voucher to the hotel before the arrival and registration of the guest.
- On registration, the front office cashier requests the guest to produce the original copy of the travel agent voucher which is tallied with the duplicate copy.
- At the time of departure of the guest, marks his folio with "**PAID**" stamp after the transaction is over.
- Finally, on departure, the front office of the hotel sends the signed copy of the guest folio along with the original copy of the voucher to the travel agent for payment.

PAYMENT THROUGH COMPANY LETTER

- Most of the multi-national companies around the world have contractual agreements with the hotels for allowing their clients and employees to register and stay on company letter settlement.
- In this type of corporate settlement, the company gives the original copy of the letter to the guest to produce the same to the hotel authorities on registration in the hotel.

- The company then sends the duplicate copy of the letter to the hotel before the arrival of the guest in the hotel.
- At the time of registration, the guest is requested to produce the original copy of the letter to tally the same with the copy received by the hotel.
- At the time of departure of the guest, marks his folio with "**PAID**" stamp after the transaction is over.
- Finally, on departure of the guest from the hotel, the original copy of the guest folio signed by the guest is sent to the company along with the original copy of the letter for settlement of the bill by the guest.

PAYMENT THROUGH TRAVELER'S CHEQUE

- Traveler's cheques are also a very famous method of settlement of bill by the guests in hotels.
- Traveler's cheques are issued in fixed denominations by major banks, travel agents and now building societies throughout the world.
- The customer buys them in their own currency, or in the currency of the country being visited.
- When they are purchased, they are to be signed, and the serial numbers are noted by the issuing bank register.
- Normally the customer pays a service charge of 1% to the bank.
- This charge covers insurance against loss or theft.
- If the traveler's cheques are stolen, the issuing company repays the customer within 24 hours. Hence, the traveler's cheques are much more secure than currency.
- When accepting payment by traveler's cheque the cashier should watch the guest sign and date of the cheque.
- If there is any doubt about the signature, the customer can be asked to sign again on the reverse of the cheque.
- Then, the front office cashier will give a receipt to the guest as a proof of receipt of payment from the guest.
- At the time of departure of the guest, marks his folio with "**PAID**" stamp after the transaction is over.
- The duplicate copy of the receipt is maintained by the front office for record purposes.
- Traveler's cheques must then be paid into the bank account of the hotel, normally with the room number of the guest noted on the reverse side so that any queries that arise can be followed up.

ANNEXURE 6.2

INFORMATION ABOUT CREDIT CARDS

JARGONS RELATED TO THE WORLD OF CREDIT CARD

- **Credit Card** – A credit card is a financial instrument, which can be used more than once to borrow money or buy products and services on credit. Banks, retail stores and other businesses generally issue these.
- **Credit limit** – The maximum amount of charges a cardholder may apply to the account.
- **Annual fee** – A bank charge for use of a credit card levied each year, which ranges depending upon the type of card one possesses. Banks usually take an initial fixed amount in the first year and then a lower amount as yearly renewal fees.
- **Revolving Line Of Credit** – This is an agreement to lend a specific amount to a borrower and to allow that amount to be borrowed again once it has been repaid. Most credit cards offer revolving credit.
- **Personal Identification Number (PIN)** - As a security measure, some cards requires a number to be punched into a keypad before a transaction can be completed. The number can usually be changed by the cardholder.
- **Teaser Rate** - Often called the "**introductory rate**", it is the below-market interest rate offered to entice customers to switch to credit cards.
- **Joint Credit** - Issued to a couple based on both of their assets, incomes and credit reports. It generally results in a higher credit limit, but makes both parties responsible for repaying the debt.

TYPES OF CARDS

- **MasterCard— MasterCard** is a product of **MasterCard International** and along with **VISA** are distributed by financial institutions around the world. Cardholders borrow money against a line of credit and pay it back with interest if the balance is carried over from month to month. Its products are issued by **23,000** financial institutions in **220** countries and territories. In **1998**, it had almost **700** million cards in circulation, whose users spent **$650** billion in more than **16.2** million locations.
- **VISA Card** – **VISA** cards is a product of **VISA USA** and along with **MasterCard** is distributed by financial institutions around the world. A VISA cardholder borrows money

against a credit line and repays the money with interest if the balance is carried over from month to month in a revolving line of credit. Nearly **600** million cards carry one of the VISA brands and more than **14** million locations accept VISA cards.

- **Affinity Cards -** A card offered by two organizations, one a lending institution, the other a non-financial group. Schools, non-profit groups, pro wrestlers, popular singers and airlines are among those featured on affinity cards. Usually, use of the card entitles holders to special discounts or deals from the non-financial group.
- **Standard Card** – It is the most basic card (sans all frills) offered by issuers.
- **Classic Card** – This is a brand name for the standard card issued by **VISA**.
- **Gold Card/Executive Card** – This is a credit card that offers a higher line of credit than a standard card. Income eligibility is also higher. In addition, issuers provide extra perks or incentives to cardholders.
- **Platinum Card** – This is a credit card with a higher limit and additional perks than a gold card.
- **Titanium Card** – This is a card with an even higher limit than a platinum card.
- **Secured Card** – This is a credit card that a cardholder secures with a savings deposit to ensure payment of the outstanding balance if the cardholder defaults on payments. It is used by people new to credit, or people trying to rebuild their poor credit ratings.
- **Smart Card** – Smart cards, sometimes called "**chip cards**", contain a computer chip embedded in the plastic. Where a typical credit card's magnetic stripe can hold only a few dozen characters, smart cards are now available with **16K** of memory. When read by special terminals, the cards can perform a number of functions or access data stored in the chip. These cards can be used as cash cards or as credit cards with a preset credit limit, or used as ID cards with stored-in passwords.
- **Charge Card** – Falls between a **debit** and **credit** card. Works like the latter and you don't have to be an accountholder. Just pay up in full when the bill arrives with the mail. No outstanding are allowed, in other words, no revolving credit facility either. **American Express** and **Diners** are providers.
- **Rebate Card** – This is a card that allows the customer to accumulate cash, merchandise or services based on card usage.
- **Co-Branded Card** – This is a marriage of convenience between two service providers who want a trade-off with the other's strengths. Specific facilities are made to members through these tie-ups. So, **Times Bank** and **Citibank** have a co-branded card that allows consessional rates for add-on cards or telephone banking. **Stanchart** and **Hindustan Lever Limited** have a co-branded card to sell **Aviance** beauty products. **SBI-GE Capital** has a co-branded card for retail loans.
- **Cash Card** – Cash cards, similar to pre-paid phone cards, contain a set amount of value, which can be read by a special cash card reader. Participating retailers will use the reader to debit the card in increments until the value is gone. The cards are like cash — they have no built-in security, so if lost or stolen, they can be used by anyone.

- **Travel Card** – These work mostly as debit cards for the limited purpose of travel. **Citibank, Dollar Card, American Express, Bob card, Global** and **Hong Kong Bank, Thomas Cook International Card** is among the players in this section.
- **Debit Card** – It is the accountholder's mobile ATM. Open an account with a bank that offers a debit card, and payments for purchases are deducted from your bank account. The retailer swipes the card over an electronic terminal at his outlet, you enter the personal identification number on a PIN pad and the money is immediately debited at the bank. **Citibank** and a few domestic banks like **Times Bank** offer this.

UNIT - VII
THE BELL DESK

UNIT VII

THE BELL DESK

Part-a (Theory)

Part - B (Practical Formats)

LEARNING OBJECTIVES

- To Study The Organization Hierarchy of Bell Desk.
- To Study The Important Functions Performed By The Bell Desk.
- To Study The Various Important Records Maintained By The Bell Desk.
- To Study The Left Luggage Handling Procedure in Bell Desk.
- To Study The Job Description of The Bell Personnel.
- To Study The Various Important Practical Formats Filled In The Bell Desk.

CHAPTER 1

AN INTRODUCTION TO THE BELL DESK

DEFINITION

Bell desk may be defined as "section or a part of the front office department of a hotel or a section or part of the uniformed department of a hotel which helps in the transportation of the luggage of the guest at the time of the arrival and at the time of departure of the guest."

ORGANISATION

- The **bell captain** is the head of the bell desk or the bell stand.
- The entire bell section is ultimately under the **Rooms Division Manager**.
- The bell captain is assisted by the bell boys and trainees who work in the desk during the various shifts.

Senior Bell Captain
↓
Bell Captain
↓
Senior Bell Boys
↓
Bell Boys
↓
Trainee

LOCATION

- The **bell desk** or the **bell stand** is located exactly on the left hand side of the lobby while entering the hotel.
- This is supposed to be the first department to come in contact with the guests on their arrival and hence is located exactly near the entrance of the hotel.

CHAPTER 2

IMPORTANT FUNCTIONS PERFORMED BY THE BELL DESK

Transportation of the Luggage of the Guest at the Time of Arrival

- The bell desk performs the important function of greeting the guests on their arrival at the hotel and helping them in unloading their luggage from the vehicles.
- Then the bell boy escorts the guest to the lobby for registration and finally transports the luggage of the guest from the lobby to the guestroom.

Transportation of the Luggage of the Guest at the Time of Departure

- The bell desk also performs the important function of transporting the luggage of the guest at the time of departure from the guestroom to the lobby.
- The bell boy then finally loads the luggage of the guest in the vehicle and wishes him a comfortable stay.

Selling of Postal Items to the Guest

- The bell desk also acts as a mini post office for the guests of the hotels and provides them with various types of postal services.
- The bell desk sells postal stamps, postcards, inlands and envelopes to the guests on their requests.
- The bell desk also arranges for various courier services for the guests in order to send their urgent mails.

Arranging for Paging Services for the Guest

- The bell desk also arranges for paging services for the guest in order to locate him in the hotel in case of any message and mails to be delivered to him.
- The paging activity is performed by the bell boy with the help of a paging board.

Delivery of Newspapers to the Guestroom

- The bellboys in the bell desk also deliver newspapers and magazines in the guestrooms early in the morning.
- The bellboys also deliver various mails, letters and faxes of the guests if the guests request for the same.

Conducting Light Housekeeping Services in the Lobby Area

- The bellboys also assist the housekeeping staff in conducting light housekeeping services in the lobby and the reception area.
- These services include light dusting of the front desk, bell desk and furniture of the lobby area and wiping the door of the entrance of the hotel.

CHAPTER 3

FORMATS AND RECORDS MAINTAINED IN BELL DESK

1) **Bell Desk Log Book: -** The bell persons maintain the bell desk logbook to keep a record of all the activities that are performed by them during a particular shift.
2) **Left Luggage Register**: - The bell persons also maintain a separate left luggage register for keeping a record of the entire left luggage within a bell desk.

(For A Detailed Look of The Left Luggage Register, Please Refer Topic -4).

3) **Scanty Baggage Register: -** The scanty baggage register is maintained by the bell persons to keep a record of all the guests who have registered in the hotel with very few luggages and are a matter of concern to the hotel as they can check-out at any time from the hotel.

(For A Detailed Look of The Scanty Baggage Register, Please Refer Topic -5).

4) **Stamp Register: -** The stamp register is maintained by the bell persons to keep a record of all the stamps that had been purchased by the guests.
5) **Bell Boy Errand Card: -** The bell boy errand card is maintained by the bell captain to keep a proper control on the activities of the bell boys.

(For A Detailed Look of The Bell Boy Card, Please Refer Topic -1).

6) **Lobby Control Sheet: -** The lobby control sheet is a summary of the total activities of the bell persons during a particular shift.

(For A Detailed Look of The Lobby Control Sheet, Please Refer Topic -2).

7) **Inventory Register : -** The inventory register keeps the record of all the inventory items of the bell desk such as: -
   - Bell Trolley
   - Wheelchair
   - Torch
   - Metal Detector
   - Paging Board
   - Stationery
   - Formats

CHAPTER 4

LEFT LUGGAGE PROCEDURE AT THE BELL DESK

LEFT LUGGAGE

- The term "**Left Luggage**" is given to the guests who have left their luggage at the hotel at the time of their departure and had wished to collect the luggage back later.
- The hotels provide the facility of left luggage to the guests as many guests who want to visit other cities in a country many find it inconvenient to carry all their baggage with them or retain the guestroom where they can keep their luggage.
- This facility is also provided to guests who check-out early from the hotel but eventually depart late from the hotel as they might be busy in sightseeing and other activities and thus, may find it difficult to cart their luggage.
- Thus, the hotel management takes the guarantee of safety and security of the luggage of the guest till the time the same is there in the luggage room.

THE BI–FOLD STEP-BY-STEP PROCEDURE OF LUGGAGE HANDLING

At the time of receipt

1. First make sure that the guest who is intending to leave his luggage at the time of departure has settled his or her bill.
2. Fix or tie luggage tags bearing numbers on each of the luggage. These tags have counterfoils.
3. The details of the left luggage are then filled in the left luggage register and the counterfoil is given to the guest.
4. These counterfoils are torn and given to the guest to possess the same as a proof of the luggage kept by the hotel front office.
5. The luggage is finally kept in the luggage room.

At the time of delivery

1. The counterfoil of the left luggage is collected from the guest and the same is tallied with that of the tag attached on the luggage.
2. The date of delivery of the luggage is then entered in the left luggage register and the bell desk personnel retain the counterfoil.

(For A Detailed Look of The Left Luggage Tag, Please Refer Topic -3).

CHAPTER 5

JOB DESCRIPTION OF BELL DESK PERSONNEL

JOB DESCRIPTION OF BELL CAPTAIN

Job Position Title	:	BELL CAPTAIN
Job Category	:	Supervisory
Reports To	:	Lobby Manager
Position Summary	:	To supervise and inspect the overall activities of the bell boys in providing efficient guest services.
Hours of Operation	:	Eight hour shift each day or according to the policy of the hotel management.

Duties and Responsibilities

- Records the attendance of the bellboys at the beginning of each shift and to brief them about their activities and conduct during the shift.
- Ensures that all the bellboys are properly groomed and geared up for providing the guest service.
- Controls the movement of the bellboys by maintaining the lobby control sheet which is a summary of the activities of all the bellboys.
- Maintains the left luggage register to keep a record of all the luggage of the various guests those have been kept at the bell desk.
- Maintains the scanty baggage register for keeping a record of all the guests who have arrived at the hotel property with a very few luggage.
- Arranges for paging service for the guests within the hotel property as and when required.
- Supervises the crew and group wake-up call procedure.

Educational Qualification	:	Graduation from any stream from a recognized college or university or One-year post graduate Diploma in Hotel Management and Catering Technology.
Experience	:	Minimum two years of hotel experience as a bellboy.

JOB DESCRIPTION OF BELL BOY

Job Position Title	:	BELL BOY
Job Category	:	Non-supervisory
Reports To	:	Bell Captain or Lobby Manager
Position Summary	:	Provide transportation services, paging services and other errands assigned by the guests.
Hours of Operation	:	Eight hour shift each day or according to the policy of the hotel management.

Duties and Responsibilities

- Transport the luggage of the guest from the porch to the lobby of the hotel during the arrival of the guest.
- Transport the luggage of the guest from the lobby to the guestroom of the guest after the process of registration.
- To bring down the luggage of the guest from the guestroom to the lobby area at the time of the departure of the guest.
- Deliver newspapers, magazines, mails and other messages of the guest to the guestrooms.
- Pages guests in the lobby area, restaurants and other public area within the hotel property.
- Properly keeps the luggage of the guests in the left luggage room on request and issue luggage tags to the guest.
- Keep a track of all the scanty baggage guests to the bell captain.

Educational Qualification	:	Graduation from any stream from a recognized college or university or One-year apprenticeship programme in bell desk and front office procedure.
Experience	:	No preliminary experience is required.

USING PRACTICAL FORMATS IN BELL DESK

Topic 1: Bell Boy Card Arrival

BELL BOY CARD ARRIVAL

(FRONT SIDE OF THE CARD)

HOTEL XYZ **BELL BOY CARD ARRIVAL**

Guest's Name ____________________

Bell Boy's Name ____________________

Rooming ____________ Room No. ____________ Date ____________

Miscellaneous ____________________

SERVICE CALL WAKE CALL ERRAND OTHERS

Bags	Briefcase	Coat	Golf Bags	Package	Trunk	Laundry	Valet	S/C	Others

(BACK SIDE OF THE CARD)

HOTEL XYZ **BELL BOY CARD-SHIFT/DEPARTURE**

Shift From ____________________ To ____________________
(Room No.) (Room No.)

B.N.P / B-IN HOLD
Amount ____________ Hold Till ____________ Room No. ____________

BELL BOY CASHIER LOBBY MANAGER

Departure: Bags Down ____________ Room No. ____________ Date ____________

INFORMATION RECEPTION CASHIER

TOPIC 1

BELL BOY CARD

GENERAL DESCRIPTION

- The **Bell Boy Card** is a very important format maintained by the bell captain or the shift in-charge of the bell during the working hours.
- The **Bell Boy Card** is maintained for controlling the activities of the bell boys when they leave the bell desk for the jobs associated with the arrival and departure of the guests in the hotel.
- Thus, each time a bell boy is assigned any job for which he or she has to leave the bell desk, a separate bell boy card is maintained for the same and is kept in a tray at the bell desk
- The **Bell Boy Card** is printed on both sides out of which, the front side is used during the arrival and up-belling of the guests as well as during the other services requested by the guests while the back side of the card is filled during room change or during the departure of the guest from the hotel.

PHYSICAL DESCRIPTION

(Bell Boy Card Arrival)

GUEST'S NAME	:	In this space, the name of the guest for whom the bell boy is serving is written.
BELL BOY'S NAME	:	In this space, the name of the bell boy going for service is written.
ROOMING	:	In this space, the time at which the rooming of the guest takes place is written.
ROOM NO.	:	In this space, the room number to which the bell is going for service is written.
TIME	:	In this space, the time at which the bell boy leaves the bell desk for the up-belling of the guest is written.
SERVICE CALL/ WAKE CALL ERRAND / OTHERS	:	In these spaces, tick marks are put according to the service for which the bell boy is leaving.

TABLE OF LUGGAGE	:	In this table, tick marks are put according to the type of luggage carried by the bell boy along with their quantity.

(Bell Boy Card Change / Departure)

SHIFT FROM —— TO	:	If the guest has changed his room, the room numbers of the previous room and the new room allotted to the guest is written in these spaces.
BILL NOT PAID / IN – HOLD	:	If the guest has not settled his bill at the time of his departure or if there is any discrepancy in his bill, his bill is kept in hold and is not cleared and so his luggage is also kept in hold by the bell desk and so the bill amount, the time till the bill will be in-hold is written along with the room number of the guest.
BELL BOY/CASHIER/LM	:	In these spaces, the bell boy, front office cashier and the lobby manager of the particular shift put their initials confirming the bill-in-hold situation.
DEPARTURE	:	This section is filled when the guest is departing from the hotel and contains important information such as baggage down time of the guest, the room number of the departing guest and the date of departure of the guest from the hotel.

Topic 2: Lobby Control Sheet

Hotel X.Y.Z

LOBBY CONTROL SHEET

CAPTAIN .... SHEET NO. ....

DATE .... SHIFT – FROM .... TO ....

ROOM NO.	ATTEN-DANT NO.	ARR.	DEP.	ROOM CHANGE TO	SERVICE CALL	TIME		COMMENT
						FROM	TO	

TOPIC 2

LOBBY CONTROL SHEET

GENERAL DESCRIPTION

- The **Lobby Control Sheet** is maintained by the bell captain during a particular shift in the hotel.
- The sheet is maintained separately in all the shifts of the hotel.
- The sheet is the summary of all the activities performed by the bell boys during a particular shift and so the sheet is prepared from the individual bell boy cards.
- The sheet is thus, a vital means of controlling the activities of the bell boys of the bell desk who continuously leave the desk for jobs allotted to them.

PHYSICAL DESCRIPTION

CAPTAIN	:	In this space, the bell captain who maintains the sheet writes his name.
SHEET NO.	:	In this space, the sheet number of the format is written which is same as the page number for a particular shift.
DATE	:	In this space, the date of maintaining the lobby control sheet is written.
SHIFT FROM —— TO	:	In these spaces, the shift in which the sheet is maintained is written.
ROOM NO.	:	In this column, the room number to which the bell boy had gone for service is written.
ATTENDANT NO.	:	In this column, attendant number *(allotted to each of the bell boys by the bell captain)* of the bell boy who had gone for service is written.
ARRIVAL / DEPARTURE ROOM CHANGE/SERVICE CALL	:	In these columns tick marks are put according to the service for which the bell boy had left. *(In case of room change, the new number of the room allotted to the guest is written)*

TIME : In these columns, the time of departure of the bell boy for the assigned task is written along with the time when the bell boy had returned back after the completion of the task.

Topic 3: Left Luggage Tag

LEFT LUGGAGE TAG

(FRONT SIDE OF THE CARD)

Date ______________ Room No ______________

Baggage Check

No: - 000345

The Management is not responsible for goods left for over 30 days.

____ Suitcase	_____ Briefcase
____ Suit Box	_____ Golf Bag
____ Umbrella	_____ Overcoat
____ Package	_____ Others

No: - 000345

The Management is not responsible for goods left for over 30 days.

Date Room No.

HOTEL XYZ

(BACK SIDE OF THE CARD)

Storage Record

Name ______________________________

Date ______________________________

The owner of the baggage or personal property indicated in this receipt assumes all risk of damage to the goods by fire, water, theft or from other causes.

The Management only undertakes to exercise that it will take proper care of the baggage left by the guest.

The left luggage will be delivered only on showing the tag to The concerned authority.

MANAGEMENT

TOPIC 3

LEFT LUGGAGE TAG

GENERAL DESCRIPTION

- The **Left Luggage Tag** or **Baggage Check** is a very important format used by the bell staff while handling the luggage of the guest during their departure from the hotel.
- The left luggage tag has two parts and is printed on both front as well as back sides.
- The first part is filled by the bell desk personnel at the time of the receipt of the luggage from the guest and is attached to the luggage, while the counterfoil is also filled by the bell desk personnel and is torn off and given to the guest as a proof of receipt of luggage from the guest which is produced by the guest when he or she would like to have his luggage back.
- Both the parts of the luggage tag have a number imprinted which is tallied when the guest produces the counterfoil to collect his luggage back from the bell desk of the hotel.

PHYSICAL DESCRIPTION

(First Part Front Side)

DATE	:	In this space, the bell desk personnel who receive the left luggage from the guest put the date of receipt of the luggage.
ROOM NO.	:	In this space, the room number of the guest from whom the left luggage has been received is written.
LUGGAGE DESCRIPTION	:	In this space, the bell desk personnel put a tick mark and writes the quantity against each type of luggage mentioned.

(First Part Back Side)

NAME	:	In this space, the name of the guest who has left his luggage in the bell desk is written.

ROOM NO. : In this space, the room number of the guest from whom the left luggage has been received is written.

(Second Part Front Side)

DATE : In this space, the bell desk personnel who receive the left luggage from the guest put the date of receipt of the luggage.

ROOM NO. : In this space, the room number of the guest from whom the left luggage has been received is written.

There is also a declaration from the management of the hotel that hotel will not be responsible for luggage kept beyond 30 days at the bell desk.

(Second Part Back Side)

- Finally, on the back side of the second half of the baggage check, there is a declaration from the management of the hotel that the guest will assume all the risk of damage caused to the left luggage from fire, water and theft and the hotel will only take care of the luggage.
- There is also a commitment from the hotel management that the bell desk will deliver the goods only when the guest will produce the counterfoil of the baggage check.

HOTEL XYZ

LEFT LUGGAGE REGISTER

DATE	ROOM NUMBER	NAME OF GUEST	NAME OF THE BELL BOY	LUGGAGE TAG NO.	DESCRIPTION OF THE LUGGAGE	DATE OF DELIVERY OF LUGGAGE	REMARKS

TOPIC 4

LEFT LUGGAGE REGISTER

GENERAL DESCRIPTION

- The **Left Luggage Register** is a very important record book maintained by the bell desk personnel.
- As the name suggests, the register keeps a record of the entire luggage left by the guest at the bell desk and thus, the register details out records of the entire luggage left by the guest at the time of departure from the hotel.

PHYSICAL DESCRIPTION

DATE	:	In this column, the date when the guest had left his/her luggage at the bell desk is written.
ROOM NUMBER	:	In this column, the room number of the guest who had left his/her luggage at the bell desk is written.
NAME OF GUEST	:	In this column, the name of the guest who had left his/her luggage at the bell desk is written.
NAME OF BELL BOY	:	In this column, the name of the guest who had received the luggage from the guest is written.
LUGGAGE TAG NO.	:	In this column, the luggage tag number of the left luggage of the guest is recorded.
DESCRIPTION OF LUGGAGE	:	In this column, a brief description of the luggage left by the guest is written and generally includes the type of baggage and quantity.
DATE OF DELIVERY OF LUGGAGE	:	In this column, the date of delivery of the luggage back to the guest is written.
REMARKS	:	In this column, any special remarks regarding the left luggage is mentioned.

Topic 5: Scanty Baggage Register

HOTEL XYZ

SCANTY BAGGAGE RECORD

SERIAL NO. ----------------------------

DATE: - ------------------------------------ SHIFT: - ---------------------------------

Sr.No.	Guest Name	Room No.	Time of Arrival	Bell Boy's Name	Baggage Description	Remarks Account Assist.	Lobby Manager/ GRE

TOPIC 5

SCANTY BAGGAGE REGISTER

GENERAL DESCRIPTION

- The **Scanty Baggage Register** is also a vital record maintained by the bell desk personnel for keeping a record of all the guests who come to the hotel with a very few baggage or without any baggage.
- The scanty baggage record is maintained in all the shifts of the hotel and is verified by the lobby manager who signs the same after the record is prepared by the bell desk and after the cashier provides billing information of all the scanty baggage guests.
- The front office sends a list of all the scanty baggage guests and circulates the copies of the list to the various departments such as the housekeeping and room service in order to keep a watch on the guests as such guests may leave the hotel anytime without settling his or her bill.

PHYSICAL DESCRIPTION

DATE	:	In this space, the date when the scanty baggage record is maintained is written.
SHIFT	:	In this space, the shift when the scanty baggage record is maintained is mentioned.
GUEST NAME	:	In this column, the name of the guest who has a scanty baggage is written.
ROOM NUMBER	:	In this column, the room allotted to the scanty baggage is written.
TIME OF ARRIVAL	:	In this column, the arrival of the scanty baggage guest in the hotel is mentioned.
BELL BOY'S NAME	:	In this column, the name of the bell boy who escorted the scanty baggage guest to the room is writ ten.
BAGGAGE DESCRIPTION	:	In this column, the type of baggage carried by the scanty baggage guest is mentioned.

REMARKS OF ACCOUNTS ASSISTANT	:	In this column, the mode of payment of bill by the scanty baggage guests at the time registration is mentioned.
LOBBY MGR / GRE	:	In this column, the **lobby manager** or **guest relation executive** who is in duty in the particular shift puts his or her signature after verifying the details of the particular scanty baggage guest.

Topic 6: Bell Desk Log Book

Hotel X.Y.Z

INDIA

LOG BOOK
(BELL DESK)

Date ________________

Day ________________

Shift ________________

Lobby Mgr./ GRE ________________

S.NO.	DETAILS	REMARKS

TOPIC 6

BELL DESK LOG BOOK

GENERAL DESCRIPTION

- The **Bell Desk Log Book** is a very important register maintained by the bell desk personnel and serves as an important mode of written communication between two consecutive shifts of the bell desk.
- The book is used by the bell desk personnel for leaving any important instructions and important piece of information for the people of the next shift.

PHYSICAL DESCRIPTION

DAY	:	In this space, the date when the log book is filled is written.
SHIFT	:	In this space, the shift when the when the log book is filled is written.
LOBBY MANAGER	:	In this column, the name of the lobby manager who is on duty during the particular shift is mentioned.
DETAILS	:	In this column, the details of the instructions and information left for the next shift is mentioned.
REMARKS	:	In this column, the follow up action taken by the bell personnel for any instructions left by the previous shift is mentioned.

UNIT – VIII

THE BUSINESS CENTER AND TELEPHONE EXCHANGE

UNIT VIII

THE TELEPHONE EXCHANGE AND BUSINESS CENTER

Part A (Theory)

Chapter 1	An Introduction to the Telephone Exchange
Chapter 2	Functions of the Telephone Exchange
Chapter 3	Job Description of Telephone Exchange Personnel
Chapter 4	The Business Center of Hotel

Part B (Practical Formats)

Topic 1	Wake-Up Call Sheet
Topic 2	Business Center Voucher

LEARNING OBJECTIVES

- ❖ To Study The Types of Telephone Exchanges Prevalent In The Hotels.
- ❖ To Study The Main Functions Performed By The Hotel Telephone Exchange.
- ❖ To Study The Job Description of Telephone Exchange Personnel.
- ❖ To Study The Operations of the Business Center of The Hotel.

CHAPTER 1

AN INTRODUCTION TO THE TELEPHONE EXCHANGE

DEFINITION

The Telephone Exchange is a very important section of the front office department that manages and places various incoming and outgoing calls of the guests and other people of the hotel property.

The Telephone Exchange is also called the "Switchboard" or the "Private Branch Exchange."

ORGANISATION

The Telephone Exchange Manager is the head of the telephone exchange section of the front office department that is generally under the Lobby Manager.

The senior telephone operators and other telephone operators assist the telephone exchange manager.

Telephone Exchange Manager

↓

Senior Telephone Operator

↓

Telephone Operator

LOCATION

- The telephone exchange section may be located on ground floor or on the first floor of the hotel.
- If the telephone exchange section is located on the ground floor, it is generally located behind the reception or the registration section of the front office department.

TYPES OF TELEPHONE EXCHANGE

Private Manual Branch Exchange (PMBX)

- The **Private Branch Exchange** is also called the "**Switchboard**" which is an equipment connected to the public telephone exchange by one or more lines and the extension telephones are placed in the various guestrooms, offices and departments.
- The equipment takes all the incoming calls to the hotels PBX's operator and the telephone operator in return sends the calls to the particular extensions of the hotel.
- Thus, in private manual branch exchange, the hotel telephone operator makes all the incoming, outgoing and internal connections.

Hotel Outward Billing Information Center (Hobic) Systems

- The **Hotel Outward Billing Information Center** are used as back up telephone exchange system for more sophisticated private automatic branch exchanges in big hotels.
- In the **HOBIC** system, the telephone companies operate the incoming and outgoing calls of the hotel and also price the outgoing calls of the guests of the hotel.
- The telephone operators of the local telephone company use to place all the outgoing calls of the guests on special HOBIC lines and use to bill the guests for making the outgoing calls and send the billing information of the guest to the hotel.

Private Automatic Branch Exchange (PABX)

- The **Private Automatic Branch Exchange** is widely used in the hotels around the world nowadays for managing the incoming and outgoing calls of the hotel.
- This system enables to place and price all the telephone calls without the assistance of the telephone company or the front desk agent.
- This system combines the telephone exchange services with the feature of automatic intercommunication facilities.
- This system has specialized software called the "**Call Accounting System**" which is interfaced with the hotel computer system and is automatically programmed to initiate the placement, pricing and posting of all the calls in the accounts of the guests.
- The operator is only used to give special services to the guests and to connect all the incoming calls, while the extensions have the convenience and speed dialing of their own calls.

CHAPTER 2

FUNCTIONS OF THE TELEPHONE EXCHANGE

- The **Telephone Exchange** is the nerve center of a hotel as it helps in routing of all the incoming and outgoing calls to and from the hotel.
- Thus, the telephone exchange acts as a vital communication hub for the hotel and helps in establishing communication links both with in the hotel as well as outside the hotel property.
- Besides acting as a communication hub, the telephone exchange of a hotel performs a number of functions and guest services.

Routing all the incoming calls to the hotel

- The telephone exchange receives all the incoming calls of the hotel for routing them properly.
- The telephone exchange of the hotel then, places the incoming calls to the hotel into the hotel guestrooms or to the appropriate department or area.

Routing all the outgoing calls from the hotel

- The telephone exchange also performs the important job of routing all the outgoing calls of the hotel.
- These outgoing calls include the calls of the hotel employees as well as that of the guests.

Placing and charging the outgoing calls of the guests

- The telephone exchange of the hotel charges the guests for the outgoing calls made by them.
- These charges are posted into the account of the guests by the telephone exchange that is settled by the guest at the time of departure of the guest from the hotel.

Performing wake-up call services for the guests

- The telephone exchange also performs the wake-up calls for the guests on their request.

- The exchange personnel then take down the wake-up time and other instructions from the guests and execute the wake-up call services at the requested time.

Executing the Do Not Disturb requests of the guests

- The telephone exchange also executes **Do Not Disturb** requests of the in-house guests of the hotel property.
- The telephone operators note down the time till when the guest wants the DND request and do not transfer any incoming calls of the guest to the hotel.

Performing screening of calls on request of the guests

- The telephone exchange also performs screening of calls of the guests on request of the guests.
- Accordingly, the telephone operator intervenes in any incoming calls of the guests to the hotel and transfers only those calls to the guests which the guest wants to attend.

Providing information services to the guests

- The telephone exchange also performs the important function of providing information services to the in-house guests of the hotel.
- The telephone exchange gives information about the various services and facilities offered by the hotel and also about the various events occurring in the hotel.

Handling general enquiry calls coming to the hotel

- The telephone exchange also handles various incoming general enquiry calls to the hotel.
- Accordingly, the telephone exchange provides information about the guestrooms and food and beverage services and facilities of the hotel.

Providing paging services to the guests and hotel employees

- The telephone exchange also provides paging services in order to locate various guests and employees of the hotel when it is required to contact them immediately.

CHAPTER 3

JOB DESCRIPTION OF TELEPHONE EXCHANGE PERSONNEL

JOB DESCRIPTION OF TELEPHONE CLERK / SWTICHBOARD OPERATOR

Job Position Title	:	TELEPHONE CLERK / SWITCHBOARD OPERATOR
Job Category	:	Non-supervisory
Reports To	:	Lobby Manager or Front Office Manager
Position Summary	:	Processes the various incoming and outgoing calls of the hotel, logs wake-up calls for the guests and effectively operate the telephone exchange.
Hours of Operation	:	Eight hour shift each day or according to the policy of the hotel management.

Duties and Responsibilities

- ❖ Has thorough knowledge about handling the various equipments of the telephone exchange such as the EPABX.
- ❖ Has proficiency and required skills in handling the entire operations of the telephone exchange.
- ❖ Replies the various incoming calls of the hotel.
- ❖ Places the various incoming calls of the guests in the guestrooms or the incoming calls of the staff in their departments.
- ❖ Places the outgoing calls of the guests.
- ❖ Receives various messages for the guest if the guest is there in his guestroom.
- ❖ Processes the screening of calls for the guests on the request of the guests.
- ❖ Processes and executes the wake-up call requests of the guests on the request of the guests.

Educational Qualification : Graduation from any stream from a recognized college or university. Excellent interpersonal and conversational skills with command in speaking, writing and reading English.

Experience	:	One year experience as a telephone operator in any reputed organization with proficiency in handling telephone equipments and incoming and outgoing calls.

A CONFERENCE ROOM OF A HOTEL

A BUSINESS CENTER OF A HOTEL

CHAPTER 4

THE BUSINESS CENTER OF HOTEL

DEFINITION

- The **Business Center** is an area where all the business services and facilities are available for the guests to meet their business needs and requirements.
- The Business Center provides a host of special business services to the guests and forms a core product of business hotels.

ORGANISATION

- The **Business Center Manager** is the head of the business center of the hotel.
- The **Business Center Secretary** and **hostesses** assist the manager in the operations of the center.
- The business center may be or may not be a part of the front office department.

Business Center Manager

↓

Business Center Secretary

↓

Business Center Hostess

LOCATION

- The business center of the hotel is located generally on the ground floor of the hotel near the office of general manager and front office manager.
- In many hotels, the business center is also located on the official floors.

MAIN FUNCTIONS PERFORMED BY THE BUSINESS CENTER

- The Business Center of the hotel is an important revenue-producing outlet of the hotel, which provides various business services and facilities for the guests to meet their needs of communication and correspondence.
- The Business Center provides the various business facilities and services to the guests on a chargeable basis.

Providing secretarial services to the guests

- The Business Center provides secretarial assistance to the guests on their request for various services such as taking dictation, setting appointment and managing various correspondences of the guests.
- The service is chargeable and the guest is charged on an hourly basis.

Providing communication services to the guests

- The Business Center also provides various communication services for the guests such as **Telex** and **FAX**, sending and receiving services.
- The service is chargeable and is based on the number pages to be sent through **FAX** or **Telex**.

Providing word-processing services to the guests

- The Business Center also provides word-processing or typing services for the guests on their request.
- The service is chargeable and the charges are based on the number of words to be typed and number of pages to be printed for the guests.

Providing photocopying services to the guests

- The Business Center also provides photocopying services to the guests according to their needs and requirements.
- The service is also chargeable and the charges are based on the number of copies photocopied from the machine.

Providing slide project facilities to the guests

- The Business Center also provides slide projections and other audio-visual services to the guests to meet their requirements of meetings and conferences.
- The service is chargeable and the charges are based on hourly basis.

Providing meeting and conference services to the guests

- The Business Center also provides meeting and conference space for the guests according to their business requirements.
- The service is chargeable and the charges are based on hourly basis.

Providing internet and computer access facilities to the guests

- The Business Center also provides computer-hiring facilities to the guests on an hourly basis.
- Many modern hotels of the world have started providing laptop facilities to the guests for their business requirements.

Settling the bill of the business center

- The Business Center provides the various services and facilities to the guests to meet their business requirements and these services are either chargeable on hourly basis or on unit basis.
- The business center hostesses prepare vouchers for the guests who avail or purchase the various services and facilities of the center. These vouchers are documents which detail the steps of the transaction between the guest and the hotel.
- These vouchers are then posted into the account of the guest if the guest is an in-house guest and the original copy of the voucher is then stapled with the folio of the guest and given to the guest on his or her departure from the hotel.
- In other case, where the guest is not an in-house guest; the main copy of the voucher is returned to the guests when he or she pays the bill.

USING PRACTICAL FORMATS IN REGISTRATION

Topic – 1: Wake-up Call Sheet

HOTEL XYZ

DATE: 16/04/10 **SHIFT:** Evening / Afternoon

SR. NO.	ROOM NUMBER	NAME OF THE GUEST	WAKE-UP CALL DATE	WAKE-UP CALL TIME	SPECIAL INSTRUCTIONS	STATUS
1.	**201**	**Roy Mr. Ram**	**16/04/10**	**0600hrs**	**Remind of meeting**	**Executed**

MAINTAINED BY: ____________________

CHECKED BY: ____________________

TOPIC 1

WAKE-UP CALL SHEET

GENERAL DESCRIPTION

- The **Wake-up Call Sheet** is a very important sheet maintained by the telephone exchange section for providing wake up calls to the guests on their request.
- The sheet contains instructions about the time of placing the wake-up calls to the guests as specified by them and also contains special instructions given by the guests to adhere to while placing the wake-up calls to the guests.

PHYSICAL DESCRIPTION

DATE	:	In this column, the date of filling of the wake-up call sheet is mentioned by the telephone operator.
ROOM NUMBER	:	In this column, the room number of the guest requesting the wake-up call service is mentioned.
NAME OF GUEST	:	In this column, the name of the guest requesting the wake-up call service is mentioned.
WAKE-UP CALL DATE	:	In this column, the date of wake-up call for the guest is mentioned.
WAKE-UP CALL TIME	:	In this column, the time of wake-up call for the guest is mentioned.
SPECIAL INSTRUCTIONS	:	In this column, the special instructions given by the guest at the time of waking him up is mentioned.
STATUS	:	In this column, the delivery status of the wake-up call sheet by the telephone operator is mentioned.
MAINTAINED BY	:	In this column, the telephone operator puts his signature after all the wake-up calls for the particular shift have been executed.
CHECKED BY	:	In this column, the telephone exchange manager puts his signature after checking the details of the wake-up call sheet prepared by the telephone operator.

Topic 2: Business Center Voucher

HOTEL XYZ

VOUCHER NO.

DATE: -

CASH / CREDIT

NAME: -

ROOM NO.: -

S.No.	SERICE	COPIES/PERIOD	RATE		AMOUNT	
			Rs.	P	Rs.	P
1.	Photocopying					
2.	Facsimile Automated Xerox Sending / Receiving					
3.	Secretarial Services					
4.	Word Processing					
5.	Personal Computer / Notebook					
6.	Hire Charges : - Office Chamber/Board Room					
7.	Miscellaneous					
	Entertainment Tax : 10% Luxury Tax : 10%					
	Ordered Received By:-					
	Total					
	Time	**Special Instructions (Incl. time by which service is required) : -**				

In case of credit bills only

Business Center In-charge

Guest

TOPIC 2

BUSINESS CENTER VOUCHER

GENERAL DESCRIPTION

- The **Business Center Voucher** is a very important source document used for detailing the transactions between the guests and the hotel when the guest purchases any service from the business center of the hotel such as secretarial services, word processing, photocopying etc.
- The business center voucher has two copies out of which the first copy is sent to the front office for posting it to the account of the guest and the second copy is retained in the business center for records.

PHYSICAL DESCRIPTION

DATE	:	In this space, the date when the voucher is generated is mentioned.
NAME	:	In this space, the name of the guest for whom the voucher has been generated is mentioned.
ROOM NUMBER	:	In this space, the room number of the guest is mentioned.
SERVICE	:	In this column, the various services provided by the business center of the hotel is mentioned such as photocopying, FAX, secretarial services, internet services, laptop services etc.
COPIES / PERIOD	:	In this column, the total number of copies generated for the guest in case of photocopying or FAX or word processing and the total period for various services such as hiring of boardroom or personal computer or internet is mentioned.
RATE	:	In this column, the price of each unit of services such as each page of FAX or each hour for hiring a computer is mentioned.

AMOUNT	:	In this column, the total price to be paid by the guest for hiring each service of the business center is mentioned.
TOTAL	:	In this box, the total price to be paid by the guest including the applicable taxes for the services of the business center is mentioned.
SPECIAL INSTRUCTIONS	:	In this space, the special instructions given by the guests regarding the hiring of any product or service of the business center is mentioned.
TIME	:	In this space, the time of the generation of the business center voucher is mentioned.
BUSINESS CENTER IN-CHARGE	:	In this space, the business center in-charge or the business center Manager puts his signature after filing up the business center voucher
GUEST	:	In this space, the guest puts his signature if the voucher is posted into the room account of the guest.

UNIT - IX
GENERAL KNOWLEDGE ABOUT THE HOSPITALITY INDUSTRY AND FRONT OFFICE

UNIT IX

GENERAL KNOWLEDGE ABOUT THE HOSPITALITY INDUSTRY AND FRONT OFFICE

LEARNING OBJECTIVES

- To Study About The Famous Personalities of Hospitality Industry.
- To Study The Important and Famous Hotels of The World.
- To Study The Important Chains of India.
- To Study The Famous International and Domestic Airlines With Their Flight Codes.
- To Gather Information About The Countries of The World With Their Capitals And Currencies.
- Too Gather Information About The Technical Terms In The Rooms Division Of The Hotels Industry.
- To Gather Information About Various Important Abbreviations Used In The Hospitality Industry.

CHAPTER 1

EMINENT PERSONALITIES OF THE HOSPITALITY INDUSTRY

Ellsworth Statler (A.D. 1863-A.D. 1928)

Ellsworth Statler is a famous name in the field of hospitality as he was one of the pioneers of this industry and contributed immensely to the development of the hospitality industry through his innovative ideas which are still applicable in the various fields of the hospitality industry.

In **A.D. 1908**, he opened an innovative hotel of its own kind during that time called the "**Buffalo Statler**" which had rooms with some modern facilities such as attached bathrooms, telephone facilities and restaurant facilities.

Statler also contributed a great deal towards the international marketing efforts in the field of the hospitality industry. Statler was also very popular among his employees as he believed in the concept of internal marketing as he used to consider his employees as internal guests.

Conrad Hilton (A.D. 1887-A.D. 1979)

Conrad Hilton is also a very famous name in the field of hospitality and was one of the pioneers of the modern hotel industry. Hilton became a famous and successful hotelier after World War I when he bought the "**Mobley hotel**" in **Texas** and built the "**Hilton Hotel**" in **Dallas, Texas** in **1925**. After the World War II, he formed the "**Hilton Hotels Corporation**" in **1946** and then he formed the "**Hilton International Company**" which had about **125** hotels under its banner.Hilton was the first major and organized hotel chain of American hotels when Conrad Hilton purchased the Statler chain of hotels in **1954**. Today Hilton Hotels are spread in most of the countries of the world and includes **Conrad International, Doubletree, Red Lion Hotels, Harrison Conference Centers, Homewood Hilton Suites** and **Embassy Suites**.

J. Willard Marriott (A.D. 1900-A.D. 1985)

J.W. Marriott was another pioneering name in the world of hospitality industry. He started the **Marriott Chain of Hotels** and thus became a frontline leader in the field of hospitality. He was thoroughly aware of the employee/customer relationship and tried to make sure that his employees were totally satisfied with their job and the working environment. He had a strong marketing brain and could forecast the importance of airline catering business for the various airline operations and was the first to enter in the field of hospitality. In today's scenario, Marriott Corporation is one of the leading companies in the field of hospitality with an annual sale of $7.5 billion and has a variety of food and beverage service operations under his banner. The lodging chain of Marriott includes **Marriott Hotels and Resorts**, **Marriott Suites**, **Residence Inns**, **Courtyards Hotels** and **Fairfield Inns**.

Ralph Hitz (A.D. 1891-A.D. 1940)

Ralph Hitz was also a very popular personality in the hospitality industry. He was the head of the largest hotel organization in U.S.A. called the "**National Hotel Company**". His hotel management company used to receive a management fee for running the day to day administration of the hotels owned by real estate investors.

Hitz had an excellent marketing brain as he was the first intellectual to develop a customer database for providing the guests of the hotel with personalized service leading to guest satisfaction and overall profitability of the hotels. Hitz also started merchandising hotel services through the in-house radio system in order to promote the various facilities of the hotels such as the restaurants. Hitz also believed in training and motivating the employees of the hotels to give more and improved service for guest satisfaction.

Ray Kroc (A.D. 1902-A.D. 1984)

Ray Kroc is famously called as the "**Father of the Fast Food Industry**". Kroc was the first franchisee of the McDonald's to synthesize a demand for a machine called the "multimixer" which could up to five different kinds of milkshakes. Thus, Kroç entered into a deal with the McDonald brother to expand the concept of restaurant which could create a greater demand for his mixers and thus their plan was very successful.

The principle of quick service, clean surroundings and inexpensive food became the base for the success of the restaurants of Kroc as these restaurants immensely attracted the younger and busier families.

Ray Kroc was intelligent enough to understand the value of public relations and thus included them in the marketing and business of McDonald's.

Thus Ray Kroc contributed immensely in making McDonald's the largest restaurant company of the world as this increased the sales of McDonald's tremendously.

Kemmons Wilson

Kemmons Wilson was the founder of the "**Holiday Inn**" chain of hotels when he opened the first **Holiday Inn property** in **Memphis, Tennessee.**

Wilson was an entrepreneur who had great achievements in the field of real estate coupled with a sound hotel management skill. Wilson even built separate chain of hotels for the travellers as well as the business public.

Wilson introduced modern hotel architecture with **high** rise and circular buildings and also started **Holidex** central reservation system in order to streamline the entire reservation process and to handle the immense volume of reservation pouring in the various properties of the chain.

Ernest Henderson and Robert Moore

Earnest Henderson and **Robert Moore** started the "**Sheraton**" Chain of hotels in the year **1937**, when they purchased the first hotel called "**The Stonehaven**" in **Massachusetts**.

The owners acquired several other hotel properties and included them in the hotel chain and at the end of its first decade; Sheraton hotel chain was the first hospitality company to be listed in the **New York Stock Exchange**.

In the year **1968**, "**ITT Corporation**" acquired **Sheraton** hotels and various corporate plans were initiated to create a global network of the properties of the chain.

The Sheraton chain is presently owned by the "**Starwood Hotels & Resorts**" worldwide and is perhaps one of the largest hotel chains of the world.

CHAPTER 2

IMPORTANT HOTELS OF THE WORLD

Name of The Country	Name of the City	Name of the Hotel Property	Year of Opening
ALGERIA	Algier	*El Djazair*	former Saint George, 1912
ARGENTINA	Buenos Aires	*Alvear Palace* *Plaza*	04.09.1932 1909
AUSTRALIA	Melbourne Victoria	*Windsor*	1883
AUSTRIA	Vienna	*Bristol*	1892
		Grand Hotel	1870 / 1994
		Imperial	1873
		Sacher	1876
	Salzburg	*Goldener Hirsch*	1671, first inn 1596
		Sacher	1866 as Oesterreichischer Hof
BAHAMAS	Paradise Island	*Ocean Club*	
BELGIUM	Brussels	*Astoria*	1909
		Métropole	1895
BRAZIL	Rio de Janeiro	*Copacabana Palace*	1923

CAMBODIA	Phnom Pen	*Le Royal*	1929
CANADA	Alberta	*Chateau Lake Louise*	1890
	Banff	*Banff Springs*	1888
	Calgary	*Palliser*	1914
	New Brunswick	*Algonquin*	1915
	Ottawa	*Chateau Laurier*	01.06.1912
	Quebec	*Chateau Frontenac*	20.12.1893
	Toronto	*Royal York*	1929
	Vancouver	*Vancouver*	1887/1939
	Victoria	*Empress*	1908
CHILE	Santiago	*Carrera*	1940
CHINA	Beijing	*Grand Hotel*	1900
CROATIA	Opatija	*Grand Hotel Kvarner -Amalia*	1884
CUBA	Habana	*Nacional de Cuba*	1930
		Plaza *Inglaterra*	29.12.1908 ca 1870
CZECH REP.	Karlovy Vary	*Grandhotel Pupp*	1701 / 1913
DENMARK	Copenhagen	*Angleterre*	1755
EGYPT	Aswan	*Cataract*	1899
	Giza, Cairo	*Mena House*	1886
	Luxor	*Winter Palace*	1887

	Cairo	*Cairo Marriott*	1865 Gezira Palace
FINLAND	Helsinki	*Kämp*	01.11.1887
FRANCE	St. Jean Cap-Ferrat	*Grand Hotel du Cap Ferrat*	1906 (Grand Hotel)
FRANCE	Antibes	*Cap Eden Rock*	1870
	Biarritz	*du Palais*	1893
	Cannes	*Martinez*	1929
	Cannes	*Carlton*	1912
	Évian	*Royal Club Evian*	1909
	Megève	*Mont Blanc*	1880
	Nice	*Negresco*	1913
	Paris	*Inter-Continental*	1878
		Westminster Opera	1846
		De Crillon	1909
		George V	1928
		Lancaster	1930
		Plaza Athénée	1867 Athénée, 1911 P.A.
		Prince de Galles	1928
		Grand Hotel Inter-Continental	1862
		Raphael	1925
		Ritz	01.06.1898

		Lotti	1910
		Meurice	1817 on diff location- 1907
		Scribe	1860
		Le Bristol	1925
		Royal Monceau	
	Sainte-Maxime	*Le Beauvallon*	built in 1913/4, started oparation in 1918/19
	Versailles	*Trianon Palace*	1907
GERMANY	Bad Reichenhall	Axelmannstein	1909, first opened 1846
	Baden-Baden	Brenner's Park-Hotel & Spa	1872
	Berlin	Adlon	1907 - 1945/ 1997
		Bristol	Kempinski, hotel in 1952, renovated 1992
	Bühl	Bühlerhöhe	
	Cologne	Excelsior Ernst	16.05.1863
		Dom	1857
	Düsseldorf	Breidenbacher Hof	1812
		Parkhotel	1902
	Frankfurt am Main	Frankfurter Hof	1876
	Hamburg	Atlantic	1909
	Hamburg	Vier Jahreszeiten	1897

	Heidelberg Hotel Europa	Europaeische Hof-	1865
	Hinterzarten	Adler-Parkhotel	1884, dating back to 1446
	Leipzig	Fürstenhof Leipzig	1889
	Munich	Bayerischer Hof	1840 / 1897 taken over by today's owning family Volkhardt
		Vier Jahreszeiten	1858
	Nürnberg	Grand Hotel Nürnberg	1897
	Weimar	Elephant	1741, mailstation in 1696
	Wiesbaden	Nassauer Hof	1830
GREECE	Athens	Grande Bretagne	1862
HAITI	Port au Prince	Splendid	1929
HONG KONG	Central	Mandarin Oriental	1963
	Tsimshatsui	Peninsula	1928
HUNGARY	Budapest	Gellert	1918
		Grand Hotel Royal	1896
INDIA	Calcutta	Grand	1890
	Delhi	Maiden's	1898
	Jaipur	Rambagh Palace	1840 hotel in 1960s
	Mumbai	Taj Mahal	1903
	New-Delhi	Imperial	1931 (fully operational in 1933)

	Rajasthan	Umaid Bhawan Palace	1971
	Udaipur	Lake Palace Hotel-Udaipur	1746 hotel in 1963
INDONESIA	Jakarta	Djalan Gadjah Mada	former Hotel des Indes 1897
	Surabaya	Majapahit	1910
IRELAND	County Mayo	Ashford Castle	1939
	Dublin	Shelbourne	1824
ISRAEL	Jerusalem	American Colony	1902
		King David	1931
ITALY	Arenzano	Genova	Grand Hotel
	Bellagio, Lago di Como	Grand Hotel Villa Serbelloni	1873
	Cernobbio	Villa D´Este	1873
	Florence	Grand Hotel	1855
		Grand Hotel Villa Medici	18th century Palazo, opened as a hotel in 1960
	Milan	Excelsior Gallia	29.02.1932
		Principe di Savoia	1927
	Montecatini Terme	Grand Hotel & La Pace	1870
	Naples	Grand Hotel Santa Lucia	1900
		Grand Hotel Vesuvio	1882

	Palermo	Grand Hotel et des Palmes	1875
		Grand Hotel Villa Igea	1900
	Santa Margherita, Portofino	Grand Hotel Miramare	1904
	Portofino	Splendido	1902
	Rapallo	Excelsior Palace	1901,1974-1995 closed
	Rome	Bernini Bristol	1870
		Excelsior	1906
		Hassler	1885
		Inghilterra D′	1845
		Grand Hotel	1894 (St. Regis, 2000)
	San Remo	Royal	1872
	Sorrento	Grand Hotel Excelsior Vittoria	1900
	Stresa	Grand Hotel Des Iles Borromées	1861
	Trieste	Grand Hotel Duch D′Aosta	1873
	Turin	Palace	1872
	Venice	Bauer Gruenwald	1949
		Cipriani & Palazzo Vendramin	1958
		Danieli	1822

		Gritti Palace	1948
	Verona	Due Torri Hotel Baglioni	
JAMAICA	Montego Bay	Half Moon Golf Tennis Beach Club	1954
JAPAN	Tokyo	Imperial	1890
	Naka-Ku	New Grand	1873, 1927 former Grand
	Nara	Nara	1909
KENYA	Nairobi	Norfolk	1904
	Nanyuki	Mount Kenya Safari Club	1959
KROATIEN	Zagreb	Esplanade	1925
LEBANON	Beirut	Le Bristol	1951
MALAYSIA	Georgetown Penang	Eastern & Oriental	1885
MEXICO	Acapulco	Las Brisas	1957
	Mérida	Gran Hotel	1901
MONTE CARLO	Monte Carlo	De Paris	1864
MOROCCO	Marrakech	La Mamounia	1923
MYANMAR	Yangon	Strand	1901
NEPAL	Kathmandu	Annapurna	1879
NETHERLANDS	Amsterdam	de L´Europe	23.09. 1896
		Amstel	1866

		Grand Hotel Krasnapolsky	1883
	Noordwijk aan Zee	Grand Hotel Huis ter Duin	1885
	The Hague	Des Indes	1881 renov 1987
NORWAY	Oslo	Grand Hotel	1874
		Continental	12.12. 1900
	Trondheim	Britannia	1897
P.R. CHINA	Shanghai	Peace	1929 (1906;)
PARAGUAY	Asuncion	Grand Hotel Del Paraguay	
PHILIPPINES	Manila	Manila	Dec-11
POLAND	Warsaw	Bristol	1901-1985, 1992 reopened after renovation
PORTUGAL	Lisbon, Estoril	Palacio	1930s
	Madeira, Funchal	Reid´s Palace	1891
RUSSIA	Moscow	Metropol	1898
	St. Petersburg	Grand Hotel Europe	1875 /1991
		Astoria	1912
SINGAPORE	Singapore City	Raffles	1887
		Goodwood Park	1900
SLOVENIA	Bled	Grand Hotel Toplice	1931
SOUTH AFRICA	Cape Town	Mount Nelson	1899

SPAIN	Barcelona	Palace	1919
	Girona	La Gavina	03.01.1932
	Madrid	Palace	1912
	Madrid	Ritz	02.10.1910
	Mallorca	Formentor	1929
	Marbella	Marbella Club	1954
	San Sebastián	Maria Cristina	1912
	Santander	Real	12.07.1917
	Seville	Alfonso XIII	1929
SRI LANKA	Colombo	Galle Face	1864
	Galle	New Oriental	1845
	Kandy	Queens	
	Kandy	Suisse	1850
	Mount Lavinia	Mount Lavinia	
	Nuwara Eliya	Hill Club	1876
SWEDEN	Stockholm	Grand Hotel	1874
SWITZERLAND	Basel	Drei Könige am Rhein	1026 (meeting of 3 kings)
	Berne	Bellevue Palace	1913
		Schweizerhof	1859
	Bürgenstock	Bürgenstock	1873
	Davos-Platz	Grand hotel Belvedere	1875

	Geneve	Des Bergues	1834
		Le Richemond	1875
	Gstaad	Palace	1913
	Interlaken	Victoria Jungfrau	1865 10. Juli
	Lausanne	Lausanne Palace	19.06.1915
		Beau-Rivage Palace	24. 03.1861
	Lugano	Splendide Royal	1887
	Luzern	Palace	1906
	Montreux	Montreux Palace	1906
	Pontresina	Grand Hotel Kronenhof	1851
	St. Moritz	Palace	1896
	Zermatt	Seiler Hotel Monte Rosa	1853 (1839 a small inn with three rooms)
	Zurich	Savoy Baur en Ville Zurich	1838
		Baur Au Lac	1844
		Dolder Grand	1899
SYRIA	Aleppo	Baron	1911
THAILAND	Bangkok	Oriental	1863 (officially 1876)
TUNESIA	Tunis	Majestic	1913
TURKEY	Istanbul	Pera Palas	1892
UNITED KINGDOM	Ayshire	Turnberry	1901
	Edinburgh	Balmoral	1902

		Caledonian	1903
	Fife	St. Andrews Old Course	
	London	Landmark	1899
		Berkeley	1899 / 1972
		Hyde Park	1908
		Langham	1865 (10.6.) -12.1940, 4.3.1991 Langham Hilton
		Ritz	1906
		Brown´s	1837
		Connought	1896
		Savoy	1889
		Dorchester	1931
		Claridge´s	1898
		Grosvenor House	1929
	Perthshire	Gleneagles	1924
	Stratford-upon-Avon	The Shakespeare Hotel	
URUGUAY	Piriapolis	Argentino	1930
USA	Abingdon	Martha Washington Inn	1935
	Asheville	Grove Park Inn	1913
	Stratford-upon-Avon	The Shakespeare Hotel	

URUGUAY	Piriapolis	Argentino	1930
USA	Abingdon	Martha Washington Inn	1935
	Asheville	Grove Park Inn	1913
	Aspen Beverly Hills	Jerome Beverly Hills	1889 1912
		Beverly Wilshire	
	Bolton Landing	Sagamore	1883
	Boston	Copley Plaza	1912
		The Lenox	1900
		Park Plaza Hotel & Towers	31.927
		Parker House	1855
		Ritz-Carlton	1927
	Charleston	Mills House	10.12.1853
	Chicago	Ambassador West	1924
		Knickerbocker	1927 (as Davis Hotel)
		Palmer House	1870
	Columbus	Great Southern	1897
	California	Del Coronado	19.02.1888
	Dallas	Adolphus	1912
	Denver	Brown Palace	1892
	Dixville Notch	Balsams Grand Resort	1866

	Estes Park	Stanley	1909
	Ft. Worth	Stockyards Hotel	1906-07
	French Lick	French Lick Springs	1902
	Galvestone Island	Galvez	10.06.1911
	Hawaii	Royal Hawaiian	1872
	Honolulu	Halekulani	1917
		Moana Surfrieder	1901
	Jekyll Island	Jekyll Island Club	1887
	Key West	Casa Marina Resort	31.12.1921
		La Concha	Jan-26
	La Jolla	La Valencia	15.12.1926
	Los Angeles	Biltmore	1923
		Chateau Marmont	1933
	Louisville	Brown	25.10.1923
	Mackinac Island	Grand Hotel Mackinac	
	Manchester Village	Equinox	
	Milwaukee	Pfister	1893
	Nashville	Union Station	1900
	Long Beach	RMS Queen Mary	1936
	Louisville	Camberley Brown	25.10.1923
	Memphis Tennessee	Peabody	1925 / reopening 9.1.1981

	Mackinac Island	Grand Hotel	1887
	Newcastle	Wentworth By The Sea	1874 (reopens 2003)
	New Orleans	Le Pavillon	1907as New Hotel Denechaud
		Pontchartrain	31.927
	New Paltz	Mohonk Mountain House	1869
	New York	Algonquin	111.902
		Chelsea	1884/1903
		Paramount	
		Pierre	1930
		Plaza	01.10.1907
		Sherry-Netherland	1927
		St. Regis	04.09.1904
		Waldorf-Astoria	1893 First W.A. /1931 (new location)
	Oregon	Timberline Lodge	1937
	Palm Beach - Florida	Breakers	Originally opened 1896, reopened 27.12.1927
	Pasadena	Huntington Hotel Ritz-Carlton	1907
	Philadelphia	Park Hyatt Philadelphia at the Bellevue	1902
	Phoenix	San Carlos	20.03.1928

		Royal Palms	1948
	Pinehurst	Pinehurst Resort & Country Club	01.01.1901
	Rhode Island-	Biltmore	1922
	Richmond	Jefferson	1895 (Halloween)
	San Antonio	Menger	01.02.1859
	San Diego	US Grant	1910
	San Francisco	Sheraton Palace	1875
		St. Francis	21.03.1904
		Fairmont	1907
	Santa Barbara	San Ysidor Ranch	1893
	Santa Monica	Shutters on the Beach	
	Skytop	Skytop Lodge	1928
	St. Louis	Mayfair	1925
		St. Louis at Union Station	
	St. Petersburg Beach	Don CeSar	1928
	Statesville	Historic Vance	1892
	Washington D.C.	Willard	1850
		Mayflower	1925
		Hay Adams	1927
		St. Regis	01.10.1926

	West Virginia	Greenbrier	01.10.1913
	Wilmington	Du Pont	1913
VIETNAM	Dalat	Dalat Palace	1922
	Ho Chi Minh City	Majestic	1925
	Hanoi	Metropole	1901
WESTERN SAMOA	Apia	Aggie Grey's	1933
ZIMBABWE	Harare	Meikles	1915
	Victoria Falls	Victoria Falls	1904

CHAPTER 3

IMPORTANT HOTEL CHAINS OF INDIA

INDIA HOTEL CORPORATION/COMPANY LIMITED

Company Background

"**INDIA HOTEL CORPORATION LIMITED**" is the parent company of the "**Taj Group of Hotels**", the leading private hotel company of India.

The **Taj Group of Hotels** was started on **April 1, 1902**, by **Mr. Jamshedji Nusserwanji Tata**. The first hotel in the chain was the "**Taj Mahal Hotel**", **Bombay** (now **Mumbai**).

The Classification of The Taj Group of Hotels

The **Taj Group of Hotels** is classified into strategic business units to get consistency across the different units in the same brand and standardize the product and service across the brands, making them distinct and identifiable. These brands have been classified as **Luxury**, **Business** and **Leisure**.

1) **Taj Luxury Hotels:** The **Taj Luxury Hotels** are located in the main political and commercial metropolitan cities of India. These hotels offer world class services to the guests with exquisitely decorated rooms and modern supplies and amenities.
2) **Taj Business Hotels:** Located in the heart of India's key commercial cities and towns, the **Taj Business Hotels** provide every modern facility at particularly attractive room rates. These international style hotels meet the growing needs of business travellers visiting cities, which are rapidly industrializing and expanding. Vibrant and progressive, they retain the warmth and spirit of India.
3) **Taj Leisure Hotels:** At the **Taj Leisure Hotels**, pleasure seekers, the curious and those simply wanting to get away from it all can do just that. These properties include idyllic beach resorts, genuine palaces, turn-of-the-century garden retreats, hotels located close to historic monuments, pilgrim centres and some of India's best wildlife sanctuaries. While offering you with experiences entirely unique in themselves, the Taj Leisure Hotels leave you with the unmistakable feeling of warmth.

LIST OF TAJ HOTELS UNDER VARIOUS CATEGORIES

Taj Luxury Hotels

The Taj Westend, Bangalore

Taj Bengal, Kolkata

Taj Coromandel, Chennai

Taj Krishna, Hyderabad

The Taj Mahal Palace & Tower, Mumbai

The Taj Mahal Hotel, New Delhi

Taj Palace Hotel, New Delhi

Taj Business Hotels

Taj Residency, Calicut

Taj Connemara, Chennai

Taj Deccan, Hyderabad

Taj Banjara, Hyderabad

Taj Residency, Ummed

Taj Residency, Aurangabad

Taj Residency, Bangalore

Taj Residency, Vadodara

Taj Residency, Thiruvanthapuram

Taj Residency, Lucknow

Taj President, Mumbai

Taj Residency, Nashik

Taj Blue Diamond, Pune

Taj Residency, Visakhapatnam

Taj Cultural-Centre Hotels

Taj Ganges, Benares

Taj Malabar, Cochin

Taj Hari Mahal, Jodhpur

Hotel Chandela, Khajuraho

The Gateway Hotel, Varkala

Gateway Hotel, Agra

Taj Other Hotels

Taj Kuteeram, Bangalore

Usha Kiran Palace, Gwalior

Taj Palace Hotels

Taj Jai Mahal Palace, Jaipur

Rambagh Palace, Jaipur

Taj Lake Palace, Udaipur

Umaid Bhawan Palace, Jodhpur

Taj Hari Mahal, Jodhpur

Taj Resort Hotels

Fisherman's Cove, Chennai

Fort Aguada Beach Resort, Goa

The Aguada Hermitage, Goa

Taj Exotica, Goa

Taj Holiday Village, Goa

Taj Green Cove Resort, Thiruvanthapuram

Taj Garden Retreats

Taj Garden Retreat, Chikmagalur

Taj Garden Retreat, Coonoor

Taj Garden Retreat, Kumarakom

Taj Garden Retreat, Madurai

Taj Gateway Hotels

Gateway Hotel on Residency Road, Bangalore

Gateway Riverview Lodge, Chiplun

The Gateway Hotel, Ummed

Gateway Hotel, Surat

The Gateway Hotel, Cochin

The Gateway Hotel, Vijayawada

Taj International Hotels

Maldives - Taj Coral Reef Resort

Maldives—Taj Exotica Resort and Spa

Ramgarh Lodge, Jaipur
Manjarun Hotel, Mangalore
The Ambassador Hotel, New Delhi
Savoy Hotel, Ooty
The Gir Lodge, Sasan Gir
The Sawai Madhopur Lodge, Sawai Madhopur
Mahua Kothi, Bandhavgarh National Park
Taj Mount Road, Chennai
Rawal-kot, Jaisalmer
SMS Hotel, Jaipur
Taj Lands End, Mumbai
Taj Wellington Mews Luxury Residences
Baghvan, Pench National Park
Australia, Sydney, Blue Sydney
Bhutan, Thimpu, Taj Tashi

Vivanta by Taj

Vivanta by Taj, Bangalore
Vivanta by Taj, Panjim, Goa

Dubai - Taj Palace
Sri Lanka, Bentota - Taj Exotica
Sri Lanka, Colombo - Airport Garden Hotel
Sri Lanka, Colombo - Taj Samudra
Malaysia, Langkawai - Rebak Island Resort
UK, London - 51 Buckingham Gate
UK, London - Crowne Plaza-St.James
Yemen, Sana'a - Taj Sheba Hotel
Zambia, Lusaka - Taj Pamodzi Hotel
Mauritius, Taj Exotica Resort and Spa
U.S.A, Boston, Taj Boston
U.S.A, New York, The Pierre
U.S.A, San Francisco, The Campton Place

EAST INDIA HOTEL LIMITED

Company Background

The history of **EIH Limited (EIHL)** and that of its founder **Rai Bahadur Mohan Singh Oberoi** is closely linked. The first major property that **Mr. M.S. Oberoi** acquired was the "**Grand Hotel**" (now the **Oberoi Grand**) in Calcutta (now **Kolkata**). The **Grand Hotel** was non-functional at that time after a bout of infection in the hotel. It was leased by **Hotels (1938)** private limited, company formed by Mr. M.S. Oberoi with two other partners. The hotel reopened in **1938**. The property was bought over in **1947** and the partnership was dissolved in **1952** with Mr. Oberoi retaining the sole ownership. Around this time Mr. M.S. Oberoi acquired "**Hotel Everest**" in **Darjeeling** and "**Palm Beach**" at **Gopalpur**, which were owned by separate companies. In **1944**, **Associated Hotels of India Limited (AHI)**, then the largest hotel chain in India, was taken over by him. The AHI properties included the **Maidens**, Delhi, the **Cecil**, Shimla and a number of properties now in Pakistan.

EIHL was established in **1949** when it leased a palace in Srinagar and AHI was merged with it. Shortly afterwards EIHL set up a wholly owned subsidiary called "**Mercury Travels Limited**", one of the first travel agencies to be set up in India. In **1956**, Mr. M.S. Oberoi decided to build a first class luxury hotel at Delhi and EIHL went public in order to raise capital for the project.

The hotel was opened in **1965** under financial and management collaboration with **Inter-continental Hotels**, one of the prominent hospitality companies in the world.

The first round of consolidation of different properties was done in **1963** when the **Palm Beach** (Gopalpur) and **Everest** (Darjeeling) merged into **Hotels (1938)** private limited. The next set was in **1968** when **Hotels (1938)** merged into **East India Hotels**.

LIST OF OBEROI HOTELS IN INDIA

The Oberoi, New Delhi
The Oberoi, Mumbai
The Oberoi Grand, Kolkata
The Oberoi, Bangalore
The Oberoi Amamvilas, Agra
The Oberoi Rajvilas, Jaipur
The Oberoi Udaivilas, Udaipur
The Oberoi Vanyavilas, Ranthambore
The Oberoi Cecil, Shimla
The Wildflower Hall, Shimla in the Himalayas

LIST OF OBEROI HOTELS IN EGYPT

Mena House Oberoi, Cairo
The Oberoi, Sahl Hasheesh, Red Sea, Egypt

LIST OF OBEROI HOTELS IN INDONESIA

The Oberoi, Bali
The Oberoi, Lombok

LIST OF OBEROI HOTELS IN MAURITIUS

The Oberoi, Mauritius

LIST OF OBEROI HOTELS SAUDI ARABIA

The Oberoi, Madina

LIST OF OBEROI CRUISES

The Oberoi Motor Vessel, Vrinda, Kerala, India

The Oberoi Philae, Nile Cruiser, Egypt

The Oberoi Zahra, Luxury Nile Cruiser, Egypt

ITC- WELCOMGROUP

Company Background

ITC-Welcomgroup, India's premier chain of luxury hotels in association with "**Sheraton Hotels Worldwide**" brings the global traveller, the best of East and West: traditional Indian hospitality with contemporary international standards.

Their presence in **41** business and tourist destinations across the country including **8** ITC-Welcomgroup Sheraton Hotels, offers you a gateway to India on business or leisure.

CLASSIFICATION OF THE ITC HOTELS

1. ITC-Welcom group Sheraton Hotels
2. ITC-Welcomgroup Hotels
3. Welcom Heritage Hotel
4. Fortune Hotels

LIST OF ITC-WELCOMGROUP HOTELS UNDER VARIOUS CATEGORIES

ITC-Welcom group Sheraton Hotels

Mughal Sheraton, Agra

ITC Hotel Windsor Sheraton & Towers, Bangalore

ITC Hotel Grand Maratha Sheraton & Towers, Mumbai

ITC Grand Central Sheraton, Mumbai

ITC Hotel Kakatiya Sheraton & Towers, Hyderabad

ITC Sonar Bangla, Kolkata

ITC Royal Gardenia

ITC Hotel Maurya Sheraton & Towers, New Delhi

ITC-Welcomgroup Hotels

Welcom Hotel Rama International, Aurangabad

Welcom Hotel Vadodara, Baroda

Chola Sheraton, Chennai

Sheraton, New Delhi

Rajputana Sheraton, Jaipur

WelcomHeritage Hotels

Bal Samand Lake Palace, Jodhpur

Bal Samand Garden Retreat,

Fortune Hotels

Fortune Hotel Landmark, Ahmedabad

Fortune Park Calicut, Calicut

Bandhavgarh Jungle Resort, Bandhavgarh
Lallgarh Palace, Bikaner
Mandir Palace, Jaisalmer
Grand Imperial, Agra
Chalets Naldhera, Naldhera
Taragarh Palace, Palampur
Kanha Jungle Lodge, Kanha
Khimsar Fort, Khimsar
Umed Bhawan Palace, Kota
Connaught House, Mount Abu
Royal Camp, Nagaur Fort
Sardar Samand Palace, Pali
Royal Camp, Pushkar, Pushkar
The Judge's Court, Pragpur
Maharani Bagh Orchard Retreat, Ranakpur
Woodville Palace, Shimla
The Fort Nalagarh, Solan
Corbett Ramganga Resort, Corbett National Park
The Palace Belvedere, Nainital, Nainital
Bassi Fort, Chittaurgarh
Bijay Niwas Palace, Ajmer
Bob' Place Nathuakhan
Burra Sahib's Baungalow, Jorhat
Calve Pondicherry
Camellia Hotek & Resort, Shantiniketan
Chinnar Plantation Bungalow Elappara, Idukki Dist.
Denzong Regency Retreat Village Tippi
Fernhills Palace Ooty
Golf View Pachmarhi
Grace Hotel, Dharamshala
Gulaab Niwas Palace, Pushkar
Gurkha Houseboat, Srinagar
Hirlicheena Nature Resort, Manan Village
Ksamanda Palace, Mussoorie

Fortune Resort Central, Darjeeling
Fortune Hotel Center Point, Jamshedpur
Fortune Chariot Resort, Mahabalipuram
Fortune Hotel The South Park, Trivandrum
Fortune Resort Bay Island, Port Blair
Fortune Global Select, Gurgaon
Fortune Select Palms, Chennai
Fortune Select Trinity, Bangalore
Fortune Select Exotica, Navi Mumbai
Fortune Select Manohar, Hyderabad
Fortune Landmark, Indore
Fortune Park Galaxy, Vapi
Fortune Murali Park, Vijayawada
Fortune Park Klassik, Ludhiana
Fortune Pandiyan Hotel, Madurai
Fortune Park Panchawati, Kolkata
Fortune Fenes, Tirupati
Fortune Inn Riviera, Jammu

Fortune Inn Jucaso, Pune
Fortune Inn Sri Kanya, Visakhapatnam
Fortune Resort Sullivan Court, Ooty

Khazanchand Mansion, Almora
Khimsar Sand Dunes Village, Khimsar
Kilar Lodge, Anandpur Sahib
Koolwal Kothi, Nawalgarh
Lal Niwas, Phalodi
Mandir Palace, Jaisalmer
Mistry Sahib's Bungalow, Jorhat
Noor-Us-Sabah Palace, Bhopal
Palace Balvedere, Nainital
Pemaling, Dirang
Pragati Resorts, Hyderabad
Rajendra Villas Palace, Mysore
Ranjit's Svaasa, Amritsar
Ranthambore Forest Resort, Sawai Madhopur
Raobagh Palace, Bundelkhand
Regency Villas, Ooty
Rosaville, Shillong
Royal Camp, Pushkar
Shalini Palace, Kolhapur
Shambha-La, Leh Ladakh
Sheikhpura Kothi, Hansi
Singhasan haveli, Mandwa
Solang Valley Resort, Manali
Taradake Cottage, Ramgarh
Thengla Manor, Jorhat
Windamere Hotel, Darjeeling
Windsor Lodge, Ranikhet

ITDC - ASHOKA GROUP OF HOTELS

The "**Ashok Group of Hotels**" has been India's gracious and regal host to leading national and international visitors. The Group is known for its unique mix of traditional Indian hospitality and modern-day systems and facilities that are beyond compare. The group has **16** hotels in **12** major destinations.

CLASSIFICATION OF THE ITC HOTELS

1. Ashok Elite Hotels
2. Ashok Classic Hotels
3. Ashok Comfort Hotels

LIST OF ITDC-ASHOKA GROUP OF HOTELS UNDER VARIOUS CATEGORIES

Ashok Elite Hotels
Askok Hotel, New Delhi
Samrat Hotel, New Delhi
Lalitha Mahal Palace, Mysore

Ashok Comfort Hotels
Lake View Ashok, Bhopal
Brahmaputra Ashok, Guwahati
Donyi Polo Ashok, Itanagar
Pondicherry Ashok, Pondicherry
Ranchi Ashok , Ranchi
Nilanchal Ashok, Puri

Ashok Classic Hotels
Hotel Janpath, New Delhi
Bharatpur Ashok, Bharatpur
Kalinga Ashok, Bhubaneswar
Jaipur Ashok, Jaipur
Jammu Ashok, Jammu

Tourist Complex
Kosi Tourist Complex

OTHER IMPORTANT HOTEL CHAINS OF INDIA

Ambassador Group of Hotels

The "**Ambassador Group of Hotels**" in India boasts of some of the best hotels in India. Ambassador believes that a great hotel should offer more than a good night's sleep. It should create an environment that awakens your senses. It's one of the many intangible qualities you'll experience at every Ambassador hotel.

Best Western Group of Hotels

The "**Best Western Group of Hotels**" in India boasts of some of the best hotels in India. The hotels are located the prime tourist locations of India like the marvelous city of **Mumbai,**

Chennai, **Kolkata**, **Hyderabad**, **Khajuraho**, **Dehradun**, **Varanasi** and **Kovalam**. The hotels run by the Best Western Group in India offer simple luxury and privacy at the same time.

Casino Group of Hotels

The "**Casino Group of Hotels**" in India boasts of some of the best hotels in India. The hotels are located the prime tourist locations of India. The Casino Group has hotels has hotels in tourists destinations like **Casino hotel** at **Cochin**, **Coconut Lagoon** at **Kumarakom**, **Spice Coast Cruises** at **Puthenangadi**, **Spice Village** at **Thekkady** and **Marari Beach Resort** at **Alleppy**.

U.P. Chain of Hotels

"**The Clarks Group of Hotels**" in India boasts of some of the best hotels in India. The hotels are located the prime tourist locations of India like the amazing city of **Agra**, **Jaipur**, **Shimla** and **Varanasi**. The hotels run by the Clarks Group offer simple luxury and privacy at the same time.

Holiday Inn Group of Hotels

The "**Holiday Inn Group of Hotels**" in India boasts of some of the best hotels in India. The hotels are located at amazing locations of the cities of **Agra**, **Jaipur** and **Goa**.

HRH Hotels

"**HRH Hotels**" is the largest owner/manager of heritage hotels in India offering world-class accommodation options for travellers. Most of these hotels are redone former palaces, mansions, and havelis of former kings and royalty of India. The royal services and luxury offered by these hotels are unmatched and an experience not easily forgotten.

K Raheja Group of Hotels

The "**K Raheja Group of Hotels**" in India boasts of some of the best hotels in India. The hotels are located at the prime tourist locations of India like the captivating destination of **Kodaikanal**, **Mumbai** and **Bangalore**.

Le Meridien Group of Hotels

The "**Le Meridien Group of Hotels**" in India boasts of some of the best hotels in India. The hotels are located at the prime tourist locations of India like the capital city of **New Delhi**, **Mumbai**, **Chennai**, **Cochin**, **Pune** and **Bangalore**.

Mansingh Group Of Hotels

The "**Mansingh Group of Hotels**" in India boasts of some of the best hotels in India. Keeping alive the old age traditions of India Mansingh group brings to you the authenticity of the historic cities of **Agra** and **Jaipur** wrapped in the fragrance of the land. The hotels run by the Mansingh Group in India offer simple luxury and privacy at the same time.

Peerless Group of Hotels

The "**Peerless Group of Hotels**" in India boasts of some of the best hotels in India. The Peerless Group is a family of hotels, resorts and inns spread out in **Kolkata**, **Port Blair** (**Andamans**), **Mukutmonipur** and **Durgapur**- four destinations off efficient hospitality.

Sarovar Park Plaza Hotels

"**Sarovar Park Plaza Hotels**" is one of the most recent but one of the fastest growing hotel chains in India. With 44 hotels already operational in different parts of the country , the chain is poised to be a big player in Indian hospitality sector. Most of the hotels managed by Sarovar Park Plaza are located in the medium sized cities, offering the travellers visiting these places better accommodation opportunities.

Sinclair Group of Hotels

The "**Sinclairs Group of Hotels**" in India boasts of some of the best hotels in India. The hotels are located at the prime tourist locations of India like the dream destination of **Darjeeling**, **Siliguri** and **Ooty**.

Tulip Star Group of Hotels

The "**Tulip Star Group of Hotels**" in India boasts of some of the best hotels in India. The hotels are located at the prime tourist locations that dot the various states of India like the gorgeous **Goa**, **Kerala**, **Maharashtra**, **Rajasthan**, **Delhi**, **Uttar Pradesh**, **Uttaranchal**, **Orissa** and **Gujarat**.

CHAPTER 4

IMPORTANT AIRLINES AND THEIR CODES

INTERNATIONAL AIRLINES

NAME OF THE AIRLINES	COUNTRY	FLIGHT CODE
Aeroflot Soviet Airways	USSR	SU
Air Alfa	Turkey	H7
Air Canada	Canada	AC
Air China	China	CA
Air France	France	AF
Air Lanka	Sri Lanka	AL
Air India	India	AI
Air Jamaica	Jamaica	JM
Air Mauritius	Mauritius	MK
Air New Zealand	New Zealand	NZ
Air Sofia	Bulgaria	CT
Air Tanzania	Tanzania	TC
Alitalia	Italy	AZ
American Airlines	USA	AA
Argentina Airlines	Argentina	AR
Asiana Airlines	South Korea	OZ
Austrian Airlines	Austria	OS
Avianca	Colombia	AV
British Airways	United Kingdom	BA
Bangladesh Biman	Bangladesh	BG
Egyptair	Egypt	MS
Emirates	United Arab Emirates	EK
Ethiopian Airlines	Ethiopia	ET

Finn Air	Finland	AY
Iberia	Spain	IB
Iran Air	Iran	IR
Iraqi Airways	Iraq	IA
Japan Airlines	Japan	JL
KLM Royal Dutch Airlines	Netherlands	KL
Kenya Airways	Kenya	KQ
Kuwait Airways	Kuwait	KU
Lan Chile	Chile	LA
Lufthansa	Germany	LH
Malaysia Airlines	Malaysia	MH
Mexicana Airlines	Mexico	MX
Nigeria Airways	Nigeria	WT
Oman Air	Oman	WY
Pakistan International Airlines	Pakistan	PK
Portugalia	Portugal	NI
Quantas Airways	Australia	QF
Qatar Airways	Qatar	QR
Royal Nepal Airlines	Nepal	RA
Royal Jordanian Airlines	Jordan	RJ
Sabena	Belgium	SN
Singapore Airlines	Singapore	SQ
Swiss Air	Switzerland	SR
Thai International Airlines	Thailand	TG
Tunisair	Tunis	TU

DOMESTIC AIRLINES OF INDIA

NAME OF THE AIRLINES	FLIGHT CODE
Air India	AI
Air India Express	IX
Air India Regional	CD
Blue Dart Aviation	BZ
Kingfisher Red	DN
Deccan Aviation	DN

Go Air	G8
Indigo Airlines	6E
Jagson Airlines	JA
Jet Airways	9W
Jet Lite	S2
Kingfisher Airlines	IT
MDLR Airlines	9H
Paramount Airways	I7
SpiceJet	SG
Hi Flying Group	H9

CHAPTER 5

LIST OF COUNTRIES WITH THEIR CAPITALS AND CURRENCIES

COUNTRY	CAPITAL	CURRENCY
Afghanistan	Kabul	Afghani
Albania	Tirana	Lek
Algeria	Algiers	Dinar
Argentina	Buenos Aires	Peso
Australia	Canberra	Dollar
Austria	Vienna	Euro
Bahrain	Manama	Dinar
Bangladesh	Dhaka	Taka
Belgium	Brussels	Euro
Bhutan	Thimphu	Ngultrum
Bolivia	La Paz	Boliviano
Brazil	Brasilia	Real
Bulgaria	Sofia	Lev
Cambodia	Phnom Penh	Riel
Canada	Ottawa	C. Dollar
Chile	Santiago	Peso
China	Beijing	Yuan
Colombia	Bogotá	Peso
Cuba	Havana	Peso
Czech Republic	Prague	Koruna
Denmark	Copenhagen	Krone
Egypt	Cairo	E. Pound
Ethiopia	Addis Ababa	Ethiopian Birr

Finland	Helsinki	Euro
France	Paris	Euro
Germany	Berlin	Euro
Ghana	Accra	Cedi
Greece	Athens	Euro
Hungary	Budapest	Forint
India	New Delhi	Rupee
Indonesia	Djakarta	Rupiah
Iran	Tehran	Rial
Iraq	Baghdad	Dinar
Ireland	Dublin	Euro
Israel	Jerusalem	Shekel
Italy	Rome	Euro
Japan	Tokyo	Yen
Jordan	Amman	Dinar
Kenya	Nairobi	K. Schilling
Kuwait	Kuwait City	Dinar
Lebanon	Beirut	L. Pound
Malaysia	Kuala Lumpur	Ringgit
Maldives	Male	Rufiyaa
Mauritius	Port Louis	M. Rupee
Mexico	Mexico City	M. Peso
Mongolia	Ulan Bator	Tugrik
Morocco	Rabat	Dirham
Nepal	Kathmandu	Rupee
Netherlands	Amsterdam	Guilder
New Zealand	Wellington	N. Dollar
North Korea	Pyongyang	Won
Norway	Oslo	Krone
Pakistan	Islamabad	P. Rupee
Peru	Lima	Nuevo Sol
Philippines	Manila	P. Peso
Poland	Warsaw	Zloty
Portugal	Lisbon	Escudo

Romania	Bucharest	Leu
Russia	Moscow	Rouble
Saudi Arabia	Riyadh	Riyal
Seychelles	Victoria	S. Rupee
Singapore	Singapore City	S. Dollar
Slovakia	Bratislava	Koruna
South Africa	Pretoria	Rand
South Korea	Seoul	Won
Spain	Madrid	Peseta
Sri Lanka	Sri Jayavadhenapurekotte	S. Rupee
Sudan	Khartoum	S. Dinar
Sweden	Stockholm	Krona
Switzerland	Berne	Swiss Franc
Taiwan	Taipei	New Taiwan Dollar
Thailand	Bangkok	Baht
Turkey	Ankara	Turkish Lira
United Arab Emirates	Abu Dhabi	Dirham
United Kingdom	London	Pound Sterling
United States Of America	Washington D.C (District Columbia)	US Dollar
Vietnam	Hanoi	Dong
Yugoslavia	Belgrade	Dinar
Zimbabwe	Harare	Z. Dollar

CHAPTER 6

JARGONS USED IN FRONT OFFICE OPERATIONS AND MANAGEMENT

A

ABA

American Bus Association is an association in U.S.A.; comprised of bus companies, operators and owners.

Account

This is a form on which, the various financial data are written or recorded or summarized.

Account aging

This is a process of tracking and tracing the various accounts guests and non-guests which are due to the hotel.

Account balance

This is a brief description of an account in the difference between the total debits and credits in an account.

Affiliate reservation network

This is a central reservation network system formed by the various hotel properties of a particular chain.

Account allowance

This is a financial transaction which reduces the outstanding balance of the guest and is caused by allowances or discounts given by the hotel management to the guest due to poor services on behalf of the hotel.

Account receivable

This is an accounting term given to the amount which is owed to the hotel.

Accounts receivable ledger

This is the term given collectively to all the accounts receivable including the guest as well as non-guest account.

Accountancy cycle

This is the total time duration or period from the origin of a financial transaction to the settlement and reconciliation and description of the same in the financial report of the hospitality property.

Accounting system

This is a standardized system followed in an organization for maintaining the various accounts created by for recording, analyzing and verifying the various financial transactions occurring in the organization.

Accounts payable

The amount of money which a hotel owes to the various suppliers of goods and services and also to the various travel agents as well as the tour operators.

Accounts receivable

The amount of money which a hotel property owes from the various individuals who are guests and various companies and organization who are non-guests.

Account receivable ledger

A summary of all the account receivable records of a hotel property.

Achievement factor

This is the percentage of the rack rate which the hotel receives in real time. It is obtained by dividing the actual average rate by the potential average rate. This is also called "**Rate Potential Percentage**".

Adds

These are the final or the last minute reservations which are added to the reservation list of a hotel on the day of arrival of the guests.

Advances

These are the petty cash amounts which the hotel front office cashier pays either to the guest or on behalf of the guest as loans or advance and are later charged to their accounts.

Advance deposit guarantee

This is a type of reservation in which guest pay an advance deposit of night's stay as a means of guaranteeing his reservation.

Affiliate reservation network

This is a type of central reservation network established for properties belonging to a single hotel chain in which all the participating properties are contractually related.

Affiliated hotel

This is a hotel which is either a property of a hotel chain or is a franchisee or a member of a referral group.

After departure

This is a charge which arrives at the front desk for posting into the guest account after the departure of the guest.

Agency Ledger

A part or a section of the city or non-guest ledger which deals with the travel agency accounts.

Allowance voucher

This is a term given to a document which is used for supporting the various account allowance transaction which either rectifies a posting error after a night audit or gives discounts to the guests for poor services.

Amenities

This is an extra product or service which is offered to the guest by the hotel authority. *E.g :- personalized stationery in the guestroom.*

Amenity creep

This is a situation when the hotels try to compete with each other by providing more numbers of amenities to the guests.

American Plan (AP)

A type of room rate which includes the price of the room, breakfast, lunch and dinner. Also known as Full Pension.

Apartment Hotel

Accommodation in apartment-style units rather than rooms; with minimum or expanded in-suite cooking facilities. Defined by legislation for licensing and classification purposes.

Arrival and departure register

This is a register in which the various guest arrivals, departures and room changes are recorded on a day to day basis.

Arrival, departure and change sheet

(*See* ***arrival and departure register***)

Arrival Time

This is the time specified by the guest by which he or she will definitely arrive at the hotel property and claim his or her reservation.

Arrivals report

This is a type of report which has a record of all the guests who have arrived in the hotel property on a particular date.

Atrium concept

This is a type of hotel design in which the guestrooms overlook the lobby from the first floor to the terrace of the hotel property.

Attendance Building

Marketing and promotional programs designed to increase attendance at conventions, trade shows, meetings and events.

Attractions

General all-inclusive term travel industry marketers use to refer to products that have visitor appeal, like museums, historic sites, performing arts institutions, preservation districts, theme parks, entertainment and national sites.

Audit

This is a process conducted to verify the accuracy and completeness of the various accounts of a particular organization.

Audit trail

This is a process of organized flow of the vouchers and other source documents detailing each step of the transaction between the guest and the hotel

Authorization code

This is a number code which is generated by a credit card company through an online authorization machine and approves the transaction of the guest.

AVHRM

Association of Vacation Home Rental Managers.

Average daily rate

This is a type of an occupancy ratio which is obtained by dividing the actual rooms revenue by the number of rooms sold. This is also called "**Sales per occupied room**".

Average rate per guest

This is an occupancy ratio which is obtained by dividing the actual rooms revenue by the total number of guests registered in the hotel.

Available sellable room

These are the number of guestrooms that are ready for sale out of the total number of rooms in the general inventory pool of the hotel.

Availability

This is the total number of rooms that are expected to be ready for sale on a particular date.

Available basis only

These are the reservations which have no claim against the block of rooms as the request made by the guest party to the hotel management was after the cut-off date.

Availability Pool

Rooms offered or are ready for sale on a particular date excluding the blocked and reserved rooms.

Average Daily Rate (ADR)

The total room revenue for a given period (day, month to date, month, year to date), divided by the number of rooms occupied for the same period. Frequently used as a measure of economic performance.

B

Back to back

A situation in which there is a continuous group departure and arrivals arranged by the tour operator so that the guestrooms of a hotel are never vacant and thus provide continuous and stable business to the hotel.

Back of the house

These are the various functional departments of the hotel which are not visible to the guest and in the working staff have about no guest contact.

Bank

The amount of money assigned to the cashier at the beginning of the shift to carry out the various transactions between the guests during the particular shift.

Bank cards

The various credit cards issued by the banks to the customers for processing the various cash transactions.

B card

This is a document which is used by the account posting machines to reconcile the cash receipts with the various source documents and summarize the total cash collected.

Bed and board

This is another name for the American plan which includes room charges, early morning tea, breakfast, lunch, evening tea and dinner.

Bed and Breakfast (B & B)

A type of room rate which includes the price of the room and breakfast. Also known as *Continental Plan.*

Bed board

This is hardboard made of wood or fiber that is provided to the guests (suffering from spondilitis or back problem) on special requests.

Bed night

This is the stay of the guest in for a night and is also called "**room night**".

Bed Tax (Transient Occupancy Tax of TOT)

City or county tax added to the price of a hotel room.

Bed occupancy

This is an occupancy ratio which is obtained by dividing the total number of beds occupied by the total number of beds available for sale. This is also called "**Sleeper occupancy**".

Bell

This is the act of calling or summoning a bell attendant.

Bell stand

The bell desk which is located in the lobby of the hotel and is located on the right hand side of the lobby while entering the hotel.

Bench mark

These are the yardsticks of performance of a hospitality property.

Best available

A reservation request requiring the best available room of the hotel property.

B folio

The individual guest folio that is used with the master folio.

Black-listed guests

These include persons whom the hotel would not like to accommodate as guests due to their bad reputation in terms of general conduct, payment of bills and other factors importance from the view-point of hotel.

Blanket reservation

This is the term given to a block of rooms demarcated for providing accommodation to a particular group for a future date.

Block

A set of rooms or a group of certain number of rooms kept aside for a Group.

Book

To sell hotel rooms to the guests or to reserve rooms ahead of time.

Booking

Term used to refer to a completed sale by a destination, convention center, facility, hotel or supplier (i.e. convention, meeting, trade show or group business booking).

Booking lead time

This is quantifiable term which means the measurement of how far in advance bookings for rooms are made by a hotel property.

Boutique Hotel

Historical, classic buildings, remodeled into boutique hotels with usually have less than 30 rooms.

Box

This is a term given to a particular date or dates in which no reservation request are entertained on the either side.

Brand standard

These are the various qualitative measures which are executed by a franchisor to ensure a minimum standard of products and service delivery and also to ensure quality of the facilities.

Breakage

This is the term given to the financial gain or profit to a hotel when an individual or a group guest does not consume services and product that was included in his or her package.

Breakeven Analysis

This is a management accounting concept which explains a detailed analysis of the relationships of costs, revenue and sales volume and is used to give accurate information about the revenue that should be earned by a hospitality property to cover all the costs. This is also called "**Cost Volume Profit Analysis**".

Brunch

This is a meal which is heavier than a breakfast but lighter than lunch and is usually served in lieu of these meals.

Bucket

It is a folio holder which is kept in the cashier's desk and is recessed on the countertop.

Bucket Check

This is a process by which the night auditor checks the posting of the room charges into the individual guest folios against the housekeeping department's occupancy report and the front desk room rack.

Building cost rate formula

This is the rule of thumb approach of pricing which states that, for every $ 1000 of construction cost, the average room rate should be $1.

Business Travel

Travel for commercial, governmental or educational purposes with leisure as a secondary motivation.

Buyer

A member of the travel trade who reserves room blocks from accommodations or coordinates the development of a travel product.

C

C of C

Chamber of Commerce

CTRLA

Car and Truck Rental and Leasing Association

CVB

Convention and Visitors Bureau

Cabana

This is a room situated by the side of a swimming pool or a beach with a shed and has various facilities for the guests to change their clothes, take shower and also take rest.

Café complet

This is coffee with snack which is served either at midmorning or at mid afternoon.

Call accounting system

This is a computerized program or software which automatically records, prices and posts the telephone charges in the individual electronic guest folio.

Call book

This is a register which is maintained by the bell boy to record their calls and activities.

Call Sheet

This is a register which is maintained by the telephone operator for recording the room numbers and the time when to place the morning calls in these guestrooms.

Cancellation

This is a request which is made by the guest to void his reservation previously made.

Cancellation hour

This is the duration or an hour stated by a hotel management after which the property is free to release and sells all the rooms with unclaimed non-guaranteed reservation to other walk-in guests.

Cancellation number

It is a number which is assigned to the guest by the property or the central reservation office as a proof that the property or the central reservation office has acknowledged the cancellation of the reservation of the guest.

Car jockey

This a uniformed service personnel who is also called "**valet parking attendant**" and his main job is to help the guests to park their cars on arrival and also performs the important function of airport pick-up of the guests.

Carrier

This is a provider of transportation to the public, such as an airline.

Cash advance

These are small amounts which are disbursed by the front office cashier either to the guest or on behalf of the guests and are later charged to their accounts. These are also called "*paid-outs*" or "*cash disbursement*".

Cash advance voucher

This is a document used to give the details and support cash advance and cash paid-outs which is disbursed either to the guest or on behalf of the guest.

Cash bank

This is the amount of money which is assigned to the cashier by the accounts division to carry out the various transactions smoothly during the shift.

Cash flow

This is the period of time between the sale of goods and services to clients and receipt of the payment of the same.

Cash voucher

This is the term given to a document which is used for supporting the various cash payment occurring in the hotel between the guest and front desk.

Cashier's drop

This is a depository which is located in the front office cashier's desk where the cashiers can deposit the total amount collected at the end of each shift.

Cashier's report

This is the cash turn-in report or form which is filled by the cashier at the end of each shift detailing the total amount of transaction and the total cash, cheques and other negotiable items collected by the cashier at the end of each shift.

Cashier's well

This is the other name for the bucket, tub or pit.

Cash paid-outs

This is the other name for the "*cash advance*" or "*advance*".

Casualty factor

The number of group reservations that fail to appear which includes the total number of cancellations and the no-shows.

Central reservation office

This is an independent or a chain affiliated office which accepts and processes the reservations of the various hotels that are coming to it.

Central reservation system

This is an extremely sophisticated combination of hardware and software with high level programming features used by the central reservation office to manage and process the various reservation requests from the travel agents, tour operators and other sources for the various member hotel properties.

Centralized electronic locking system

This is a sophisticated electronic system which is operated though a master console installed at the front desk and connected to all the guestrooms through wires.

Chain hotel

A hotel property which is owned by or affiliated with other properties.

Chambers of Commerce

Typically, a Chamber of Commerce will specialize in local economic development that can include tourism promotion.

Chance business

This is also called "*Chance Trade*" and is the term given for the business which is done with the walk-in or chance guests who arrive at a property without any reservation.

Change

This is a process by which a group or an individual guest is moved from one guestroom to another or it can also be a change in the applied or charged room rate.

Chargeback

This is the credit card charges which is not approved by the credit card company and are refused by the credit card company due to some particular reason.

Charge voucher

This is a document which is used to track the various charge purchases or deferred payment transactions occurring at the various point-of-sales other than the front office.

Charter Group

Group travel in which a previously organized group travels together, usually on a custom itinerary.

Check-in

This is a process which combines the entire process of receiving the guest and registering him by assigning him the required room.

Check-out

This includes all the procedures associated with the departure of the guest and his account settlement.

Check-out hour

This is the time stated by the hotel management by which the guest must vacate his room and check-out. This is generally 1200 hrs.

City Ledger

This is the collection or summary of all non-guest accounts and other receivable accounts.

City ledger journal

This is a form on which the entire city ledger is recorded and summarized.

Clefs d'Or

This is the international association of the concierges which actually means "**Keys of Gold**".

Close to arrival

This is a revenue management strategy through which a hotel accepts reservations for a particular date so long as the guest arrives before that date.

Closeout hour

This is an arbitrary stopping point for the business day of a hotel for separating out the records of one day from another.

Closing

This is a process of concluding the sale of a room.

Colored transparency

This is a colored celluloid strip placed as an indicator of the room status in the room rack pocket.

Commissions

A percent of the total product cost paid to travel agents and other travel product distributors for selling the product to the consumer.

Commissionaire

This is uniformed service personnel who is also called a "**Doorman**" and whose job is to open and close the main doors or the entrance of the hotel.

Commissionable

This is an indication that the hotel is paying a commission or amount of fee to the travel agents for the potential business referred by the travel agents to the hotels.

Commissioned trade

This is term given to the business which is generated by the intermediary agents (travel agents, tour operators and airlines who provide business to the hotel) for the hotel and for which the hotel has to pay commission.

Comp

This means complimentary; a service or a product which is provided without charging the guest for the same.

Company made

This is a type of guaranteed reservation in which a company enters into a contract with the hotel and guarantees to pay on behalf of the guest in case the guest does arrives and stay at the hotel.

Compressed work schedule

This is a deviation of the regular work schedule and allows an employee to work the equivalent of standard working hours in fewer than the traditional five days.

Complimentary Room

An occupied guest room for which no price is charged. This may include a room occupied by a hotel employee.

Concessionaire

This the term given to the various shops and emporiums which are operating in the premises of a hotel but are not owned by the hotel. These are also called "**Rentals**" or "**Business Arcade**".

Condominium Hotels

Customers purchase fee-simple equity in the units-the hotel's guestrooms. Unit owners may live in the hotels permanently or use them as second and third homes. Depending on the hotel's policy, unit owners may rent their units independently or through the management company's rental program and derive income through a revenue-sharing.agreement. Unit owners also incur budgeted maintenance and operating expenses. Depending on the management company, unit owners have varying degrees of access to their hotel's amenities and services.

Confirmation notification

This is the process of notification of reservation confirmation provided to the guests through letter, phone, fax, e-mail etc.

Confirmation number

This is a number or code which is given to the guest as a proof of reservation confirmation and is also used by the reservation section for tracking the various reservations for modification and cancellation.

Confirmed reservation

This is a hotel's acknowledgement or agreement in writing to the guest's reservation request.

Construction cost

This is the total cost incurred by the property on the construction of the entire hospitality property.

Contribution margin

This is the mathematical difference between the sales of a department or a product and the cost of sales of the department or the product. This also shows the amount of contribution of a department or a product towards the total revenue of a hotel property.

Control folio

This is an accounting department document used internally by the front office computer to support and document all the account postings by department during a system update routine.

Convertible bed

This is a sofa bed.

Convention and Visitors Bureau

These organizations are local tourism marketing organizations specializing in developing conventions, meetings, conferences and visitations to a city, county or region.

Conventions and Trade Shows

Major segment of travel industry business. Trade shows differ from conventions in that they have exhibit space that provides product exhibition and sales opportunities for suppliers, as well as information gathering and buying opportunities for customers.

Conversion Study

Research study to analyze whether advertising respondents actually were converted to travellers as a result of advertising and follow-up material.

Co-op Advertising

Advertising funded by two or more destinations and /or suppliers.

Cooperative Marketing

Marketing programs involving two or more participating companies, institutions or organizations.

Cooperative Partner

An independent firm or organization which works with a tourism office by providing cash or in-kind contributions to expand the marketing impact of the tourism offices program.

Corkage

This refers to the charges of providing various equipments and soda charged by the hotel authorities to the guests who bring their own alcoholic beverages and consume in the hotel or any licensed establishment.

Corner

This is a guestroom which is situated in the corner of the residential floor and has two exposures.

Corporate guaranteed

This is a type of guaranteed reservation where a company enters into a contract with the hotel and agrees to accept the financial responsibilities in case the guest does not turn up in spite of having a confirmed reservation.

Correction sheet

This is a format on which the various posting errors are recorded by the front office machines for reconciliation by the night auditor during the night audit.

Correction voucher

This is a voucher which is used to track and support an account correction which is generally a rectification of a posting error.

Cost center

This is a term which is given to all the non-revenue earning department of the hotel such as the personnel department, the engineering and maintenance department as these departments incur cost to the hotel management.

Cost per occupied room

This is the variable or the added cost of selling a product that is incurred only if the rooms are sold.

Coupon

This is a voucher which is issued by the travel agencies to the guests against payment for settling the accounts in the hotel during their stay and at the time of departure. This can also be a sort of ticket which is issued by the tour operator to the members of the group so that various meals and services can be purchased by the guest and later charged in to the master folio.

Cover

Each diner at a restaurant

Credit

This is a financial accounting term which indicates a decrease in the account receivable.

Credit authorization

This is the maximum amount of charges that have been authorized by the credit card company to be made on the credit card of the guest.

Credit card guaranteed

This is a type of guaranteed reservation where a credit card company accepts the financial responsibilities in case the guest is a no-show and thus guarantees payment to the hotel for unoccupied reserved rooms.

Credit Card Commissions

A fee paid to credit card companies based upon a contracted percentage of credit card charges accepted.

Current account

A due city ledger account which is within the current billing period of 30 days.

Cut-off date

This is an agreed upon date between a group and the hotel after which all the unclaimed reservation in the group block are released into the general inventory pool for resale.

Cut-off hour

This is also called the "**cancellation hour**" and is the stated hotel time after which all the unclaimed non-guaranteed reservations are cancelled and the room is made available for sale to the walk-in guests.

D

Daily rooms report

This is a report which is prepared daily night for recording the room status of the guestrooms of the hotel. This report is used for reconciliation of any room status discrepancy and is used as a means of verifying the room statistics.

Daily operations report

This is a report which is prepared by the night auditor which focuses on the total financial transactions that occurred in the hotel during the last 24-hours and includes the various operating statistics, revenue and receivables.

Daily transcript

This is a sheet which is the summary report of all the guest accounts and also gives detailed information the various transactions affecting the balance of the guest account and is thus is a very important report used for detecting the posting errors during the process of night audit.

Date and time punching machine

This is an equipment which is kept at the front desk and is used for stamping the date and time on mails, parcels and other important documents.

Day rate

This is a reduced type of room rate that is charged from the guests who do not stay overnight at the hotel; i.e. guests who arrive and depart the same day from the hotel.

D card

This is the night auditor's report used in the semi-automated front office accounting system and is a form on which the totals of the front office posting machine are summarized and posted.

Dead move

This is a process of physical change of the room made by the hotel authority in the absence of the guest and is generally done in case of emergency. This is also called "**Dead room change**".

Debit

This is an accounting term which indicates that there is an increase in the account receivable.

Delinquent account

This is a term given to an unsettled city ledger or non-guest account which has crossed the acceptable settlement period of 90 days.

Denial code

This is a code which is generated by an on-line authorization service stating that the particular transaction that has been requested for has declined and has not been approved.

Density control chart

This is a type of reservation control system where the number of rooms committed is controlled by room types.

Departmental control sheet

This is a form which is maintained by all the departments and the point of sale for recording from the various departmental source documents or the vouchers to be sent to the front desk for posting.

Departure notification slip

This is an important intimating slip which is prepared at the time of the departure of the guests in order to inform the other departments about the departure of the particular guest.

Deposit reservation (See advance deposit reservation).

Destination Clubs

The newest entrant to lodging, this niche most closely resembles country clubs in ownership structure. While developers of destination clubs expect to branch out into other price segments, for now this niche targets the most affluent of travellers. Customers pay initiation fees that can run as high as $ 500,000 and annual dues running as high as $ 25,000. In return, customers get to stay for weeks at a time in multi-million dollar residences and villas in prime urban and resort locations and enjoy a full range of amenities and services.

Destination: A hotel, resort, attraction, city, region, or state.

Destination Marketing

Marketing a city, state, country, area or region to consumers and trade.

Destination Marketing Organization

Local tourism marketing organizations, such as convention and visitors bureaus or chambers of commerce.

Did not stay

This means that the guest departed from the hotel very soon after registering in the hotel.

Difference returnable

This is a situation which occurs when a cashier pays out more cash than what he actually receives in cash and the difference is due back to the cashier's bank. This is also called "**Due Back**" or "**Exchange**".

Direct billing

This a type of credit arrangement in which the hotel bills the company for the charges incurred by a corporate guest during his stay at the property provided there is pre-established correspondence between the hotel and the company for the same.

Discount grid

This is a chart which displays a matrix which shows the occupancy percentage which a hotel should achieve to generate equivalent net revenue with the various levels of discounts provided.

Discounted Fare

Negotiated air fare for convention, trade show, meeting, group and corporate travel.

Discover America

Theme used by the Travel Industry Association and its marketing partners to market travel within the United States.

Double up

This is situation when a room is occupied by two guests who are not related to each other and separate room rack slip has been maintained for each of these guests.

Due back

This is a typical situation which occurs in the front office cash section when a front office cashier is not able to restore his initial cash bank due to the receipt of a large number of cheques and large bills and thus in this situation he pays out more than that he actually receives in cash and thus the difference is due back to the cashier's cash bank.

Due-out

This is a term which states that a guest is expected after the following day's check-out time.

Dunning letters

These are the official letters accompanied with outstanding bills which are sent to guests with delinquent accounts.

E

Eco-tourism

This is a modern concept which amalgamates the development of the various tourism related activities in a tourist destination along with a proper preservation of the natural environment and the various other natural and cultural heritages.

Economic / Limited service

This a level or type of service provided by small hotels and emphasizes clean, comfortable, inexpensive room fulfilling the basic needs and requirements of the guests and is generally targeted towards the budget minded people.

Employee folio

This is a folio used for recording the various transactions of an employee of a hotel who has been given charge purchase privileges.

Essential functions

This is term is used in association with the Americans with Disability Act and are the duties and responsibilities of an individual holding a particular position in an organization must be able to do unaided or do it by changing the usual pattern of doing of performing the duties and the responsibilities.

Emergency Key

This is a type of special key which opens the doors of all the guestrooms even if they are double locked and is generally handled by the executive housekeeper or the general manager. This key is also called the "**Grand master key**".

Employee folio

This is a type of folio which records the transactions of the account assigned to the employees which credit or charge purchase privileges.

Express check-out

This is a type of pre-departure activity performed by the front desk for all the guests expected to depart on a particular morning and involves the proper distribution of the updated folios in the individual guestrooms early in the morning.

End-of-day

A random or capricious stopping of the formalities for a particular business day.

Equivalent Occupancy

This is the occupancy percentage required to obtain the same net revenue as was obtained from the old price and occupancy percentage in case of change in the average room rate.

F

Facilities

Core physical features: accommodation, restaurants, bars, and meeting rooms.

Fair market rate

This is the ratio of the guestrooms available in a hotel and the total number of market existing.

Family room

This is a term given to a twin double room which has two separated double beds and is especially assigned to the families.

Fam trip

This is the term given to the various familiarization trips undertaken by the various travel agents or the tour operators at a very little or no cost (at the expense of the suppliers like hotels) in order to get themselves familiar with the facilities and services of the hotel properties for potential referral business.

Farm out

This is the process of assigning of guests with reservation to other properties when the hotel is fully occupied or is full house.

Feeder Airport/City

An outlying city which feeds travellers to hubs or gateway cities.

Fenced rates

This is a special addition to the reservation tools of a hotel and includes the various rules and regulations for the guests associated with the reservation process such as the mode of payment, nonrefundable, cut-off-dates for groups etc.

Financial transactions

This is the term given to the process of sale of goods and services in return for cash or any other deferred mode of settlement such as credit card, voucher etc.

Fixed costs

This is the term given to the costs which remains constant and so does not change in the short term with the change total sales volume.

Flat rate

This is a special rate applied to the groups and is generally half the rack rate with a single, flat price applicable to any room with the exception of suites. This rate is also called the "**Run-of-the-house rate**".

Flextime

This is a type of flexible work schedule in which the employee is free to vary his timc of starting and ending a particular shift but has to complete a minimum of eight hours in the shift.

Float

This is a term describing a situation when there is a delay in payment from an account after using a credit card or a cheque.

Floor limit

This is the maximum amount of credit charges that are allowed to the credit card user in a hotel property without prior permission or clearance. This limit is established by the credit card company for the hotel property.

Folio

This is a form on which the various financial transactions are recorded and summarized.

Folio header

This is the top portion or section of the folio which shows various personal details of the guest such as name of the guest, room number of the guest, date of arrival, date of departure, room tariff, pax, etc.

Folio well

This is a type of front office cash equipment which is used for storing the various guest and non-guest folios.

Foot patrol

This is the process of guarding a hotel property by walking across the halls, floors, and corridor and out of the building in order to ensure the safety and security of the guests.

Forecast

This is the process of predicting or estimating the future business of a particular firm or company.

Forecast scheduling

This is the process of scheduling the various jobs and tasks of an organization on the base of the forecasts made.

Forfeited deposit

This is a reservation deposit which is retained by the reservation department of the hotel property in case the guest does not register at the hotel on the particular date of arrival neither cancels his reservation. This deposit is called "**Lost Deposit**".

Franchising

This is a method of doing business where one organization which has developed a particular pattern method of doing a business, a "**Franchisor**", grants the right to another organization, the "**Franchisee**" to conduct the same business provided it follows the rules and regulations maintained by the "**Franchisor**".

Franking machine

This is a machine which is used for printing the postage stamp value on the envelope.

Free sale

This is a situation when a travel agent or any other intermediary agent confirms accommodation for guest without prior confirmation with the hotel property.

Frequency

The number of times an advertisement appears during a given campaign.

Frequent Independent Traveler (FIT)

A term which applies to visitors who arrive on their own as opposed to being a part of an organized group.

Front of the house

These are the departments and outlets of the hotel which are in extensive guest contact such as front office and food and beverage outlets.

Front Office

This is a term given to entire front desk and personnel working in the desks who are involved with the duties and responsibilities in the salc of the guestrooms and providing efficient services to the guests during their entire stay.

Front office accounting formula

This is the term given to the formula which used by the front office cash sections in order to post the various transactions in to the front office accounts.

Previous Balance + Debits – Credits = Net Outstanding Balance

Front office cash sheet

This is am important form which is maintained by the front office cashiers and is used for recording all the transactions of the front office which resulted in the receipt and disbursement of cash during a particular shift and is thus used as an important means of control for verifying the cash in hand with the recorded transactions during a particular shift.

Fulfillment

This is process of servicing consumers and trade who request information as a result of advertising or promotional programs. Service often includes an 800 number, sales staff and distribution of materials.

Fully automated hotel

This is a hotel where the general operations and management are carried with the help of computers which are used for the purpose of electronic data processing.

Full day

This is the term given to the entire hotel day for which a guest is charged and is thus extremely useful for front office accounting.

Full house

This is a situation when all the guestrooms of a hospitality property are occupied by guests.

Futon

This is a term given to a Japanese sleeping arrangements consisting of many layers of cotton-quilted batting which can be rolled when not in use.

G

Gateway or Gateway City

A major airport, seaport, rail or bus center through which tourists and travellers enter from outside the region.

Global distribution system

This is a reservation network which provides worldwide reservation information in the various hotel properties and is established by connecting the hotel reservation system with the airline reservation system.

GIT (Groups Independent Travel)

Group travel in which individuals purchase a group package in which they will travel with others along a pre-set itinerary.

Group booking speed

This is the rate at which the group reservations for rooms are accepted at a hotel and are executed.

Group Rate

Negotiated hotel rate for convention, trade show, meeting, tour or incentive group.

Group resume

This is a term given to report containing the summary of all the activities of a group which includes arrival and departure dates and times, food and beverage service requirements, recreational requirements, billing arrangements and other important information.

Guaranteed reservation

This is a type of reservation in which the hotel management guarantees to keep a room for a guests for 24 hours following the guest's scheduled date of arrival in return for guarantee given by the guest to pay for the same either through cash advance deposit, credit card, voucher, letter from company and other methods of guarantee.

Guest cycle

This is a concept which identifies the various stages of the guest contact with the hotel staff and also identifies the financial transactions between the guest and the hotel during these stages.

Guest history file

This is the term given to a manual file which is created with the information generated from expired registration cards or electronic file which is created through sophisticated computerized software in which all the information from the guest registration file is automatically transferred to the guest history data base file.

Guest history record

This is the term given to the record of the financial and personal information about the various guests of the hotel and is used by the front office department and the sales and marketing division for anticipating the various needs of the guests in order to serve them in a better way.

Guest account

This is a term given to the form on which the various transactions between a guest and the hotel are recorded and summarized.

Guest Amenities

Not to be confused with "amenities", this is the term given to the range of disposable items provided in guest room bathrooms and includes such items as shampoo, lotion, conditioner, soap, toothpaste, toothbrush, shower caps, etc... The costs of these items are built into room rate.

Guest Check (Restaurant)

The invoice presented to restaurant and bar patrons for food and beverage consumed during a visit. Also referred to as a waiter's check or restaurant check.

Guest House

A personal residence with a small amount of overnight accommodation sometimes limited by legislation and residence constraints. Typically provides breakfast which is included within the room rate but no other meals. Not licensed to provide alcoholic beverages commercially.

Guest ledger

This is a term given to the summary of all the accounts of the guests presently registered in the hotel. This also called "**Rooms ledger**", "**Front Office ledger**" or "**Transient ledger**".

Guest Service Directory

A documented listing of all of the features of a hotel together with general and pertinent information about the community within which the property is located. Directories are usually provided within each guest room.

H

Head in Beds

Industry slang referring to the primary marketing objective of accommodations and most destinations - increasing the number of overnight stays.

High balance account

This is an account of the guest whose charge purchases are either approaching the credit limit or have crossed the credit limit decided for the guest by the hotel property at the time of registration.

High balance report

This is a report which summarizes all the high balance guests and the amount due on them for settlement.

Hospitality Industry

Another term for the travel industry.

Hospitality

This is a term which describes friendly and cordial treatment to a guest with proper provisions for a sophisticated service.

Hotel

This is defined as a lodging establishment whose primary purpose is to provide accommodation services to the guests and can even provide various other services such as food and beverage services, housekeeping services and uniformed services in return of payment from the guests and thus is also called "**A House of Taxes and Endless Luxury**".

Hot list

This is a list of stolen credit cards or lost credit cards which are sent by the credit card company to the hotels so that the hotels do not accept such cards. This list is also called the "**Cancellation bulletin**".

Hotel Broker

The person who sells various packages of hotels and resorts to the corporate clients, promoters and event management companies.

Hotel Information System

This is an organized information system which helps in the collection of various data important from the point of view of the various level of management and thus help in the decision making process of the hotel management.

House count

This is a front office statistics giving information about the total number of guests registered and residing in a particular hospitality property.

House limit

This is a credit limit established by the hotel for the guests and thus is the maximum limit up to which the hotel can accept charge purchase privileges for the guests.

House phone

This is a telephone which is located in the lobby of the hotel from where a visitor can call and contact a guest in his room.

House profit

This is the gross profit earned by the hotel on the sale of goods and services before the deduction of the taxes.

Housekeeper's report

This is report prepared by the housekeeping department and is sent to the front desk during each shift and contains information about the room status of all the guestrooms of the hotel property in that particular shift and thus is based on thorough physical check. This report is also called "**Housekeeping status report**".

Housing bureau

This is an intermediary agency which processes the guestroom bookings of guests who are either in groups or are a part of a large convention and thus act similarly as central reservation office.

Hub

An airport or city which serves as a central connecting point for aircraft, trains or buses from outlying feeder airports or cities.

Hub and Spoke

Air carriers use of selected cities as "hubs" or connected points for service on their systems to regional destinations.

Hubbart formula

This is a formula used for computing and determining the average room rates on the base of a bottom-up approach to pricing and considers various factors such as the operating expenses, average price per room, desired profit, desired return on investment, expected rooms sold and income from various departments of the hotel.

Iurdle rate

This is the lowest possible room rate that has been accepted for a particular category of room n a particular date.

I

con

A facility or landmark which is visually synonymous with a destination.

n-balance

This a term used to describe an accounting situation when the total debit amounts and the ›tal credit amounts of an account are equal.

ncentive travel

This is a type of travel in which the traveller or the guest is generally sponsored by an rganization as a motivational effort on the part of the company and includes a complimentary ay at a hotel property; generally awarded to the travel agents and tour operators for their outstanding erformance in bringing guests to the hotel.

nclusive Tour

A tour program that includes a variety of feature for a single rate (airfare, accommodations, ghtseeing, performances, etc.)

ncome statement

This is a report or statement summarizing the financial performance of a hotel property for particular financial year.

ndependent hotel

This is a type of hotel without any management or chain affiliation and is neither associated th a franchise and thus has its own management and norms for operation.

formation directory

This is a book or a directory which contains information about the city where a particular tel property is situated and contains maps, important addresses and telephone numbers of banks, vernment and corporate offices, hospitals, car companies, travel agents, places of sight seeing and so on and is thus serves as an important information tool for the front desk agents which helps them to answer the various queries of the guests within a hotel property.

Information rack

This a front office equipment with aluminum slots which holds information slips of various guests registered in the hotel in an alphabetical manner and thus is used by the front desk to place telephone messages and visitor enquiries of the in-house guests.

In-house guest

This is a term given to guest who is registered to a hospitality property and has currently occupies a guestroom.

In-room guest check out

This is an exclusive feature provided by the property management system in fully automated hotel systems which allows the in-house guest to check out of the hotel through an in-house guestroom television.

Interdepartmental communication

This is the flow of the communication process between the various departments of a hospitality property.

Interface

This a term which describes the connection of one computer with another through LAN or WAN wires for the process of information dissemination and communication of the information generated in an organization.

Interhotel property referrals

This is a system in which one hotel which is a member of the hotel referral group recommends another hotel property which is also the member of the group to the guests incase of an overbooking situation.

Internal control

This is the process of verification of the various financial transactions by reconciliation with the sources documents such as vouchers and sales summary sheet.

Intersell cards

These are credit cards issued by the various hotel corporations and act same as normal credit cards.

Intradepartmental communication

This is the flow of the communication process between the various sections within a particular department.

Ingress and Egress

Ingress/Egress relates to the Civil Authority coverage part of the Business Income/EE forms. If one is unable to enter or exit by direction of civil authority.

Innkeepers Statutes

Statutes that limit the common law liability of innkeepers

Intelligent Hotels

Hotels that have the state of the art technology systems for their operations. These hotels have replaced the traditional systems to reduce their energy cost and usually have integrated systems which join analog and digital systems to achieve an effective communication in their hotels. The return on investment is reflected in the energy-cost savings and the comfort they provide to their guests.

International Marketing

Marketing a destination, product or service to consumers and traders outside the country.

J

Job Analysis

This is a process of collecting, analyzing and synthesizing information about the job and is thus examining a job to identifying its component parts and circumstances in which it is to be performed.

Job description

This is a broad statement of the purpose, duties and responsibilities of a job or a position and is thus is a listing of the job title, pay, tasks, reporting relationships and working conditions required to perform a particular job.

Job evaluation

This is a process of establishing the value of jobs in a job hierarchy.

Job redesign

These are the attempts and strategies developed by the hotel property to improve the quality of work performance of the employees of the property.

Job sharing

This is a process of sharing the duties and responsibilities of a full-time position employee by two or more part-time employees.

Job specification

This is a list of personal qualifications which includes skills, knowledge, abilities and other characteristics regarded as necessary for the satisfactory performance of a job.

K

Key card

This is a folder which is used for enclosing the key in its pocket and is given by the front desk agent to guest at his registration. The card also contains general information about the property which includes accommodation facilities, food and beverage facilities and other facilities.

Key fob

This is a term given to an attractive, decorative and descriptive metal, plastic or wooden tag which is attached to the key and bears the logo of the hotel with the guestroom number.

King

This is an extra-long, extra-wide double bed which measures about 78 inches by 80 inches.

L

Lanai

This is a guestroom with a porch or a balcony and is thus a famous **Hawaiian** term which is used for the guestrooms of a resort.

Last

This is a designation for a bell person who has completed a rooming assignment or other errand.

Last room availability

This is a modernized and sophisticated reservation system that provides real-time access between the chain's central reservation system and the hotel's in-house property management system through internet.

Late arrival

This is a guest who has a confirmed reservation and notifies the hotel that he or she will be arriving at the property after the stated cancellation hour or cutoff hour of the hotel.

Late charge

This is an outstanding charge which has not been posted into the account of the guest and reaches the front desk after the guest has already checked out of the hotel.

Late check-out

This is a guest who has requested the hotel authorities that he or she will be checking out of the hotel after the hotel's standard check-out time and thus is generally not assessed any charge from the hotel.

Late check-out fee

This is a fee which is charged from the guests who continue to occupy the guestrooms and do check-out by the standard time established by the hotel for check-out.

Least Cost Router (LCR)

This is special telephone equipment that routes the outgoing calls of the guest over the least expensive lines available. This equipment is also called **Automatic Route Selector**.

Ledger

This is an accounting terminology which denotes a group or a set of accounts.

Leisure Travel

Travel for recreational, educational, sightseeing, relaxing and other experiential purposes.

Light Baggage

This is a guest who arrives at the hotel property with a very few baggage and is thus requested to pay in advance of his stay. This guest is also called **Scanty Baggage**.

Lightning call

This is a term which is given to the most urgent incoming and outgoing calls of a hotel.

Liquidity

This is gauging of the ability of hotel to meet the current financial and non-financial obligations by the maintenance of sufficient.

Limited Service Hotels

Brand hotels with franchise memberships of recognized hotels, built within limited areas without a restaurant. These hotels are located near business areas such as industrial parks, cities, and airport terminals.

Lockout

This is a situation when the guest is not allowed by the hotel authorities to enter his room and generally occurs when the guest does settle his bill in spite repeated requests made by the front office.

Log Book

This is a register which is maintained by all the operating departments of a hotel and thus acts as an important means of communication between the shifts.

Loss of Attraction

"Loss of Attraction" falls under the Business Income and Extra Expense coverage form although coverage is rarely included as it is hard to prove. For example, if a fire occurred at a hotel in Las Vegas, there may be other hotels in the surrounding area that will have lost income as a result of the reduction in tourism. For those hotels that have not suffered direct damage to the property, Business Income claims would fall under "Loss of Attraction."Loss of Attraction coverage is not common and can be difficult to identify the loss resulting from a disaster and that which could have resulted from poor management or other uninsured factors. Physical damage to insured property is the primary trigger for business interruption claims; however, additional triggers of coverage outside of physical damage include acts of civil authority, ingress/egress, contingent business interruption and loss of attraction.

Loss leader

This is the term which is given to product which is priced below the break-even price.

Low (off-peak) season

The consecutive months during which the lowest revenues, room/suite occupancy and average room rates are generated. In the Rajasthan this is generally April to September.

Luggage pass

This is a pass which gives the authority to the guest luggage to be taken away from the hotel.

M

Maid's Report

This is a report prepared by the room attendant or the chambermaid and summarizes the occupancy status of the guestrooms on a single floor and thus is consolidated with the maid's report of the other floor to form the Housekeeper's Report.

Mail and key rack

This is wooden front office equipment which is used for the storage of mail and messages and keys of the guests according to the room number.

Management contract

This is a business agreement established between a hotel owner lacking sufficient knowledge to management a particular hotel property and a hotel management company to run the day to day administration and operations of the hotel in return for a management fee which will be provided to the company by the hotel owner.

Manager's report

This is a report which is generally prepared by the night auditor during the night auditing process and it includes information such as the average daily rate, Rev PAR, occupancy percentage, yield percentage and other important guest related statistics of the previous day.

Managerial report

This is a report prepared by the department managers and thus gives proper information about the financial status and the operational effectiveness of the respective departments of the hotel.

Market condition pricing

This is an approach towards establishing prices of particular products and advocates that a particular hospitality should base the prices of products and services on the prices charged by its competitive firms within the same geographical region.

Market segment

This is a term given to distinguished group of customers or guests or target market with a similar type of needs and wants for products and services.

Market Share

The percentage of business within a market category.

Market Volume

The total number of travellers within a market category.

Marketing

This is a process of creation of satisfied customer and is thus a social and managerial process by an individual or a group to obtain what they need and want by creating and exchanging services with tech other.

Marquee

This is a term given for the message board which is placed in the lobby bearing the logo of the hotel and displays the various messages allocated in the space.

Master account / master folio

This is a main folio or account which is prepared for the group members which accumulates all the charges of the group members according to the contract made between the group and the hotel.

Master key

This is a key which is used for opening several guestroom doors except the rooms which are double locked. This key is also called **Floor Key**.

Message lamp

This is an electronic light which is generally placed near the telephone and is used for informing the guests that the telephone operator at the exchange has a message to deliver.

Micro-fitted electronic locking

This is a sophisticated electronic locking system with each door of the guestroom having its own microprocessor with a preprogrammed code sequence stored by a central console at the front desk.

Middle class service

This is a type of hotel with a sufficient level of service being provided to its target market consisting of businesspeople and families and generally offers uniformed service, food and beverage service, a fine dining restaurant, coffee shop and sometimes special rates to guests.

Mini Bar

A specially designed small floor mounted refrigerator containing a variety of beverages and snacks located in guest rooms, with individual guest room key access. This amenity serves as a more credible and profitable substitute for room service.

Minimum length of stay

This is a type of revenue management strategy that is followed and practiced by a hotel management and according to it a reservation request for rooms should have a minimum length (covering some minimum nights) according to the policies of the hotel in order to be accepted for further execution.

Minor departments

These are the less important operating departments of a hotel which include the valet, beauty parlor and laundry.

Miscellaneous Charge Order

This is a voucher which is issued by an airline company and thus authorizes the mentioned guests to avail the facilities of accommodation and food and other facilities according to the contract with the payment due to the airline company.

Mission (Sales)

A promotional and sales trip coordinated by a state travel office, conventional and visitors bureau or key industry member to increase product awareness, sales and to enhance image. Target audiences may include tour operators, wholesales, incentive travel planners, travel agents, meeting planners, convention and trade show managers and media. Missions often cover several international or domestic destinations and include private and public sector participants. Mission components can include receptions, entertainment representatives of the destination, presentations and pre-scheduled sales and media calls.

M.O.D.

Manager On Duty

Mom and Pop

This was a type of lodging establishment which was operated by the members of a single family and so there was no need to hire employees as the operations were conducted by the members of the family.

Money wire

This is a term given to an electronic message which authorizes money from one person to another person.

Morning call

This is also called a **wake-up call** and is made by the telephone operator for the guests at their requests.

Motel

Overnight accommodation originally targeted to automobile travellers and therefore, situated at roadside locations. A more contemporary definition would be the provision of accommodation only, with no other amenities and services provided by the motel.

Motorcoach

Deluxe equipment used by most tour operators in group tour programs. Amenities include reclining seats, bathrooms, air conditioning, good lighting and refreshment availability.

Multiple occupancy

This is a situation when a guestroom is occupied by more than one guest.

Multiple occupancy percentage

This is a front office management statistic found out by dividing the total number of rooms occupied by more than one guest by the total number of guestrooms occupied by guests. (x 100)

Multiple occupancy ratio

This a front office management statistic which is derived from multiple occupancy percentage or from average number of guests per room sold and is used for forecasting the product and service requirements of the food and beverage production and service divisions and also for the linen requirements of the housekeeping department.

Murphy bed

This is a standard double bed which folds into the closet made in the wall.

N

NCR

This is a special type of paper which is used for NCR which is so treated that it can produce copies without carbon.

NCR 2000

This is an account posting machine which was manufactured by the NCR Company for the semi-automated accounting systems but is obsolete nowadays.

NCR 4200

This is also an account posting machine which was manufactured by the NCR Company for the semi-automated accounting systems but is obsolete nowadays. This was famously called "**42**".

Net cash receipts

This is the total amount of cash, cheques, and other negotiable items in the cashier's drawer excluding the cash bank.

Net rate

This is the room rate after the deduction of the commission charges that is paid to the travel agents or airline or other intermediary agents.

Networking

This is a process of creating contact with prospective clients that might prove to be valuable for the hotel in selling the guestrooms and meeting spaces of the hotel.

Night Audit

This is a process of verification of the various guest accounts for their accuracy and completeness conducted by the night auditor during the night shift in at the front desk.

Night Auditor

The person who performs the important function of night audit at the front desk is called the night auditor.

Night auditor's report

This is a report prepared by the night auditor during the night auditing process and summarizes the revenue earned by the front office along with the list of VIP guests and sale summary of the various outlets of the hotel.

Night Manager

Evening Manager

No-show

This is a term given to guests who fail to register in a hotel inspite of having a confirmed reservation.

Non-affiliate reservation network

This is a type of central reservation network established by various independent hotels and connects them for process the various reservation requests.

Non-group displacement

This is a type of strategy adopted by the front office management in which the transient guest or individual guests are turned or bounced away due to lack of rooms caused by accepting group reservation or business.

Non-guest account

This is an accounting term given to a form which is used for recording the financial transaction of a former guest with an outstanding balance or a local agency with charge purchase privileges or a business group sponsoring a meeting at the hotel.

Non-guest folio

This is an accounting term given to a folio which is a statement of record of the financial transaction of a former guest with an outstanding balance or a local agency with charge purchase privileges or a business group sponsoring a meeting at the hotel.

NTA

National Tour Association, comprised of domestic tour operators.

O

Occupancy percentage

This is the total number of rooms occupied in the hotel divided by the total number of rooms available in a hotel for sale. (x 100)

Occupancy ratios

This is a term given collectively all the statistical ratios which are used for gauging the success of a hotel property in selling the guestrooms and includes average room revenue, revenue per available room, average rate per guest, multiple occupancy statistics and occupancy percentage.

Occupancy report

This is a report which is prepared by the front desk agent and gives information about all the guestrooms occupied on a particular and also gives information about the guests who are expected to check-out the next day.

Off-season rate

This is a reduced or discounted rate which is offered to guests to hotels and resorts which are located in destinations with extreme climatic conditions.

On change

This is a room status which states that the room has been vacated by the guest but has not been cleaned by the housekeeping department for occupancy by a new guest.

On-the-job-training

This is a type of training practice which is very famous in the hospitality industry in which an individual employee observes and practices a task while performing his duties and responsibilities.

Operating departments

These are the departments of the hotel which are directly involved in providing various products and valuable services to the guests.

Operating ratios

This is the term given collectively to all the statistical ratios which are essentially used for analyzing the operating performance and efficiency of a hospitality property.

Operational reports

These are the various reports generated by the various departments of a hotel in a conjunction with the accounts department as these reports include important financial information which is critical to the operations of the hotel.

Organization chart

This is a schematic representation of the various positions within an organization and also denotes to working relationships and the line of authority.

Orientation

This is a process of introducing the new recruit to the company and its working environment so that the new employee gains information about the practices and policies of the company.

Out-of-balance

This is a accounting situation which describes that the total debit amounts and credit amounts are equal and thus shows absence of any discrepancy.

Outside room

This is a room located on the outer side and perimeter of the hotel building and thus has an outward facing with a desirable exposure.

Outsourcing

This is a process of hiring an outside agency for the purpose of providing certain services to the hotel or any other hospitality organization.

Outstanding balance

This is an accounting term given to the amount which the guest owes to the hotel.

Outstanding balance report

This is a report generated by the front office department and provides information about all the guests with their account or folio balances.

Overage

This is a type of discrepancy which occurs at the front office cash section when after removing the initial cash bank, the total amount of cash, cheques and other negotiable items in the cashier's drawer is more than the net cash receipts.

Overbooking

This is a process of reserving or booking more number of guestrooms than that are actually available in the hotel property. This process is also called **Overselling**.

Overdue account

This is a term which is given to an unsettled city ledger or non-guest account that has exceeded the current billing period of 30 days but has not yet crossed the billing period of 90 days.

Overflow facility

This is a term given to a hotel property participating in the central reservation network system and receives reservation requests only when all the hotels of the particular chain in the same region are booked for a particular requested date.

Override

This is an extra commission that is offered by the hotel property to the intermediary agents such as travel agents and tour operators for encouraging more number of bookings.

Overstay

This is a term given to a guest who has extended his stay at the hotel property and thus continues to stay even after his scheduled date of departure from the hotel.

P

Package

This includes a number of services offered by the hotel and other principal suppliers purchased separately but put together and sold at a reduced price either by the supplier or by the intermediary agents to the guests.

Paid in advance

This is a room charge which has been collected from a guest at the time registration on his arrival and the procedure is generally performed by the hotel authority when a guest registers in a hotel with a very few or no luggage. The paid-in-advance guests are generally denied credit facilities due to their chance of being skipper.

Parlor

This is the term given to a living room or a sitting room and is always the first part of a suite room. This is also called a **Salon**.

Permanent (guest)

This is a term given to a guest who has been staying in a hotel property for a very long duration with or without a formal lease agreement.

Petty cash

These are small cash payments that are made by the hotel authority on behalf of the guest and later collect the same from the guests. This is also called **Paid out**.

Pick-up error

This is a type of error which is prevalent in the night auditing process in the semi-automated and non-automated front office systems and occurs when the night auditor mistakenly enters the closing balance of the previous day wrongly as the opening balance of the next day.

Picture Tel

This is a process of using the telephone lines to send audiovisual information to the guests in their respected guestrooms.

Plus

This term generally denotes the room position of a hotel property and thus a plus positions means that a hotel property still has rooms available for sale on a particular date.

Point of sale

This is the term given either to the revenue centers or any outlets of hotels that sells products and services to the guests.

Point-of-sale terminal (POS)

This a computerized equipment which is used for posting of the various guest charges at the various outlets or point-of-sales of a hotel and is directly connect to the front office computer for the automatic recording of the charges incurred by the guest.

Policy and procedure manual

This is a book or a manual which is issued by the personnel department to the newly recruit in order to gain information about the procedures to do specific jobs and duties in his or her concerned department.

Posting

The process of recording the various transactions between the guest and the hotel by debiting and crediting charges and payments to a guest account.

Potential average rate

This is a revenue management statistic which combines the various other statistics such as potential average single rate, potential average double rate, multiple occupancy percentage and rate spread to generate the average rate that would be achieved if all the rooms of a hotel are sold at their rack rates.

Predicted house count

This is a process of forecasting and predicting the number of guests registering in a hotel property on a particular date and is generally developed on the base of previously collected occupancy statistics.

Prepayment guaranteed

This is a type of confirmed guaranteed reservation in which a full payment (of the total number of days the guest will stay in the hotel) from the guest is accepted prior to the date of arrival of the guest.

Prior approved credit

This is the process of using a credit card to establish credit worthiness with an organization such as hotels.

Private Branch Exchange

This is a term given to the telephone switchboard of a hotel.

Private label cards

These are the credit cards issued by the various retail outlets such as petrol pumps.

Property

This is a general term given to a hotel including its personnel and physical facilities and infrastructure.

Property Management System (PMS)

This is the term given to the entire computer network installed or commissioned in a hotel property in order to manage the day to day operations and management of a hotel property.

Published rate

This is the maximum possible rate which is charged by the hotel from the guest for overnight accommodation. This is also called the **Rack Rate**.

Q

Quality assurance

This is a special philosophy applicable in large hospitality organizations which advocates a high consistency in the delivery of the services to the guests.

Quality circles

Quality circle is an important part of **Total Quality Management** program running in a hotel property and consists of executives of the various departments meeting together to solve the various organization problems regarding quality management.

Quality control

This is a process of assigning the staffs, the responsibility of maintaining the quality of the products and services at the time of their delivery to the guests.

Queuing theory

This is a mathematical theory implied by the hotel management to arrive at an optimum rate of customer flow in the hotel property.

R

Rack rate

This is the standard and the maximum possible rate that is established for a particular category of guestroom charged by a hotel property from the guests for overnight accommodation.

Rate spread

This is the term given to the arithmetical difference between a hospitality property's potential average single rate and potential average double rate.

Reach

The percentage of people within a specific target audience reached by an advertising campaign.

Reader board

This is a term given to a display board which is kept in the lobby in order to display and communicate the latest events in the hotel on a daily event.

Reasonable accommodation

This is a term used for describing a process of changing the usual way of performing a particular job so that any qualified person with disability cab perform the same taking care that it does not cause any inconvenience to the employer.

Recap sheet

This is a summary sheet generated by the front office cash section and shows the total of all the transcripts of a particular day to obtain the grand total of that particular day.

Receptive Operator

Specialists in handling arrangements for incoming visitors at a destination including airport transfers, local sightseeing, restaurants, accommodations, etc. Receptive operators can be a travel agent or tour operator.

Referral group

This is a term given to the independent hotel banded together for business profitability and market recognition as these hotels refer business to each other in terms of reservation.

Registration

This is term given to the entire procedure followed by the hotel authorities on the arrival of the guests to confirm the stay of the guest at the hotel and includes the process of signing of the guests on the registration card.

Registration card

This is a form which is completed by the guests on arrival or by the front office staff on behalf of the guests but is signed by the guests as it is an important document which acknowledges the visiting patron as an in-house guest.

Registration record

This is a term given collectively to all the essential information taken from the guest by the hotel at the time registration and includes the name and address of the guest, type of room and rate offered, method of payment and other special instruction by the guests.

Repeat Business

Business that continues to return, thereby generating increased profits.

Reservation

This is a mutual agreement between the guest and the hotel in which the guest hires accommodation from the hotel at a given for a given time.

Reservation code

This is also called a **reservation number** and is a combination of alphabets and numbers that provides a guest a reference or proof for his reservation confirmation with the hotel.

Reservation file

This is a file in which the various reservation slips are properly stored. The term is also used for computerized electronic file with a collection of reservation records.

Reservation rack

This is a rack in the expected arrivals (guests) are listed alphabetically or chronologically on the basis of their date of arrival.

Reservation record

This is a term given collectively to the data which is collected from the guest at the time of reservation and includes the date of arrival and departure of the guest, type of room requested, rate offered, reservation status, special instructions and other miscellaneous information.

Reservation referral system

This is a term given to an organization operating worldwide that processes reservation requests of a member property of the reservation referral system.

Reservation status

This is a terminology which is used for indicating the availability of a guestroom to be given to be given on hire to the guest on a particular night.

Reservation Systems (Automation Vendors)

Computerized systems leased to travel agencies offering airline, hotel, car rental and selected tour availability and bookings. Systems are affiliated with major carriers, including American (Sabre),

United (Apollo), Eastern (System One), TWA (PARS), and Delta (DATAS II) and feature flight schedules of the sponsoring and other carriers, plus additional travel products.

Reservations control book

This is a loose leaf binder which is used in non-automated hotels for tracking the room availability and reservations of the present day.

Reservations manager

The reservations manager is a person who is in-charge of the reservations section of the front office department and supervises the main functions of his section which is maintaining an accurate room inventory, confirming reservations to individual guests and groups and communicating and co-coordinating with the marketing and sales division of a hotel.

Resident manager

This is a senior manager who stays in the hotel and who has been given the responsibility of the general management of the hotel by the general manager in absence and during night.

Retail Agent

A travel agent.

Retailer

Another term for travel agents who sell travel products directly to consumers.

Revenue center

This is the term given to the various departments of a hotel property which sell goods and services to the guests and in return generates revenue for the hotel such as front office, gift shops, and food and beverage service outlets.

Revenue management

This is a management strategy based on the magnitude of demand and supply and aims to maximize the revenue of a hotel property by increasing the prices during the periods of high demands and by lowering the prices during the period of low demands to increase the revenue generation.

Revenue per available room (Rev PAR)

This is a very important ratio used for determining the financial success of a property and is determined by dividing the total rooms revenue received on a particular day by the total number of guestrooms available in the property for sale.

Rollaway (bed)

This is a movable or portable bed which measures about 30 inches in breadth and 72 inches in length and is generally supplied by the hotels on request the guests in the guestrooms.

Room

This is the most important product sold by a hotel offering accommodation to a guest.

Room Block

A predetermined number of rooms reserved in advance for group (conference, tour) use.

Room Service

Food and beverage delivered and served in a guest room.

Room charge sheet

This is a report which is prepared by the front desk every night and is a record of the room rack for a particular night and is thus used for verifying the accuracy of the room status.

Room inspection report

This is a report prepared by the floor supervisor when the room attendant has finished cleaning a particular guestroom.

Room pick up

This term denotes the number of guestrooms that have been confirmed by the members of a particular for occupancy for a particular forthcoming event.

Room rack

This a front office equipment mostly used in the semi-automated systems and is a wooden framework with an array of metallic pockets in which various colored room rack slips are inserted to show the occupancy status of the guestrooms.

Room rack slip

This is a small form which is prepared from the registration card of the guests and is inserted in the guestrooms and shows some important information about the guest such as name of the guest, date of arrival and departure and rate offered to the guest.

Room rate

This is the term which is given to the price that is charged by the hotel from the guests for providing overnight accommodations.

Room rate variance report

This is an important front office management report which details all the rooms that have been sold at a discounted rate and not at rack rate for that particular day.

Room revenue

This is the total amount received by the sale of guestrooms of a hotel.

Room sales figure

This is the daily sum total of the guestroom charges for the in-house guests of a hospitality property.

Room sales projections

This is a weekly report prepared by the front office managers in conjunction with the lobby managers of a hotel and contains a summary of the expected number of arrivals, departures, cancellations, no-shows, overstays and under stays.

Room status

This is an information on the availability of a guestroom for a particular guest for occupancy – reservation (confirmed guaranteed, confirmed non-guaranteed, repair,) or housekeeping (vacant and ready, not cleared, out of order)

Room status discrepancy

This is a term used to describe a situation when the housekeeping room status information does not tally or coincide with the room status information maintained by the front desk.

Room status report

This is a report which is prepared by the front office assistant as a part of the night auditing process and thus is gives a thorough information about the room status of all the guestrooms of a hospitality property which helps the front office assistant to know about the vacant and ready rooms.

Room variance report

This is a report which gives information about all the discrepancies between the front office and housekeeping room status that have been found in the night auditing process.

Rooming

This is the entire procedure of greeting of a newly arrived guest, assigning him a room and his escort to the guestroom by the bell staff.

Rooming list

This is a list which includes the rooming details of the various guests coming in group and is thus used by the front office staff to pre-register the guests of the group.

Rooming slip

This is a form which is issued by the front desk to the bell persons when in turn leaves the same with the guest to verify the name, rate and room.

Rooms division

This is the most important functional and revenue earning division of a hotel and includes the front office department, housekeeping department and the uniformed service department.

Rooms forecast

This is a process of estimating the room sales of a particular hospitality property for a specific period in the future.

Rule-of-the-thumb rate

This is a type of method used for setting the rack rates for the guestrooms and according to this method; a hotel will charge $1 for each $1,000 of construction costs.

Ryokan

This is term given to a traditional and authentic Japanese inn and is pronounced as **Leo Gan**.

S

Safe-deposit boxes

These are individual vaults which are either placed at the guestrooms or in the back of the front office and are used for keeping the valuable items of the guests.

Sales Mission

Where suppliers from one DMO travel together to another state of country for the purpose of collectively promoting travel to their area. Sales missions may include educational seminars for travel agents and tour operators.

Sales rack

These are front-office spaces for the storage and control of sales tickets.

Sales Seminar

An educational session in which travel agents, tour operators, tour wholesales or other members of the travel trade congregate to receive briefings about tourism destinations.

Sample room

This is a standard or model guestroom which is used for displaying the merchandises and accommodation facilities and services of a hospitality property.

Seamless connectivity

This term describes the ease with which the various intermediary agents such as travel agents, tour operators having on-line subscription through internet can access the room availability of a hospitality property to the last available room for sale.

Season rate

This is the maximum room rate this is charged by the resort owners to the guests when the demand is highest.

Self check-out terminal

This is a fully computerized machine or terminal located in the lobby of hotels and allows the guest to personally review his account or folio and settle the account balance through a credit card.

Self-registration

This is a sophisticated registration system where a computerized self-registration terminal checks-in the guest on the base of credit card information and also dispenses a guestroom key to complete the registration process.

Sell through

This is a revenue management strategy which does not allow any reservation to be accepted for a particular for particular days although the reservations for the previous days will be accepted and allowed to stay through the date.

Service charge

This is a percentage (generally 5% to 10%) of the total bill which is added to the same and charged from the guests and is later on distributed the services employees in place of tipping.

Service elevators

This is the term given to the elevators which are situated at the back of the lobby and are used by the employees for various official purposes such as transportation of luggage and goods.

Service strategy statement

This is a formal declaration and commitment made by the hotel management that the hotel will strive hard to deliver superior quality products and services to the guests in order to meet their expectations and provide them with total satisfaction.

Shells

A marketing and sales promotional piece that depicts a destination, accommodation or attraction on the cover and provides space for copy to be added at a later date. Usually shells fit a #10 envelope.

Shortage

This is a type of accounting error or imbalance which occurs when after removing the initial cash bank, the total amount of cash, cheques, drafts and other negotiable items in the cashier's drawer are more than the net cash receipts.

Shoulder period

This is a period of the year when the occupancy of the hotel is neither high nor low and thus is a famous marketing term which denotes the period between the peaks and valleys of demand.

Shoulder Season

The period between peak and low season.

Siberia

This is an industrial jargon or term which means a very undesirable guestroom and is the last room to be offered to the guest by the hotel property.

Site Inspection

An assessment tour of a destination or facility by a meeting planner, convention or trade show manager, site selection committee, tour operator, wholesaler or incentive travel manager to see if it meets their needs and requirements prior to selecting a specific site for an event. After site selection, a site inspection may be utilized to make arrangements.

Size

This is the total capacity of the hospitality property to house guests and is determined by the total number of guestrooms present in the hotel.

Skipper

This is a term used to describe a guest who leaves the hotel without making arrangements to settle his bill account.

Slide

This is an error which occurs during transcription and is caused by the misplacement of decimal point between figures. E.g. 38.60 is mistakenly written or typed as **3.68**.

Special attention list

This is a list prepared by the front office to identify the guests who are VIPs and who require special attention and treatment by the front office and other departments and also includes those guests who have special rooming requirements (Disabled room).

Split folio

This is a term given to guest folio in which the charges of the guests have been split into different folios on request of the guest.

Split rate

This is the process of division of the total rate of a guestroom in between several occupants (guest) of the room.

Split shift

This is the division of a particular working shift into two shifts with a long separation period or time between the same. This is also called **Break shift** and is generally performed by the food and beverage service personnel working in specialty restaurants.

Spouse Program

Special activities planned for those who accompany an attendee to a convention, trade show or meeting. Note that programs today are not simply for women, but rather for men and women, spouses and friends. Programs must be creatively designed to interest intelligent and curious audiences.

Spread rate

This is the process of assigning the guests in groups a standard room rates with the prices of the guestrooms less than the **rack rate**.

Star categorization

This is the process of categorization of the hotels into different ranks of stars and is thus is widely accepted and applied by the hotel industry around the whole world.

Star Ratings

Five Star Hotel

Luxury hotels; most expensive hotels/resorts in the world; numerous extras to enhance the quality of the client's stay (for example: some have private golf courses and even a small private airport).

Four Star Hotel

First class hotels; expensive (by middle-class standards); have all of the previously mentioned services; has many "luxury" services (for example: massages or a health spa).

Three Star Hotel

Middle class hotels; moderately priced; has daily maid service, room service, and may have dry-cleaning, Internet access, and a swimming pool.

Two Star Hotel

Budget hotels; slightly more expensive; usually has maid service daily.

One Star Hotel

Low budget hotels; inexpensive; may not have maid service or room service.

No Category Hotel

These hotels include motels, cottages, bungalows and others with limited services. Nevertheless, these hotels represent 41% of the total hotel market share.

Stayover

This is a room occupancy status which states that the guest is not departing the present day and will continue to stay for at least one more night and thus continues to occupy a particular guestroom from his date of arrival to his date of departure.

Supplier

Those businesses that provide industry products like accommodations, transportation, car rentals, restaurants and attractions.

Supplemental transcript

This is a report which summarizes all the non-guest accounts and displays the transactions which affected the balances of the each of the non-guest account and thus is used in the night auditing process for the detection of posting errors.

Support center

This is the term given to all the departments of the hotel which do not generate revenue for the hotel but help the revenue centers to generate revenue for the hotel such as housekeeping, food and beverage production division, stores, personnel division, engineering and maintenance division.

Swing

This is the evening or the afternoon shift which lies between the morning shift or the day shift and the night shift or the graveyard shift.

System update

This is the term give to the night audit routine followed in fully-automated or computerized system and thus includes preparing back-up copies of the reports generated, file re-organization, system maintenance, generation of the reports and providing an end-of-day time frame.

T

Target market

This is the term given to distinctly identified group of customers towards whom a hotel would target its marketing efforts and develop products and services to be accepted by them.

Target Rating Points

TRPÕs are a statistical measurement which allows one to evaluate the relative impact of differing advertising campaigns.

Tariff

Rate of fare quoted and published by a travel industry supplier (i.e. hotels, tour operators, etc.) Usually an annual tariff is produced in booklet form for use in sales calls at trade shows.

TIA

Travel Industry Association of America.

Timeshare (Vacation Ownership)

A marketing and equity financing concept which permits participants to enjoy vacation accommodation for a fixed, one time amount for life, or shorter contracted period. According to the American Resort Development Association (ARDA), timeshare consumers make a one-time purchase of furnished resort accommodations, at a fraction of whole ownership costs, and pay an annual maintenance fee. Each condominium, or unit, of a vacation ownership resort is divided into intervals, either by the week or points equivalent, which are sold separately.

The accommodations are priced according to a variety of factors, including size of the unit, resort amenities, location, and season. The purchaser owns the vacation accommodations, but only for the amount of time he or she plans to use it - typically one or two weeks each year. With time-share, the owner has all the benefits of a vacation home without the year-round costs. From its origin, the idea behind time-sharing was to give people the ability to purchase their future vacation - at current prices.

Fractionals are a variation of timeshare in which the purchaser owns longer intervals, from four to 12 weeks a year. Costs of fractionals are significantly higher, ranging to more than $600,000. Major branded hotel companies participate in fractional timeshare, though not to the extent of independent operators.

TOT

Transient Occupancy Tax.

Total Quality Management

This is a modern philosophy which is accepted around the world and is a process of bringing about a continuous improvement in the operations and management of all the divisions of an organization with the help of productive human resource and a financial resource.

Touch screen

This is a type of sophisticated computer monitor screen which allows the user to feed or input the data by touching the screen.

Tour Operator

An organization or individual who actively manages and escorts tours and tour packages to FIT and group visitors.

Tour Wholesaler

An individual or company that sells tour packages and tour products to travel agents. Tour wholesalers usually receive a 20% discount from accommodations, transportation companies and attractions and pass on a 10 to 15% discount to the retail agent.

Tourism

Leisure travel.

Tourist/Visitor/Traveler

Any person who travels either for leisure or business purposes more than 100 miles (round-trip) in a day or who stays overnight away from his/her primary domicile.

Trade advertising contract

This is an agreement between a hospitality property and advertising media in which the hotel property pays for the advertising of its product and services to the advertising media (pays for the advertising space in print media and for broadcast time in broadcast media).

Traditional Lodging

Guests pay nightly rates for single rooms or suites and have full access to the hotels' range of amenities and services. Rates begin at "rack," but vary widely, based on time of week and season and nearby events and attractions.

Trial balance

This is a process of balancing all the front office transactions against departmental transaction and is thus is used for balancing the revenue center departments and is thus a very important function in the night auditing process.

Transcript

This is a form prepared by the night auditor and is used for accumulating and segregating the charges of the day by departments and guests.

Transfer

This is an accounting method of moving the numerical figures from one account or folio to another. This term is also given to the movement or shift of guest and luggage from one place at the property to another.

Transfer folio

This is a special unnumbered folio which is used for carrying the account of the guest beyond the first week when the original folio of the guest was numbered and verified with the registration card of the guest.

Transfer journal

This is a front office accounting form which is used for recording the transfer entries between different accounts and ledgers.

Transfer voucher

This is a document which is used for the tracking the account transfer transaction and is used for transfers between guest accounts and for transfers from guest accounts to non-guest accounts settled either by credit card, letter from company or through miscellaneous charge order.

Transient guest

This is a guest who stays in a hotel for a short duration or period.

Transmittal form

This is a form provided by the credit card companies to the hotel for summarizing and dispatching the credit card charges to the companies for payment.

Transposition error

This is a common error during the process of transcription when the cashier or the auditor mistakenly interchanges the sequence of the digits. E.g. Rs. 698 instead of Rs. 689.

Travel

Leisure and other travel including travel for business, medical care, education, etc. All tourism is travel, but not all travel is tourism.

Travel agent

This is an intermediary agent which books or reserves accommodation and other facilities for the guests in the various hotel properties and also books space for travellers in various transport carriers and returns receives commission from the hotels and transport operators for providing with guests and passengers.

Travel agent guaranteed

This is a method of guaranteeing a confirmed reservation and is established by a correspondence between a hotel property and a travel agent in which the travel agent accepts the financial responsibilities of the guests in case the guest is a no-show and thus agrees to pay for the unoccupied reserved rooms.

Travel directories

This is a directory which provides detailed information about the methods of doing reservations with the hospitality properties and also gives a brief description (location, accommodation and other facilities) of the various famous hotels in a particular country.

Travel Management Company

This is a large travel agency which provides a bulk reservation and business to the hotel and thus has significant room rate negotiating power.

Travel Product

Refers to any product or service that is bought by or sold to consumers of trade including accommodations, attractions, events, restaurants, transportation, etc.

Travel Seasons

Travel industry business cycles including: Peak: Primary travel season Off Peak: Period when business is slowest Shoulder: Period between peak and off peak periods when business is stronger, but has room for growth.

Travel Trade

The collective term for tour operators, wholesalers and travel agents.

Traveler

Definitions very, but in general a traveller is someone who leaves their own economic trade area, (usually going a distance of a minimum of fifty to one hundred miles) and stays overnight.

Traveler's checks

These are prepaid checks that are issued by banks and other financial institutions to the visitors and guests and thus are an important means of account settlement.

Turn-downs

This is the term given to the evening service provided by the housekeeping to the guestroom in which the soiled linen is changed, the room is cleaned and the bed is prepared for night.

Turn-in

This is the amount pf money deposited by the front office cashier in the accounts division after the end of a particular shift.

U

Understay

This is a guest who leaves the hotel before his scheduled date of departure.

Unpaid account balance

This is a term collectively given to all the charges which are left in the account of the guest after the guest has left the hotel.

Upgrade

This is a process of offering or moving a registered guest to a better category of rooms than what he had actually asked for and the guest is assessed no charge for the same and is thus a promotional effort of the hotel to increase goodwill and future business.

Upsell

This is the process of offering a better accommodation to the guest than what he or she had asked for during the time of reservation or registration and thus encourage the guest to buy a higher priced product i.e. guestroom or any other hospitality product.

User friendly

This is a quality of computer hardware and software programs to increase the confidence of the customers and employees in the operation of computers so that the users can find it easy to operate the computers.

V

Vacancy

This is a situation when guestrooms are available for sale in a property as all the rooms are not occupied and thus are vacant.

Very Important Person (VIP)

This is a status which is given to guests such as state guests, dignitaries, ambassadors and other important guests who require special care and attention and special service by the hotel management.

Visitors Center

Travel information center located at a destination to make it easier for visitors to plan their stay; often operated by a convention and visitor's bureau, chamber of commerce or tourism promotion organization.

Voice mailbox

This is an electronic device or equipment which is used for recording, storing and playing back telephone messages for the guests in their absence.

Voucher

This is a document generated by the various point of sales and other revenue centers for notifying the front office about the occurrence of a particular transaction and thus is a source document detailing each steps of transaction.

W

Walk

This is the process of turn away a guest having a confirmed reservation from a particular property due to unavailability of guestrooms due to overbooking taken by the reservation staff.

Walk-in

This is a term given to a guest who arrives at a hospitality property without any reservation and demands a guestroom.

Walked Guests

When a hotel is overbooked and a guest room is not available for a confirmed guest, the hotel has "walk the guest" to a nearby hotel.This usually includes paying for transportation to the hotel and covering any difference in the room rate at the hotel the guest was "walked" to.

Walk-through

This is the process of thoroughly inspecting the entire property and its facilities by a prospective owner or an inspection team of the Franchisor or FHRAI or any other classification and approval body.

Washing

This is the process of removing all the unreserved rooms within a group block in to the general inventory pool after the cut-off-date for reselling them to other groups or guests. This is also called **Wash Factor**.

Watch

This is an industrial jargon used for defining a work-shift of the employees.

Who

This is the term given to an unidentified guest occupying a guestroom in a hotel that is shown as vacant in the front office room rack.

Wholesaler

This is the term given to an entrepreneur who purchases tours and packages from hospitality suppliers such as hotels and airlines and sells the same to either directly to the customers or to the travel agents and other retail agencies.

Wide Area Telephone Services

This is the term given to long-distance telephone line connections offered to hotels and wholesalers at subsidized rates with separate charges imposed for the incoming and outgoing WAT lines.

World-class service

This is a term given to the famous international hotels with personalized service being offered to the guests and also have fine dining restaurant, lounges, guestrooms with exquisite décor and furnishings and above all a high staff-guest ratio.

X

Xenodogheionology

This is the study of the history, stories and myths about the hospitality establishments such as inns, hotels and motels.

Y

Yield

This is statistical information that gives information about the general performance of the hotel and is the product of the occupancy of the hotel on a particular date and the average daily rate.

Yield management

This a management strategy that is increasingly used by the most of the hospitality companies and is a process of maximizing the revenue of a property by increasing the room rates during the periods of high occupancy and decreasing the room rates during the period of low occupancy.

Yield percentage

This is the statistical figure that determines the effectiveness and efficiency of the hotel in selling all the rooms at the rack rate which is the highest possible room rate available to prospective guests.

Yield statistic

This is the term given to the ratio of the actual rooms' revenue of a hotel property and the potential rooms' revenue of the hotel property.

Z

Zero out

This is the process of balancing the guest accounts by the front office cashier during the process of check-out of the guests and making arrangements for the settlement of the folio.

Zip

This is the term given to the postal code assigned to the various cities, towns and districts of the country.

Zip-out

This is the term given to the process of express check-out and has generally become an obsolete technical term.

CHAPTER 7

ABBREVIATIONS OF HOSPITALITY INDUSTRY

1.	**AAA**	American Automobile Association
2.	**AAUI**	Automobile Association of Upper India
3.	**ADA**	Americans With Disabilities Act
4.	**ADR**	Average daily Revenue
5.	**AHL**	Asian Hotels Limited
6.	**AH&LA**	American Hotel and Lodging Association
7.	**AII**	Air India International
8.	**ANS**	Arrival Notification Slip
9.	**ARR**	Average Room Revenue
10.	**ASTA**	American Society of Travel Agent
11.	**ATA**	Air Transport Authority
12.	**BTC**	Bill to Company
13.	**CAS**	Call Accounting System
14.	**CIP**	Commercially Important Person
15.	**CRO**	Central Reservation Office
16.	**CRS**	Central Reservation System
17.	**DFIT**	Domestic Free Individual Traveler
18.	**DGCA**	Director General Of Civil Aviation
19.	**DNA**	Did Not Arrive
20.	**DNCO**	Did Not Check Out
21.	**DND**	Do Not Disturb

22.	**DNS**	Did Not Stay
23.	**DOT**	Department Of Tourism
24.	**ECO**	Express Check Out
25.	**ECR**	Electronic Cash Register
26.	**EIHL**	East India Hotel Limited
27.	**ELS**	Electronic Locking System
28.	**EMS**	Energy Management System
29.	**FAX**	Facsimile Automated Xerox
30.	**FEMA**	Foreign Exchange Monetary Act
31.	**FFIT**	Foreign Free Individual Traveler
32.	**FH&RAI**	Federation Of Hotel And Restaurant Association Of India
33.	**FIT**	Free Individual Traveler
34.	**FMCG**	Fast Moving Consumer Goods
35.	**FRRO**	Foreigner's Regional Registration Office
36.	**GATT**	General Agreement For Tariff And Trade
37.	**GDS**	Global Distribution System
38.	**GIT**	Group Inclusive Travel
39.	**GOI**	Government Of India
40.	**HCI**	Hotel Corporation Of India
41.	**HCIMA**	Hotel And Catering International Management Association
42.	**HIS**	Hotel Information System
43.	**HOBIC**	Hotel Outward Bound Information Center
44.	**HRACC**	Hotel And Restaurant Approval And Classification Committee
45.	**HRANI**	Hotels And Restaurants Associations Of North India
46.	**HSMA**	Hotel Sales Management Association
47.	**IAAI**	International Airports Authority Of India
48.	**IAC**	Indian Airlines Corporation
49.	**IATA**	International Air Transport Association
50.	**IATO**	International Air Transport Association

51.	**ICAO**	International Civil Aviation Organization
52.	**ICICI**	Industrial Credit And Investment Corporation Of India
53.	**IHCL**	Indian Hotel Company Limited
54.	**IDBI**	Industrial Development Bank Of India
55.	**IDD/ISD**	International Direct Dialing / International Subscriber Dialing
56.	**IHA**	International Hotel Association
57.	**IMF**	International Monetary Fund
58.	**IRO**	Instant Reservation Office
59.	**IRS**	Instant Reservation System
60.	**IRTC**	Indian Railways and Tourism Corporation
61.	**ITDC**	India Tourism Development Corporation
62.	**IUOTO**	International Union Of Official Travel Organization
63.	**IYHF**	International Youth Hostel Federation
64.	**MTG**	Mobil Travel Guide
65.	**NB**	No Baggage
66.	**NC**	Not Cleaned
67.	**NCR**	National Cash Register
68.	**NR**	No Reservation
69.	**O**	Occupied
70.	**OOI**	Out Of Inventory
71.	**OOO**	Out Of Order
72.	**OS**	Off The Street
73.	**PABX**	Private Automatic Branch Exchange
74.	**PATA**	Pacific Air Travel Association
75.	**PBX**	Private Branch Exchange
76.	**PIA**	Paid In Advance
77.	**PIP**	Politically Important Person
78.	**POS**	Point Of Sale
79.	**RNA**	Room Not Assigned

80.	**SAARC**	South Asian Association For Regional Co-operation
81.	**SATC**	South Asia Travel Commission
82.	**SB**	Scanty Baggage
83.	**SIDBI**	Small Industrial Development Bank Of India
84.	**SITA**	Student International Travel Association
85.	**SITS**	Special Interest Tours
86.	**SPATT**	Special Attention Guest
87.	**STD**	Subscriber Trunk Dialing
88.	**TAAI**	Travel Agents' Association Of India
89.	**TIPS**	To Insure Prompt Service
90.	**UFTAA**	Universal Federation Of Travel Agent Association
91.	**UR**	Under Repair
92.	**V**	Vacant and Ready
93.	**VPO**	Visitor's Paid Out
94.	**VPP**	Value Payable Post
95.	**VTL**	Visitor's Tabular Ledger
96.	**WATS**	Wide Area Telephone Service
97.	**WTO**	World Tourism Organization
98.	**WTV**	Worldwide Travel Vouchers
99.	**YMCA**	Young Men's Christian Association
100.	**YWCA**	Young Women's Christian Association

Index

K

L

M

O

P

R

S

T